The SECRET *of* THE AGES

The SECRET *of* THE AGES

ROBERT COLLIER

A TarcherPerigee Book

tarcherperigee

An imprint of Penguin Random House LLC
375 Hudson Street
New York, New York 10014

The Secret of the Ages was originally published in 1925 under the title *The Book of Life*. It appeared under its current title in 1926 and later in a revised and expanded version in 1948.
First Jeremy P. Tarcher/Penguin edition 2007

ISBN 978-1-58542-629-4

Printed in the United States of America

CONTENTS

CHAPTER I

THE WORLD'S GREATEST DISCOVERY

You can do as much as you think you can,
But you'll never accomplish more;
If you're afraid of yourself, young man,
There's little for you in store.
For failure comes from the inside first,
It's there if we only knew it,
And you can win, though you face the worst,
If you feel that you're going to do it.

—EDGAR A. GUEST*

What, in your opinion, is the most significant discovery of this modern age?

The finding of Dinosaur eggs on the plains of Mongolia, laid—so scientists assert—some 10,000,000 years ago?

*From "A Heap o' Livin'." The Reilly & Lee Co.

The unearthing of ancient tombs and cities, with their confirmation of the Scriptural story, and their matchless specimens of bygone civilizations?

The radioactive time clock by which Professor Lane of Tufts College estimates the age of the earth at 1,250,000,000 years?

Radio? Airplanes? Atomic energy? The Hydrogen Bomb? No—not any of these. The really significant thing about them is that from all this vast research, from the study of bygone ages, men are for the first time beginning to get an understanding of that "Vital Force" which—somehow, some way—was brought to this earth thousands or millions of years ago. They are beginning to get an inkling of the infinite power it puts in their hands—to glimpse the untold possibilities it opens up.

This is the greatest discovery of modern times—that every man has within him a particle of "Creative Force" endowed with infinite Intelligence, infinite Resource; that he can call upon this Power at will; that it is as much the servant of his mind as was ever Aladdin's fabled "Genie-of-the-Lamp" of old; that he has but to understand it and work in harmony with it to get from it anything he may need—health or happiness, riches or success.

To realize the truth of this, you have but to go back for a moment to the beginning of things.

IN THE BEGINNING

It matters not whether you believe that mankind dates back to the primitive apeman of 500,000 years ago, or sprang full-grown from the mind of the Creator. In either event, there had to be a First Cause—a Creator. Some Power had to bring to this earth the first germ of Life, and the creation is no less wonderful if it started with the lowliest form of plant life and worked up through countless ages into the highest product of today's civilization, than if the whole were created in six days.

In the beginning, this earth was just a fire mist—six thousand or a billion years ago—what does it matter which?

The one thing that does matter is that some time, some way, there came to this planet the germ of Life—the Vital Force which animates all Nature—plant, animal, man. If we accept the scientists' version of it, the first form in which Life appeared upon earth was the humble Algae—a jelly-like mass which floated upon the waters. This, according to the scientists, was the beginning, the dawn of life upon the earth.

Next came the first bit of animal life—the lowly Amoeba, a sort of jelly fish, consisting of a single cell, without vertebrae, and with very little else to distinguish it from the water round about. But it had *life*—the first bit of *animal* life—and sufficient Intelligence and Resource to find the means of sustaining life, and to PROGRESS. From that life, according to the scientists, we can trace everything we have and are today.

All the millions of forms and shapes and varieties of plants and animals that have since appeared are but different manifestations of *life*—formed to meet differing conditions.

For millions of years this "Life Germ" was threatened by every kind of danger—from floods, from earthquakes, from droughts, from desert heat, from glacial cold, from volcanic eruptions—but to it each new danger was merely an incentive to finding a new resource, to putting forth Life in some new shape.

To meet one set of needs, it formed the Dinosaur—to meet another, the Butterfly. Long before it worked up to man, we see its unlimited resourcefulness shown in a thousand ways. To escape danger in the water, it sought land. Pursued on land, it took to the air. To breathe in the sea, it developed gills. Stranded on land, it perfected lungs. To meet one kind of danger it grew a shell. For another, a sting. To protect itself from glacial cold, it grew fur. In temperate climes, hair. Subject to alternate heat and cold, it produced feathers. But ever, from the beginning, it showed its power to meet every changing condition, to answer every creature need.

Had it been possible to kill this "Life Germ," it would have perished ages ago, when fire and flood, drought and famine followed each other in quick succession. But obstacles, misfortunes, cataclysms, were to it merely new opportunities to assert its power. In fact, it required obstacles to awaken it, to show its energy and resource.

The great reptiles, the monster beasts of antiquity, passed on. But the "Life Principle" stayed, changing as each age changed, always developing, always improving.

Whatever Power it was that brought this "Life Germ"

to the earth, it came endowed with unlimited resource, unlimited energy, unlimited LIFE! No other force can defeat it. No obstacle can hold it back. All through the history of life and mankind you can see its directing intelligence—call it Nature, call it Providence, call it what you will—rising to meet every need of life.

THE PURPOSE OF EXISTENCE

No one can follow it down through the ages without realizing that the whole purpose of existence is GROWTH—*expression*. Life is dynamic—not static. It is ever moving forward—not standing still. The one unpardonable sin of nature is to stand still, to stagnate. The Gigantosaurus, that was over a hundred feet long and as big as a house; the Tyrannosaurus, that had the strength of a locomotive and was the last word in frightfulness; the Pterodactyl or Flying Dragon—all the giant monsters of Prehistoric Ages—are gone. They ceased to serve a useful purpose. They did not know how to meet the changing conditions. They stood still—stagnated—while the life around them passed them by.

Egypt and Persia, Greece and Rome, all the great Empires of antiquity, perished when they ceased to grow. China built a wall about herself and stood still for a thousand years. Today she is oppressed by Communism. In all Nature, to cease to grow is to perish.

It is for men and women who are not ready to stand still, who refuse to cease to grow, that this book is written. It will give you a clearer understanding of your own potentialities, show you how to work with and take advantage of the infinite energy all about you.

The terror of the man at the crossways, not knowing which road to take, will be no terror to you. Your future is of your own making. For the only law of Infinite Energy is the law of supply. The "Life Principle" is your principle. To survive, to win through, to triumphantly surmount all obstacles has been its everyday practice since the beginning of time. It is no less resourceful now than ever it was. You have but to supply the urge, to work in harmony with it, to get from it anything you may need.

For if this Vital Force is so strong in the lowest forms of animal life that it can develop a shell or a poison to meet a need; if it can teach the bird to circle and dart, to balance and fly; if it can grow a new limb on a spider to replace a lost one, how much more can it do for *you*—a reasoning, rational being, with a mind able to *work with* this "Life Principle," with an energy and an initiative to urge it on!

The evidence of this is all about you. Take up some violent form of exercise—rowing, tennis, swimming, riding. In the beginning your muscles are weak, easily tired. But keep on for a few days. The Vital Force flows into them more strongly, strengthens them, toughens them, to meet their new need. Do rough manual labor—and what happens? The skin of your hands becomes tender, blisters, hurts. Keep it up, and does the skin all wear off? On the contrary, the Vital Force provides extra thicknesses, extra toughness—calluses, we call them—to meet your need.

All through your daily life you will find this "Life Force" steadily at work. Embrace it, work with it, take it to yourself, and there is nothing you cannot do. The mere fact that you have obstacles to overcome is in your favor, for when there is nothing to be done, when things run along too smoothly, this "Life Force" seems to sleep. It is when you need it, when you call upon it urgently, when you seem to have used up every bit of Vital Force in you, that it is most on the job.

It differs from "Luck" in this, that fortune is a fickle jade who smiles most often on those who need her least. Stake your last penny on the turn of a card—have nothing between you and ruin but the spin of a wheel or the speed of a horse—and it's a thousand to one "Luck" will desert you! But it is just the opposite with the "Life Principle." As long as things run smoothly, as long as life flows along like a song, this "Life Principle" seems to slumber, secure in the knowledge that your affairs can take care of themselves.

But let things start going wrong, let ruin and disgrace stare you in the face—*then* is the time this "Life Force" will assert itself if you but give it a chance.

THE "OPEN, SESAME!" OF LIFE

There is a Napoleonic feeling of power *that insures success* in the knowledge that this invincible Life Force is behind your every act. Knowing that you have working with you a power which never yet has failed in anything it has undertaken, you can go ahead in the confident knowledge that it will not fail in your case, either. The ingenuity which overcame every obstacle in making you what you are, is not likely to fall short when you have immediate need for it. It is the reserve strength of the athlete, the "second wind" of the runner, the power that, in moments of great stress or excitement, you unconsciously call upon to do the deeds which you ever after look upon as superhuman.

But they are in no wise superhuman. They are merely beyond the capacity of your conscious self. Ally your conscious self with that sleeping giant within you, rouse him daily to the task, and those "superhuman" deeds will become your ordinary, everyday accomplishments.

W. L. Cain, of Oakland, Oregon, wrote: "I know that there is such a power, for I once saw two boys, 16 and 18 years of age, lift a great log off their brother, who had been caught under it. The next day, the same two boys, with another man and myself, tried to lift the end of the log, but could not even budge it."

How was it that the two boys could do at need what the four were unable to do later on, when the need had passed? Because they never stopped to question whether or not it *could* be done. They saw only the urgent need. They called upon all their vital forces—never doubting, never fearing—and the Genie which is in all of us waiting only for such a call, answered their summons and gave them the strength—not of two men, but of ten!

Medical men would explain it by saying that, under the stress of excitement, their glands pumped such stimulants into their blood that they were capable of almost any effort. But whether you call it glands or the answer to prayer, the fact remains that there is a Power in each of us capable of superhuman effort, and that under the stress of urgent need, we can call it forth.

It matters not whether you are Banker or Lawyer, Business Man or Clerk. Whether you are the custodian of millions, or have to struggle for your daily bread. The "Life Force" makes no distinction between rich and poor, high and low. The greater your need, the more readily will it respond to your call. Wherever there is an unusual task, wherever there is poverty or hardship or sickness or despair, *there* is this Servant of your Mind, ready and willing to help, asking only that you call upon him.

And not only is it ready and willing, but it is always ABLE to help. Its ingenuity and resource are without limit. It is Mind. It is Thought. It is the Telepathy that carries messages without the spoken or written word. It is the Sixth Sense that warns you of unseen dangers. No matter how stupendous and complicated, nor how simple your problem may be—the solution of it lies within yourself. And since the solution is there, this Mental Giant can call it forth. It can KNOW, and it can DO, every right thing. Whatever it is necessary for you to know, whatever it is necessary for you to do, you can know and you can do if you will but seek the help of this Genie-of-Your-Mind and work with it in the right way.

CHAPTER II

THE GENIE-OF-YOUR-MIND

It matters not how strait the gate,
How charged with punishment the scroll,
I am the Master of my Fate;
I am the Captain of my Soul.

—Henley

First came the Stone Age, when life was for the strong of arm or the fleet of foot. Then there was the Iron Age—and while life was more precious, still the strong lorded it over the weak. Later came the Golden Age, and riches took the place of strength—but the poor found little choice between the slave drivers' whips of olden days and the grim weapons of poverty and starvation.

Now we are entering a new age—the Atomic Age, which is really the Age of Mind—when every man can be his own master, when poverty and circumstance no longer hold power and the lowliest creature in the land can win a place side by side with the highest.

To those who do not know the resources of mind, these

will sound like rash statements; but science proves beyond question that in the well springs of every man's mind are unplumbed depths—undiscovered deposits of energy, wisdom and ability. Sound these depths—bring these treasures to the surface—and you gain an astounding wealth of new power.

From the rude catamaran of the savages to the giant liners of today, carrying their thousands from continent to continent, is but a step in the development of Mind. From the lowly cave man, cowering in his burrow in fear of lightning or fire or water, to the engineer of today, making servants of all the forces of Nature, is but a measure of difference in mental development.

Man, without reasoning mind, would be as the monkeys are—prey of any creature fast enough and strong enough to pull him to pieces. At the mercy of wind and weather. A poor, timid creature, living for the moment only, fearful of every shadow.

Through his superior mind, he learned to make fire to keep himself warm; weapons with which to defend himself from the savage creatures round about; habitations to protect himself from the elements. Through mind he conquered the forces of Nature. Through mind he has made machinery do the work of millions of horses and billions of hands. What he will do next, no man knows, for man is just beginning to awaken to his own powers. He has split the atom—now he is harnessing its power. He is beginning to get an inkling of the unfathomed riches that are buried deep in his own mind. Like the gold seekers of '49, he has panned the surface gravel for the gold swept down by the streams. Now he is starting to dig deeper to the pure vein beneath.

We bemoan the loss of our forests. We worry over our dwindling resources of coal and oil. We decry the waste in our factories. But the greatest waste of all, we pay no attention to—the waste of our own potential mind power. Professor Wm. James, the world-famous Harvard psychologist, estimated that the average man uses only 10 percent of his mental power. He has unlimited power—yet he uses but a tithe of it. Unlimited wealth all about him—and he doesn't know how to take hold of it. With God-like powers slumbering within him, he is content to continue in his daily grind—eating, sleeping, working—plodding through an existence little more eventful than the animals', while all of Nature, all of life, calls upon him to awaken, to bestir himself.

The power to be what you want to be, to get what you desire, to accomplish: whatever you are striving for, abides within you. It rests with you only to bring it forth and put it to work. You must learn *how* to do that, of course, but the first essential is to *realize* that you *possess* this power, your first objective to get acquainted with it.

Psychologists and Metaphysicians the world over are agreed on this—that Mind is all that counts. You can be whatever you make up your mind to be. You need not be sick. You need not be unhappy. You need not be poor. You need not be unsuccessful. You are not a mere clod. You are not a beast of burden, doomed to spend your days in unremitting labor in return for food and housing. You are one of the Lords of the Earth, with unlimited potentialities. Within you is a power which, properly grasped and directed, can lift you out of the rut of mediocrity and place you among the Elect of the earth—the lawgivers, the writers, the engineers, the great industrialists—the DOERS and the THINKERS. It rests with you only to learn to use this power which is yours—this Mind which can do all things.

Your body is for all practical purposes merely a machine which the mind uses. This mind is usually thought of as consciousness; but the *conscious part* of your mind is in fact the *very smallest part of it.* Ninety percent of your mental life is subconscious, so when you make active use of only the conscious part of your mind you are using but a fraction of your real ability; you are running on low gear. And the reason why more people do not achieve success in life is because so many of them are content to run on low gear all their lives—on SURFACE ENERGY. If these same people would only throw into the fight the resistless force of their subconscious and superconscious minds, they would be amazed at their undreamed-of capacity for winning success.

Religion has always taught us to look upon God as a triplicity—as Three in One—but seems to have forgotten that man is likewise three in one, made in the image and likeness of God. For man's mind is a triplicity, the conscious mind, the subconscious, and the subliminal or superconscious mind.

THE CONSCIOUS MIND

When you say "I see—I hear—I smell—I touch," it is your conscious mind that is saying this, for it is the force governing the five physical senses. It is the phase of mind with which you feel and reason—the phase of mind with which everyone is familiar. It is the mind with which you do business. It controls, to a great extent, all your voluntary muscles. It discriminates between right and wrong, wise and foolish. It is the generalissimo, in charge of all your mental forces. It can plan ahead—and get things done as it plans. Or it can drift along haphazardly, a creature of impulse, at the mercy of events—a mere bit of flotsam in the current of life.

For it is only through your conscious mind that you can reach the subconscious and the superconscious mind. Your conscious mind is the porter at the door, the watchman at the gate. It is to the conscious mind that the subconscious looks for all its impressions. It is on it that the subconscious mind must depend for the teamwork necessary to get successful results. You wouldn't expect much from an army, no matter how fine its soldiers, whose general never planned ahead, who distrusted his own ability and that of his men, and who spent all his time worrying about the enemy instead of planning how he might conquer them. You wouldn't look for good scores from a ball team whose pitcher was at odds with the catcher. In the same way, you can't expect results from the subconscious when your conscious mind is full of fear or worry, or when it does not know what it wants.

The most important province of your conscious mind is to center your thoughts on the thing you want, "Believe that you receive," and then shut the door on every suggestion of fear or worry or failure.

If you once gain the ability to do that, nothing else is impossible to you.

For the subconscious mind does not reason inductively. It takes the thoughts you send in to it and works them out to their logical conclusion. Send to it thoughts of health and strength, and it will work out health and strength in your body. Let suggestions of disease, fear of sickness or accident, penetrate to it, either through your own beliefs or the talk of those around you, and you are very likely to see the manifestation of disease working out in yourself.

Your mind is master of your body. It directs and controls every function of your body. Your body is in effect a little universe in itself, and mind is its radiating center—the sun which gives light and life to all your system, and around which the whole revolves. And your *conscious thought* is master of this sun center.

THE SUBCONSCIOUS MIND

Can you tell me how much water, how much salt, how much of each different element there should be in your blood to maintain its proper specific gravity if you are leading an ordinary sedentary life? How much, and how quickly these proportions must be changed if you play a fast game of tennis, or run for your car, or chop wood, or indulge in any other violent exercise?

Do you know how much water you should drink to neutralize the excess salt in salt fish? How much you lose through perspiration? Do you know how much water, how much salt, how much of each different element in your food should be absorbed into your blood each day to maintain perfect health?

No? Well, it need not worry you. Neither does any one else. Not even the greatest physicists and chemists and mathematicians. But your subconscious mind knows.

And it doesn't have to stop to figure it out. It does it almost automatically. It is one of those "Lightning Calculators." And this is but one of thousands of such jobs it performs every hour of the day. The greatest mathematicians in the land, the most renowned chemists, could never do in a year's time the abstruse problems which your subconscious mind solves every minute.

And it doesn't matter whether you have ever studied mathematics or chemistry or any other of the sciences. From the moment of your birth your subconscious mind solves all these problems for you. While you are struggling with the three R's, it is doing problems that would leave your teachers aghast. It supervises all the intricate processes of digestion, of assimilation, of elimination, and all the glandular secretions that would tax the knowledge of all the chemists and all the laboratories in the land. It planned and built your body from infancy on up. It repairs it. It operates it. It has practically unlimited power, not merely for putting you and keeping you in perfect health, but for acquiring all the good things of life. Ignorance of this power is the sole reason for all the failures in this world. If you would intelligently turn over to this wonderful power all your business and personal problems, no goal would be too great for you to strive for.

Dr. Geo. C. Pitzer sums up the power of the subconscious mind very well in the following:

"The subconscious mind is a distinct entity. It occupies the whole human body, and, when not opposed in any way, it has absolute control over all the functions, conditions, and sensations of the body. While the objective (conscious) mind has control over all of our voluntary functions and motions, the subconscious mind controls all of the silent, involuntary, and vegetative functions. Nutrition, waste, all secretions and excretions, the action of the heart in the circulation of the blood, the lungs in respiration or breathing, and all cell life, cell changes and development, are positively under the complete control of the subconscious mind. This was the only mind animals had before the evolution of the brain; and it could not, nor can it yet, reason inductively, but its power of deductive reasoning is perfect. And more, it can see without the use of physical eyes. It perceives by intuition. It has the power to communicate with others without the aid of ordinary physical means. It can read the thoughts of others.

It receives intelligence and transmits it to people at a distance. Distance offers no resistance successful missions of the subconscious mind."

In "Practical Psychology and Sex Life," by David Bush, Dr. Winbigler is quoted as going even further. To quote him:

"It is this mind that carries on the work of assimilation and upbuilding whilst we sleep. . . .

"It reveals to us things that the conscious mind has no conception of until the consummations have occurred.

"It can communicate with other minds without the ordinary physical means.

"It gets glimpses of things that ordinary sight does not behold.

"It makes God's presence an actual, realizable fact, and keeps the personality in peace and quietness.

"It warns of approaching danger.

"It approves or disapproves of a course of conduct and conversation.

"It carries out all the best things which are given to it, providing the conscious mind does not intercept and change the course of its manifestation.

"It heals the body and keeps it in health, if it is at all encouraged."

It is, in short, a powerful and beneficent force, but like a live electric wire, its destructive force is equally great. It can be either your servant or your master. It can bring to you evil or good.

The Rev. William T. Walsh, in a book published some years ago, explained the idea clearly:

"The subconscious part in us is called the subjective mind, because it does not decide and command. It is a subject rather than a ruler. Its nature is to do what it is told, *or what really in your heart of hearts you desire.*

"The subconscious mind directs all the vital processes of your body. You do not think consciously about breathing. Every time you take a breath you do not have to reason, decide, command. The subconscious mind sees to that. You have not been at all conscious that you have been breathing while you have been reading this page. So it is with the mind and the circulation of blood. The heart is a muscle like the muscle of your arm. It has no power to move itself or to direct its action. Only mind, only something that can think, can direct our muscles, including the heart. You are not conscious that you are commanding your heart to beat. The subconscious mind attends to that. And so it is with the assimilation of food, the building and repairing of the body. In fact, all the vital processes are looked after by the subconscious mind."

"Man lives and moves and has his being" in this great subconscious mind. It supplies the "intuition" that so often carries a woman straight to a point that may require hours of cumbersome reasoning for a man to reach. Even in ordinary, everyday affairs, you often draw upon its wonderful wisdom.

But you do it in an accidental sort of way without realizing what you are doing.

Consider the case of "Blind Tom." Probably you have heard or read of him. You know that he could listen to a piece of music for the first time and go immediately to a piano and reproduce it. People call that abnormal, but as a matter of fact he was in this respect more normal than any of us. We are abnormal in that we cannot do it, because our subconscious minds retain a perfect record of everything we have ever heard or seen, and if appealed to in the proper way, they will recall these images to consciousness.

Consider the case of these "lightning calculators" of whom one reads now and then. It may be a boy seven or eight years old; but you can ask him to divide 7,649.437 by 326.2568 and he will give you the result in less time than it would take you to put the numbers down on a piece of paper. You call him phenomenal. Yet you ought to be able to do the same yourself. Your subconscious mind can.

Dr. Hudson, in his book "The Law of Psychic Phenomena," tells of numerous such prodigies. Here are just a few instances:

"Of mathematical prodigies there have been upwards of a score whose calculations have surpassed, in rapidity and accuracy, those of the greatest educated mathematicians. These prodigies have done their greatest feats while but children from three to ten years old. In no case had these boys any idea how they performed their calculations, and some of them would converse upon other subjects while doing the sum. Two of these boys became men of eminence, while some of them showed but a low degree of objective intelligence.

"Whateley spoke of his own gift in the following terms:

" 'There was certainly something peculiar in my calculating faculty. It began to show itself at between five and six, and lasted about three years. I soon got to do the most difficult sums, always in my head, for I knew nothing of figures beyond numeration. I did these sums much quicker than anyone could upon paper, and I never remember committing the smallest error. When I went to school, at which time the passion wore off, I was a perfect dunce at ciphering, and have continued so ever since.'

"Professor Safford became an astronomer. At the age of ten he worked correctly a multiplication sum whose answer consisted of thirty-six figures. Later in life he could perform no such feats.

"Benjamin Hall Blyth, at the age of six, asked his father at what hour he was born. He was told that he was born at four o'clock. Looking at the clock to see the present time, he informed his father of the number of seconds he had lived. His father made the calculation and said to Benjamin, 'You are wrong 172,000 seconds." The boy answered, 'Oh, papa, you have left out two days for the leap years 1820 and 1824,' which was the case.

"Then there is the celebrated case of Zerah Colburn, of whom Dr. Schofield writes:

"'"Zerah Colburn could instantaneously tell the square root of 106,929 as 327, and the cube root of 268,336,125 as 645. Before the 'question of the number of minutes in forty-eight years could be written he said 25,228,810. He immediately gave the factors of 247,483 as 941 and 263, which are the only two; and being asked then for those of 36,083, answered none; it is a prime number. He could not tell how the answer came into his mind. He could not, on paper, do simple multiplication or division.'"

The time will come when, as H. G. Wells visioned in his "Men Like Gods," schools and teachers will no longer be necessary except to show us how to get in touch with the infinite knowledge our subconscious minds possess from infancy.

"The smartest man in the world," wrote Dr. Frank Crane in an article in *Liberty*, "is the Man Inside. By the Man Inside I mean that Other Man within each one of us that does most of the things we give ourselves credit for doing. You may refer to him as Nature or the Subconscious Self or think of him merely as Force or a Natural Law, or, if you are religiously inclined, you may use the term God.

"I say he is the smartest man in the world. I know he is infinitely more clever and resourceful than I am or than any other man is that I ever heard of. When I cut my finger it is he that calls up the little phagocytes to come and kill the septic germs that might get into the wound and cause blood poisoning. It is he that coagulates the blood, stops the gash, and weaves the new skin.

"I could not do that. I do not even know how he does it. He even does it for babies that know nothing at all; in fact, does it better for them than for me.

"No living man knows enough to make toenails grow, but the Man Inside thinks nothing of growing nails and teeth and thousands of hairs all over my body; long hairs on my head and little fuzzy ones over the rest of the surface of the skin.

"When I practice on the piano I am simply getting the business of piano playing over from my conscious mind to my subconscious mind: in other words, I am handing the business over to the Man Inside.

"Most of our happiness, as well as our struggles and misery, comes from this Man Inside. If we train him in ways of contentment, adjustment, and decision he will go ahead of us like a well trained servant and do for us easily most of the difficult tasks we have to perform."

Dr. Jung, celebrated Viennese specialist, claimed that the subconscious mind contains not only all the knowledge that it has gathered during the life of the individual, but that in addition it contains all the wisdom of past ages. That by drawing upon its wisdom and power the individual may possess any good thing of life, from health and happiness to riches and success.

You see, the subconscious mind is the connecting link between the Creator and ourselves, between Vital Force all about us and our own bodies and affairs. It is the means by which we can appropriate to ourselves all the good gifts, all the riches and abundance which Universal Mind has created in such profusion.

Berthelot, the great French founder of modern synthetic chemistry, once stated in a letter to a close friend that the final experiments which led to his most wonderful discoveries had never been the result of carefully followed and reasoned trains of thought, but that, on the contrary, "they came of themselves, so to speak, from the clear sky."

Charles M. Barrows, in "Suggestion Instead of Medicine," tells us that:

"If man requires another than his ordinary consciousness to take care of him while asleep, not less useful is this same psychical provision when he is awake. Many persons are able to obtain knowledge which does not come to them through their senses, in the usual way, but arrives in the mind by direct communication from another conscious intelligence, which apparently knows more of what concerns their welfare than their ordinary reason does. I have known a number of persons who, like myself, could tell the contents of letters in their mail before opening them. Several years ago a friend of mine came to Boston for the first time, arriving at what was then the Providence railroad station in Park Square. He wished to walk to the Lowell station on the opposite side of the city. Being utterly ignorant of the streets as well as the general direction to take he confidently set forth without asking the way, and reached his destination by the most direct path. In doing this he trusted solely to 'instinctive guidance,' as he called it, and not to any hints or clews obtained through the senses."

The geniuses of literature, of art, commerce, government, politics and invention are, according to the scientists, but ordinary men like you and me who have learned how to draw upon their subconscious minds.

Sir Isaac Newton is reported to have acquired his marvelous knowledge of mathematics and physics with no conscious effort. Mozart said of his beautiful symphonies that "they just came to him." Descartes had no ordinary regular education. To quote Dr. Hudson:

"This is a power which transcends reason, and is independent of induction. Instances of its development might be multiplied indefinitely. Enough is known to warrant the conclusion that when the soul is released from its objective environment it will be enabled to perceive all the laws of its being, to 'see God as He is,' by the perception of the laws which He has instituted. It is the knowledge of this power which demonstrates our true relationship to God, which confers the warranty of our right to the title of 'sons of God,' and confirms our inheritance of our rightful share of his attributes and powers—our heirship of God, our joint heirship with Jesus Christ."

The subconscious mind is the seat of memory. Every thought or impression we have ever had is registered there. The conscious mind remembers nothing beyond what is held in its thought. It must draw upon the files of the subconscious for everything it wishes to recall.

"Considered from the standpoint of its activities," says Warren Hilton in "Applied Psychology," "the subconscious is that department of mind, which on the one hand directs the vital operations of the body, and on the other conserves, subject to the call of interest and attention, all ideas and complexes not at the moment active in consciousness.

"Observe, then, the possibility that lies before you. On the one hand, if you can control your mind in its subconscious activities, you can regulate the operation of your bodily functions, and can thus assure yourself of bodily efficiency and free yourself of functional disease. On the other hand, if you can determine just what ideas shall be brought forth from subconsciousness into consciousness, you can thus select the materials out of which will be woven your conscious judgments, your decisions and your emotional attitudes.

"To achieve control of your mind is, then, to attain (a) health, (b) success, and (c) happiness."

Few understand or appreciate, however, that the vast storehouse of knowledge and power of the subconscious mind can be drawn upon at will. Now and then through intense concentration or very active desire we do accidentally penetrate to the realm of the subconscious and register our thought upon it. Such thoughts are almost invariably realized. The trouble is that as often as not it is our negative thoughts—our fears—that penetrate. And these are realized just as surely as the positive thoughts. What you must manage to do is learn to communicate only such thoughts as you wish to see realized to your subconscious mind, for it is exceedingly amenable to suggestion. You have heard of the man who was always bragging of his fine health and upon whom some of his friends decided to play a trick. The first one he met one morning commented upon how badly he looked and asked if he weren't feeling well. Then all the others as they saw him made similar remarks. By noon time the man had come to believe them, and before the end of the day he was really ill.

That was a glaring example, but similar things are going on every day with all of us. We eat something that someone else tells us is bad for us and in a little while we think we feel a pain. Before we know it we have indigestion, when the chances are that if we knew nothing about the supposed indigestible properties of the food, we could eat it the rest of our days and never feel any ill effects.

Let some new disease be discovered and the symptoms described in the daily paper. Hundreds will come down with it at once. They are like the man who read a medical encyclopedia and ended by concluding he had everything but "housemaid's knee." Patent medicine advertisers realize this power of suggestion and cash in on it. Read one of their ads. If you don't think you have everything the matter with you that their nostrums are supposed to cure, you are the exception and not the rule.

You see, the subconscious takes those things that are handed to it as facts and works them out to a logical conclusion. You read or hear that doing such and such will bring on a cold or fever or some other ailment. The subconscious accepts this as fact unless you actively combat the belief, and if you do the things proscribed, it will proceed to give you a cold or fever, even though you had never given the matter a second conscious thought.

That is the negative side of it. Emile Coué based his system on the positive side—that you suggest to your subconscious mind that whatever ills it thinks you have are getting better. And it is good psychology at that. Properly carried out, it works wonders. But this method has its weaknesses. Suggestion will cure many ills, but not all. When you try to suggest something to the subconscious that is contrary to a long-held or deep-seated belief, you will fail. The subconscious will not accept it. You have to DO something to change its beliefs. You have to CONVINCE it, and in later chapters, we shall show you how.

Suffice it now to say that your subconscious mind is exceedingly wise and powerful. That it knows many things that are not in books. That when properly used it has infallible judgment, unfailing power. That it never sleeps, never tires.

Your conscious mind may slumber. It may be rendered impotent by anesthetics or a sudden blow. But your subconscious mind works on, keeping your heart and lungs, your arteries and glands ever on the job.

Under ordinary conditions, it attends faithfully to its

duties, and leaves your conscious mind to direct the outer life of the body. But let the conscious mind meet some situation with which it is unable to cope, and, if it will only call upon the subconscious, that powerful Genie will respond immediately to its need.

You have heard of people who had been through great danger tell how, when death stared them in the face and there seemed nothing they could do, things went black before them and, when they came to, the danger was past. In the moment of need, their subconscious mind pushed the conscious out of the way, the while it met and overcame the danger. Impelled by the subconscious mind, their bodies could do things absolutely impossible to their ordinary conscious selves.

For the power of the subconscious mind is unlimited. Whatever it is necessary for you to do in any right cause, it can give you the strength and the ability to do.

Whatever of good you may desire, it can bring to you. "The Kingdom of Heaven is within you."

But remember this: The subconscious works beneath the surface, and it reasons logically, deductively, from the facts that are given it. It will not go contrary to those facts. If you want to change it, you must give it new and stronger facts to work upon. Not only that, but you must nullify the original facts.

THE UNIVERSAL MIND

Have you ever dug up a potato vine and seen the potatoes clustering underneath? How much of intelligence do you suppose one of these potatoes has? Do you think it knows anything about chemistry or geology? Can it figure out how to gather carbon gas from the atmosphere, water and all the necessary kinds of nutriment from the earth round about to manufacture into sugar and starch and alcohol? No chemist can do it. How do you suppose the potato knows? Of course it doesn't. It has no sense. Yet it does all these things. It builds the starch into cells, the cells into roots and vines and leaves—and into more potatoes.

"Just old Mother Nature," you will say. But old Mother Nature must have a remarkable intelligence if she can figure out all these things that no human scientist has ever been able to solve. There must be an all-pervading Intelligence behind Mother Nature—the Intelligence that first brought life to this planet—the Intelligence that evolved every form of plant and animal—that holds the winds in its grasp—that is all-wise, all-powerful. The potato is but one small manifestation of this Intelligence. The various forms of plant life, of animals, of man—all are mere cogs in the great scheme of things.

But with this *difference*—that man is an active part of this Universal Mind. That he partakes of its creative wisdom and power and that by consciously drawing to him its vital power, and then working in harmony with Universal Mind, he can *do* anything, *have* anything, *be* anything.

There is within you—within everyone—this mighty resistless force with which you can perform undertakings that will dazzle your reason, stagger your imagination. There constantly resides within you a Mind that is all-wise, all-powerful, a Mind that is entirely apart from the mind which you consciously use in your everyday affairs—the superconscious mind or Higher Self.

Your subconscious mind partakes of this wisdom and power, and it is through your subconscious mind that you can reach the superconscious and draw upon it in the attainment of anything you may desire. When you can intelligently use your subconscious mind in this way, you can be in communication with that Higher Self in you which is part of the Universal Mind.

Remember this: the Universal Mind is omnipotent. And when the subconscious mind is in tune with the Higher Self, there is no limit to the things that it can do. Given any desire that is in harmony with the Universal Mind, and you have but to hold that desire in your thought with confident and serene faith to attract from the invisible domain the things you need to satisfy it.

You see, there is just as much of the Creative Force around you today as there was when the world was made. And the Universal Mind, of which your superconscious is a part, is just as capable of making from it anything it desires.

"In the beginning was the Word," says the Gospel of St. John. What is a "Word"? A mental image, is it not? So all that God had in the beginning was a mental image. That was His mold, and into it He poured the Creative Force all about Him and formed the world and everything upon it.

If you are like most of us, you are not too well satisfied with your world as it is. What shall you do to improve it? RE-CREATE it! All you need is the mental image, and the faith to put the Creative Force all about you into it.

An understanding of this explains the power of prayer. The results of prayer are not brought about by some special dispensation of Providence. God is not a finite being to be cajoled or flattered into things as you desire.

When you pray earnestly, you form a mental image of the thing you desire and you hold it strongly in your thought. Then, if you have the necessary faith that you ARE RECEIVING the thing asked for, your superconscious mind (which is part of the Universal or God Mind) draws to you enough of the Creative Force to fill out the image you are holding in thought and to bring it into being.

Throughout the Old and the New Testament, you find the assurance that we are Sons of God, partaking of all His power—that nothing is impossible to us. And from earliest recorded times, a few have proved this to be so.

Jesus cured the sick, He raised the dead, He brought gold from the fish's mouth, He fed thousands with a handful of loaves and fishes. He showed His followers how to perform similar wonders, and everything that He did, He assured us that we could do also—"And greater things than these shall ye do!"

Whence comes such power? Where but from our part of Divinity—from the superconscious mind which is part of the Universal or God Mind.

Most of us think of mind as being merely the conscious part of us, but from the earliest Greek religious writings we have been taught that man is a triune being: 1st, the physical or conscious self; 2nd, the subconscious, sometimes called the "Inner Mind" because it is latent within you; 3rd, the superconscious or "Higher Self."

Go back 2,000 years before Christ to the Upanishads or earliest religious books of India and you find a similar teaching. Study the religion of the Egyptians, and you find the same belief. The great pyramids were triangular on each side, exemplifying the idea you find on many of their monuments. The Egyptians believed that the "Ka" or "Higher Self" could separate itself from the body at will and perform any service that was required of it, regardless of distance.

You can send your Higher Self to do your will, as Jesus sent His to cure the Centurion's servant. Through it, you can protect your loved ones, you can heal, you can help in all ways.

To do so, however, you must charge it with your own Vital Force. You can never help another without giving something of your self. You must consciously GIVE of your Vital Force. You must have the faith to SEE your Higher Self doing the things you direct it to do. You must BELIEVE it IS doing them. Given such faith, all things are possible to you.

All around you is the Vital Force of the Universe—the material of which everything is made. And YOU are a Creator, with the God-given power to use that Vital Force as you please, to make of it what you will.

But to create anything of good requires four things:

1. The mental image of what you want. That is the mold.
2. Knowledge of your power, so you can consciously draw to you all the Vital Force you need—breathe it in—and then pour it into your mental mold.
3. Faith in your creative power, faith to crystallize the Vital Force in your mold, until it is manifest for all to see.
4. Doing something to convince your subconscious mind—and through it, the superconscious—that you do believe you HAVE received. For instance, a woman who prayed for a house got a board and nail and kept them before her, affirming that they were the beginning of the house.

As I see it, the Universal Mind is the Supreme Intelligence and Creator of the Universe and we are partakers of the Divine Attributes. You are part of it, I am part of it, and anything we do that is for the good of all has the support of this Universal Mind—*provided we call upon it.*

To bring you to a realization of the power latent in you, to teach you simple, direct methods of drawing upon it, is the beginning and the end of this book.

There are two kinds of people on earth today,
Just two kinds of people, no more, I say.

Not the good and the bad, for 'tis well understood
The good are half bad, and the bad are half good.

Not the rich and the poor, for to count a man's wealth
You must first know the state of his conscience and health.

Not the humble and proud, for in life's busy span
Who puts on vain airs is not counted a man.

No, the two kinds of people on earth I mean
Are the people who LIFT and the people who LEAN!

Wherever you go, you will find the world's masses
Are ever divided in just these two classes.

And strangely enough you will find, too, I ween,
There is only one LIFTER to twenty who LEAN.

In which class are you? Are you easing the load
Of overtaxed LIFTERS who toil down the road?

Or are you a LEANER who lets others bear
Your portion of worry and labor and care?

—ELLA WHEELER WILCOX

CHAPTER III

THE PRIMAL CAUSE

This city, with all its houses, palaces, steam engines, cathedrals and huge, immeasurable traffic and tumult, what is it but a Thought, but millions of Thoughts made into one—a huge immeasurable Spirit of a Thought, embodied in brick, in iron, smoke, dust, Palaces, Parliaments, coaches, docks and the rest of it. Not a brick was made but some man had to think of the making of that brick.

—CARLYLE

The measure of your success in life can be forecast by just one factor—the extent to which you work directly with first causes, rather than with conditions.

What is a "First Cause"? Judge Troward gave so clear an answer to this question in his Edinburgh Lectures that we quote it here:

If a lighted candle is brought into a room, the room becomes illuminated; if the candle is taken away, it be-

> comes dark again. Now the illumination and the darkness are both *conditions,* the one positive resulting from the presence of the light, the other negative resulting from its absence. A condition, whether positive or negative, is never a *primary cause,* and the primary cause of any series can never be negative, for negation is the condition which arises from the absence of active causation.

How can you know whether you are working with first causes or not? To quote Troward again:

> If we regard the fulfilment of our purpose as contingent upon any *circumstance,* past, present or future, we are not making use of first cause. We have descended to the level of secondary causation, which is the region of doubts, fears and limitations.

When you are in need and creditors are hounding you on every side, what they may do is not the important thing. They are mere secondary causes—the result of conditions or circumstances. You must get back to the first cause—SUPPLY! And that first cause lies in your thought-pattern, just as the first cause of a house lies in the thought-pattern of the architect. What kind of thought-patterns are you making?

For thousands of years the riddle of the universe has been this question of causation. Did the egg come first, or the chicken? "The globe," says an Eastern proverb, "rests upon the howdah of an elephant. The elephant stands upon a tortoise, swimming in a sea of milk." But then what?

It has been said that every man is either a materialist or an idealist. The materialist, roughly speaking, declares that nothing exists but matter and the forces inherent therein. The idealist declares that all is mind or energy, and that matter is necessarily unreal.

The time has come when people have become dissatisfied with these unceasing theories which get them nowhere. And today, as the appreciation of a Primal Cause becomes more clearly defined, the spiritual instinct asserts itself determinedly.

"Give me a base of support," said Archimedes, "and with a lever I will move the world."

And the base of support is that all started with *mind,* with a mental image. In the beginning was nothing—a fire mist. Before anything could come of it there had to be an idea, a model on which to build. *Universal Mind* supplied that idea, that model. Therefore the primal cause is mind. Everything must start with an idea. Every event, every condition, every thing is first an idea in the mind of someone.

Before you start to build a house, you draw up a plan of it. You make an exact blueprint of that plan, and your house takes shape in accordance with your blueprint. Every material object takes form in the same way. Mind draws the plan. Thought forms the blue-print, well drawn or badly done as your thoughts are clear or vague. It all goes back to the one cause. The creative principle of the universe is mind, and thought is the eternal energy.

But just as the effect you get from electricity depends upon the mechanism to which the power is attached, so the effects you get from mind depend upon the way you use it. We are all of us dynamos. The power is there—unlimited power. But we must connect it with something—set it some task—give it work to do—else are we no better off than the animals.

The "Seven Wonders of the World" were built by men with few of the opportunities or facilities that are available to you. They conceived these gigantic projects first in their own minds, pictured them so vividly and worked at them so earnestly that their superconscious minds came to their aid and showed them how to overcome obstacles that most of us would regard as insurmountable. Imagine building the Pyramids of Gizeh, enormous stone upon enormous stone, with nothing but bare hands. Imagine the labor, the sweat, the heart-breaking toil of erecting the Colossus of Rhodes, between whose legs a ship could pass! Yet men built these wonders, in a day when tools were of the crudest and machinery was undreamed of, by using the unlimited power of Mind.

Mind is creative, but it must have a model on which to work. It must have thoughts to supply the power.

There are in Universal Mind ideas for millions of wonders greater far than the "Seven Wonders of the World." And those ideas are just as available to you as they were to the artisans of old, as they were to Michelangelo when he built St. Peter's in Rome, as they were to the architect who conceived the Empire State Building, or the engineer who planned the Golden Gate Bridge.

Every condition, every experience of life is the result of our mental attitude. We can *do* only what we think we can do. We can *be* only what we think we can be. We can *have* only what we think we can have. What we do, what we are, what we have, all depend upon what we think. We can never express anything that we do not first have in mind. The secret of all power, all success, all riches, is in first thinking powerful thoughts, successful thoughts, thoughts of wealth, of supply. We must build them in our own mind first.

William James, the famous psychologist, said that the greatest discovery in a hundred years was the discovery of the power of the subconscious mind. It is the greatest discovery of all time. It is the discovery that man has within himself the power to control his surroundings, that he is not at the mercy of chance or luck, that he is the arbiter of his own fortunes, that he can carve out his own destiny. He is the master of all the forces round about him. As James Allen puts it:

"Dream lofty dreams, and as you dream, so shall you become. Your vision is the promise of what you shall one day be; your Ideal is the prophecy of what you shall at last unveil."

Matter in the ultimate is but a product of thought. Even the most material scientists admit that matter is not what it appears to be. According to physics, matter (be it the human body or a log of wood—it makes no difference which) is made up of an aggregation of distinct minute particles called atoms. Considered individually, these atoms are so small that they can be seen only with the aid of a powerful microscope, if at all.

MATTER— DREAM OR REALITY?

Until comparatively recently, these atoms were supposed to be the ultimate theory regarding matter. We ourselves—and all the material world around us—were supposed to consist of these infinitesimal particles of matter, so small that they could not be seen or weighed or smelled or touched individually—but still particles of matter *and indestructible.*

Now, however, these atoms have been further analyzed, and physics tells us that they are not indestructible at all—that they are mere positive and negative buttons of force or energy called protons and electrons, without hardness, without density, without solidity, without even positive actuality. In short, they are vortices in the ether—whirling bits of energy—dynamic, never static, pulsating with life, but the life is *spiritual!* As one eminent British scientist put it—"Science now explains matter by *explaining it away!*"

And that, mind you, is what the solid table in front of you is made of, is what your house, your body, the whole world is made of—*whirling bits of energy!*

To quote the New York *Herald-Tribune:* "We used to

believe that the universe was composed of an unknown number of different kinds of matter, one kind for each chemical element. The discovery of a new element had all the interest of the unexpected. It might turn out to be anything, to have any imaginable set of properties.

"That romantic prospect no longer exists. We know now that instead of many ultimate kinds of matter there are only two kinds. Both of these are really kinds of electricity. One is negative electricity, being, in fact, the tiny particle called the electron, familiar to radio fans as one of the particles vast swarms of which operate radio vacuum tubes. The other kind of electricity is positive electricity. Its ultimate particles are called protons. From these protons and electrons all of the chemical elements are built up. Iron and lead and oxygen and gold and all the others differ from one another merely in the: number and arrangement of the electrons and protons which they contain. That is the modern idea of the nature of matter. *Matter is really nothing but electricity.*"

Can you wonder then that scientists believe the time will come when mankind *through mind* can control all this energy, can be absolute master of the winds and the waves, can literally follow the Master's precept—"If ye have faith as a grain of mustard seed, ye shall say unto this mountain, Remove hence to yonder place; and it shall remove; and nothing shall be impossible unto you."

For Modern Science is coming more and more to the belief that what we call *matter is a force subject wholly to the control of mind.*

How tenuous matter really is, is perhaps best illustrated by the fact that a single violin string, tuned to the proper pitch, might start a vibration that would shake down the Brooklyn Bridge! Oceans and mountains, rocks and iron, all can be reduced to a point little short of the purely spiritual. Your body is 85 percent water, 15 percent ash, phosphorus and other elements. And they in turn can be dissipated into gas and vapor. Where do we go from there?

Is not the answer that, to a great degree at least, and perhaps altogether, this world round about us is one of our mind's own creating? And that we can put into it, and get from it, pretty much what we wish? You see this illustrated every day. A panorama is spread before you. To you it is a beautiful picture; to another it appears a mere collection of rocks and trees. A girl comes out to meet you. To you she is the embodiment of loveliness; to another all that grace and beauty may look drab and homely. A moonlit garden, with its fragrant odors and dew-drenched grass, may mean all that is charming to you, while to another it brings only thoughts of asthma or rose fever or rheumatism. A color may be green to you that to another is red. A prospect may be inviting for you that to another is rugged and hard.

The fact is that our limited human senses take in but a small fraction of the infinite life around us. Our ears, for instance, are attuned to only a few of the sound waves that are constantly beating upon our eardrums. Very short waves and very long ones are entirely imperceptible to us. Waves of sound that the radio and other mechanical devices catch perfectly, make no impression on our unaided eardrums.

The same with light. Light waves of very high or very low frequency cannot be detected by our unaided eyes. Yet they are there all the time, as you will find if you turn upon any object the "black" light of the ultra violet ray. Entirely different aspects show themselves, weird and unbelievable colors. There they are, but our limited senses cannot detect them, any more than they can detect the pictures which are being wirelessed through the air by television. Some people, of course, can see more than others. Some eyes have a species of ultra violet ray of their own, which accounts for so-called "color blindness." It is not blindness at all. It is simply that their eyes happen to refract the light rays a bit differently from the average, so they get a different angle of color.

The fact is that the physical senses are so limited, that to accept their verdict without question is like believing you see the sun go down of an evening. You can SEE it go down, yet every school-boy knows that this is merely an optical illusion—that the sun is standing still and it is the earth that is moving.

Feelings, sensations, all are just as illusory. To quote "Applied Psychology," by Warren Hilton:

"The same stimulus acting on different organs of sense will produce different sensations. A blow upon the eye will cause you to 'see stars'; a similar blow upon the ear will cause you to hear an explosive sound. In other words, the vibratory effect of a touch on eye or ear is the same as that of light or sound vibrations.

"The notion you may form of any object in the outer world depends solely upon what part of your brain happens to be connected with that particular nerve-end that receives an impression from the object.

"You see the sun without being able to hear it because the only nerve-ends tuned to vibrate in harmony with the ether-waves set in action by the sun are nerve-ends that are connected with the brain center devoted to sight. 'If,' says Professor James, 'we could splice the outer extremities of our optic nerves to our ears, and those of our auditory nerves to our eyes, we should hear the lightning and see the thunder, see the symphony and hear the conductor's movements.'

"In other words, the kind of impressions we receive from the world about us, the sort of mental pictures we form concerning it, in fact, the character of the outer world, the nature of the environment in which our lives are cast—all these things depend for each one of us simply upon how he happens to be put together, upon his individual mental make-up."

It would seem to come back to the old fable of the three blind men and the elephant. To the one who caught hold of his leg, the elephant was like a tree. To the one who felt of his side, the elephant was like a wall. To the one who seized his tail, the elephant was like a rope. The world is to each of us the world of *his individual perceptions.*

You are like a radio receiving station. Every moment

thousands of impressions are reaching you. You can tune in on whatever ones you like—on joy or sorrow, on success or failure, on optimism or fear. You can select the particular impressions that will best serve you, you can hear only what you want to hear, you can shut out all disagreeable thoughts and sounds and experiences, or you can tune in on discouragement and failure and despair.

Yours is the choice. You have within you a force against which the whole world is powerless. By using it, you can make what you will of life and of your surroundings.

"But," you will say, "objects themselves do not change. It is merely the difference in the way you look at them." Perhaps. But to a great extent, at least, we find what we look for, just as, when we turn the dial on the radio, we tune in on whatever kind of entertainment or instruction we may wish to hear. And who can say that it is not our thoughts that put it there? Who, for the matter of that, can prove that our surroundings in waking hours are not as much the creature of our minds as are our dreams?

You have often heard how artists, in trying to renovate some cracked old painting, have scraped off the outer coating of paint, and underneath discovered a masterpiece.

The masterpiece had fallen into the hands of a mediocre artist who, trying to improve the original or else failing to appreciate its perfection, painted over it a picture of his own. But once his amateurish daubing had been removed, the work of the great painter stood out in all its pristine glory.

We are all of us daubers, painting our poor pictures over the finest masterpieces ever conceived.

For what is life but a picture—a moving picture thrown by mind upon the screen of the ether? God paints a perfect picture of our bodies, of our surroundings—a picture of beauty and love and harmony and plenty.

But we fail to see it. Like the artist who cannot appreciate the grandeur of a Master's work, we paint our own cubist pictures over it, concealing the perfect original—and then complain because of the very conditions we painted!

You have seen pictures of men and scenes which had been telegraphed from distant points. You know that they are made up of a great number of dots. But do you know that is all your body is, all any material thing is, a great number of dots—tiny buttons or waves of force?

There is nothing stable about them. They are constantly shifting, constantly changing, even in the most solid objects. They are merely pictures cast upon the air by mind. True, we can feel them, sometimes taste and smell them as well as see them, but that merely indicates their relative properties and densities. It does not make the pictures any more real or permanent. Look at these same pictures under the invisible light of the ultra violet ray, and you see something entirely different.

In the first verse of Genesis, we are told that God created the heaven and the earth. And in the last verse of that chapter, we are also told that God saw every thing that He had made, and *it was very good.*

How are we to reconcile this with the experiences of everyday life—the poverty, the hardship, the evil we see all around? Didn't God create them? Or did He consider them good for us?

Our answer is that He not only did not create them, but that they are not real! They are the pictures we ourselves have painted over His perfect masterpiece.

God formed the perfect picture of earth and heaven and all that in them is. He made a perfect picture of you, with perfect surroundings, abounding in happiness, peace and plenty. But almost from the very beginning, mankind has thought that it knew better the kind of picture it wanted, and it has painted over His masterpiece its daubs of poverty and sickness and woe.

How can we get back to the original? How can we uncover God's masterpiece of ourselves and the conditions and circumstances around us?

You have seen these pseudo-artists on the stage, who paint a picture in half a minute by the simple expedient of rubbing from a picture already on the board, the coating of wax or other stuff which conceals the picture from you. Well, that is all you have to do. The Master Painter has already made His perfect picture of you and your surroundings. All you have to do is to rub away your belief in what seem to be wrong conditions—*and let His perfect picture show!*

Throw away all the pictures you have which show poverty or sickness or unhappiness. Know that they are no part of His perfect picture. See in your mind's eye the perfect picture that should be there. Then CLAIM it! Believe that you have it! *And as your faith is, so will it be unto you.*

Just as the most powerful forces in nature are the invisible ones—heat, light, air, electricity—so the most powerful forces of man are his invisible forces, his thought forces. And just as electricity can fuse stone and iron, so can your thought forces control your body, so can they make or mar your destiny.

THE PHILOSOPHER'S CHARM

There was once a shrewd necromancer who told a king that he had discovered a way to make gold out of sand. Naturally the king was interested and offered him great rewards for his secret. The necromancer explained his process. It seemed quite easy, except for one thing. Not once during the operation must the king think of the word Abracadabra. If he did, the charm was broken and the gold would not come. The king tried and tried to follow the directions, but he could not keep that word Abracadabra out of his mind. And he never made the gold.

Dr. Winbigler puts the same idea in another way: "Inspiration, genius, power, are often interfered with by the conscious mind's interposing, by man's failing to recognize his power, afraid to assist himself, lacking the faith in himself necessary to stimulate the subconscious so as to arouse the genius asleep in each."

From childhood on we are assured on every hand—by scientists, by philosophers, by our religious teachers, that "ours is the earth and the fullness thereof." Beginning with the first chapter of Genesis, we are told that "God said, Let us make man in our image, after our likeness; and let them have dominion over the fish of the sea, and over the fowl of the air, and over the cattle, and over all the earth—and over every living thing that moveth upon the earth." All through the Old and the New Testament, we are repeatedly adjured to use these God-given powers. "He that believeth on me," said Jesus, "the works that I do shall he do also; and greater works than these shall he do." "If ye abide in me, and my words abide in you, ye shall ask what ye will, and it shall be done unto you." "For verily I say unto you, that whosoever shall say unto this mountain, Be thou removed, and be thou cast into the sea; and shall not doubt in his heart, but shall believe that those things which he saith shall come to pass; he shall have whatsoever he saith." "The kingdom of God is within you."

We hear all this, perhaps we even, think we believe, but always, when the time comes to use these God-given talents, there is the "doubt in our heart."

Baudouin expressed it clearly: "To be ambitious for wealth and yet always expecting to be poor; to be always doubting your ability to get what you long for, is like trying to reach east by travelling west. There is no philosophy which will help a man to succeed when he is always doubting his ability to do so, and thus attracting failure.

"You will go in the direction in which you face. . . .

"There is a saying that every time the sheep bleats, it

loses a mouthful of hay. Every time you allow yourself to complain of your lot, to say, I am poor; I can never do what others do; I shall never be rich; I have not the ability that others have; I am a failure; luck is against me;' you are laying up so much trouble for yourself.

"No matter how hard you may work for success, if your thought is saturated with the fear of failure, it will kill your efforts, neutralize your endeavors, and make success impossible."

And that is responsible for all our failures. We are like the old lady who decided she wanted the hill behind her house removed. So she got down on her knees and prayed the good Lord to remove it. The next morning she got up and hurried to the window. The hill was still in its same old place. "I knew it!" she snapped. "I gave Him His chance. But I knew all the time there was nothing to this prayer business."

Neither is there, as it is ordinarily done. Prayer is not a mere asking of favors. Prayer is not a paean of praise. Rather prayer is a realization of the God-power within you—of your right of dominion over your own body, your environment, your business, your health, your prosperity. It is an understanding that you are "heir of God and coheir with Christ." And that as such, no evil has power over you, whereas you have all power for good. And "good" means not merely holiness. Good means happiness—the happiness of everyday people. Good means everything that is good in this world of ours—comforts and pleasures and prosperity for ourselves, health and happiness for those dependent upon us. There are no limits to "Good" except those we put upon it ourselves.

What was it made Napoleon the greatest conqueror of his day? Primarily his magnificent faith in Napoleon. He had a sublime belief in his destiny, an absolute confidence that the obstacle was not made which Napoleon could not find a way through, or over, or around. It was only when he lost that confidence, when he hesitated and vacillated for weeks between retreat and advance, that winter caught him in Moscow and ended his dreams of world empire. Fate gave him every chance first. The winter snows were a full month late in coming. But Napoleon hesitated—and was lost. It was not the snows that defeated him. It was not the Russians. It was his loss of faith in himself.

THE KINGDOM OF HEAVEN

"The Kingdom of Heaven is within you." Heaven is not some far-away state—the reward of years of tribulation here. Heaven is right here—here and now! When Christ said that Heaven was within us, He meant just what He said—that the power for happiness, for good, for everything we need of life, is within each one of us.

That most of us fail to realize this Heaven—that many are sickly and suffering, that more are ground down by poverty and worry—is no fault of His. He gave us the power to overcome these evils; He stands ready and waiting to help us use it. If we fail to find the way, the fault is ours. To enjoy the Heaven that is within us, to begin here and now to live the life eternal, takes only a fuller understanding of the Power-that-is-within-us.

Even now, with the limited knowledge at our command, we can control circumstances to the point of making the world without an expression of our own world within, where the real thoughts, the real power, resides. Through this world within you can find the solution of every problem, the cause for every effect. Discover it—and all power, all possession is within your control.

For the world without is but a reflection of that world within. Your thought *creates* the conditions your mind images. Keep before your mind's eye the image of all you want to be and you will see it reflected in the world without. Think abundance, feel abundance, BELIEVE abundance, and you will find that as you think and feel and believe, abundance will manifest itself in your daily life. But let fear and worry be your mental companions, thoughts of poverty and limitation dwell in your mind, and worry and fear, limitation and poverty will be your constant companions day and night.

Your mental concept is what counts. Its relation to matter is that of idea and form. There must be an idea before it can take form. As Dr. Terry Walter says:

"The impressions that enter the subconscious form indelible pictures, which are never forgotten, and whose power can change the body, mind, manner, and morals; can, in fact, revolutionize a personality.

"All during our waking hours the conscious mind, through the five senses, acts as constant feeder to the subconscious; the senses are the temporal source of supply for the content of the soul mind; therefore, it is most important that we know and realize definitely and explicitly that every time we think a thought or feel an emotion, we are adding to the content of this powerful mind, good or bad, as the case may be. Life will be richer or poorer for the thoughts and deeds of today."

Your thoughts supply you with limitless energy which will take whatever form your mind demands. The thoughts are the mold which crystallizes this energy into good or ill according to the form you impress upon it. You are free to choose which. But whichever you choose, the result is sure. Thoughts of wealth, of power, of success, can bring only results commensurate with your idea of them. Thoughts of poverty and lack can bring only limitation and trouble. As one successful writer tersely warned—"If you don't want it, don't think it!"

"A radical doctrine," you may say, and think me wildly optimistic, because the world has been taught for so long to think that some must be rich and some poor, that trials and tribulations are our lot, that this is at best a vale of tears.

In the ages to come man will look back upon the poverty and wretchedness of so many millions today, and think how foolish we were not to take advantage of the abundance all about us. Look at Nature; how profuse she is in everything. Do you suppose the Mind that imaged such profuseness ever intended you to be limited, to have to scrimp and save in order to eke out a bare existence?

There are hundreds of millions of stars in the heavens. Do you suppose the Mind which could bring into being worlds without number in such prodigality intended to stint you of the few things necessary to your happiness?

What is money but a mere idea of mind, a token of exchange? The paper money you have in your pockets is supposed to represent so much gold or silver currency. There are billions upon billions of this paper money in circulation, yet all the gold in the world amounts to only a few billions. Wealth is in ideas, not in money or property. You can control those ideas through mind.

Reduced to the ultimate—to the atom or to the electron—everything in this world is an idea of mind. All of it has been brought together through mind. If we can change the things we want back into mental images, we can multiply them as often as we like, possess all that we like.

"TO HIM THAT HATH"

Take as an example the science of numbers. Suppose all numbers were of metal—that it was against the law to write figures for ourselves. Every time you wanted to do a sum in arithmetic you'd have to provide yourself with a supply of numbers, arrange them in their proper order, work out your problems with them. If your problems were too abstruse you might run out of numbers, have to borrow some from your neighbor or from the bank.

"How ridiculous," you say. "Figures are not things; they are mere ideas, and we can add them or divide them or multiply them or subtract them as often as we like. Anybody can have all the figures he wants."

To be sure he can. And when you get to look upon money in the same way, you will have all the money you want.

"To him that hath shall be given, and from him that hath not shall be taken away even that which he hath." To him that hath the right idea everything shall be given, and from him who hath not that right idea shall be taken away even that which he hath.

Thought externalizes itself. What we are depends entirely upon the images we hold before our mind's eye. Every time we think, we start a chain of causes which will create conditions similar to the thoughts which originated it, Every thought we hold in our consciousness for any length of time becomes impressed upon our subconscious mind and creates a pattern which the mind weaves into our life or environment.

All power is from within and is therefore under our own control. When you can direct your thought processes, you can consciously apply them to any condition, for all that comes to us from the world without is what we have already imaged in the world within.

Do you want more money? Money, you must remember, is merely a medium of exchange. It is the equivalent of so many hours of labor, so much skill, so many ideas. Your mind is possessed of unlimited ideas, and any idea of service to your fellow man can be turned into money. Since your mind is part of Universal Mind, there is no such thing as limitation or lack. Somewhere, somehow, the ideas that shall bring you all the money you need for any right purpose are available for you. You have but to put it up to your Higher Self to find these ideas, have utter faith in its willingness and its ability to do it—and then, when the ideas come, ACT upon them.

"What things soever ye desire, when ye pray, believe that ye receive it and ye shall have it." Don't forget that *"believe that ye receive it."* This it is that images the thing you want on your subconscious mind, and through it upon the super conscious. This it is that brings it to you. Once you can image the belief clearly on your subconscious mind, "whatsoever it is that ye ask for . . . ye shall have it."

For the source of all good, of everything you wish for, is the Universal Mind, and you can reach it only through the subconscious and your Higher Self—your part of the God-Mind.

Universal Mind will be to you whatever you believe it to be—the kind and loving Father whom Jesus pictured, always looking out for the well-being of his children—or the dread Judge that so many dogmatists would have us think.

When a man realizes that his mind is part of Universal Mind, when he realizes that he has only to take any right aspiration to this Universal Mind to see it realized, he loses all sense of worry and fear. He learns to dominate instead of to cringe. He rises to meet every situation, secure in the knowledge that everything necessary to the solution of any problem is in Mind, and that he has but to take his problem to Universal Mind to have it correctly answered.

Take a drop of water from the ocean, and you know that it has the same properties as all the rest of the water in the ocean, the same percentage of sodium chloride. The only difference between it and the ocean is in volume. Take a spark of electricity, and you know that it has the same properties as the thunderbolt, the same power that moves trains or runs giant machines in factories. Again the only difference is in volume. It is the same with your mind and Universal Mind. The only difference between them is in volume. Your mind has the same properties as the Universal Mind, the same creative genius, the same power over all the earth, the same access to all knowledge. Know this, believe it, use it, and "yours is the earth and the fulness thereof." In the exact proportion that you believe yourself to be part of Universal Mind, sharing in Its all-power, in that proportion can you demonstrate the mastery over your own body and over the world about you.

All growth, all supply is from the world-within. If you would have power, if you would have wealth, you have but to image it on this world within, on your subconscious mind, through belief and understanding.

If you would remove discord, you have but to remove the wrong images—images of ill health, of worry and trouble from within. The trouble with most of us is that we live entirely in the world without. We have no knowledge of that inner world which is responsible for all the conditions we meet and all the experiences we have. We have no conception of "the Father that is within us."

The inner world promises us life and health, prosperity and happiness—dominion over all the earth. It promises peace and perfection for all its offspring. It gives you the right way and the adequate way to accomplish any normal purpose. Business, labor, professions, exist primarily in thought. And the outcome of your labors in them is regulated by thought. Consider the difference, then, in this outcome if you have at your command only the limited capacity of your conscious mind, compared with the boundless energy of the subconscious and the Universal Mind. "Thought, not money, is the real business capital," said Harvey S. Firestone, "and if you know absolutely that what you are doing is right, then you are bound to accomplish it in due season."

Thought is a dynamic energy with the power to bring its object out from the invisible substance all about us. Matter is inert, unintelligent. Thought can shape and control. Every form in which matter is today is but the expression of some thought, some desire, some idea.

You have a mind. You can originate thought. And thoughts are creative. Therefore you can create for yourself that which you desire. Once you realize this you are taking a long step toward success in whatever undertaking you have in mind.

More than half the prophecies in the Scriptures refer to

the time when man shall possess the earth, when tears and sorrow shall be unknown, and peace and plenty shall be everywhere. That time will come. It is nearer than most people think possible. You are helping it along. Every man who is honestly trying to use the power of mind in the right way is doing his part in the great cause. For it is only through Mind that peace and plenty can be gained. The earth is laden with treasures as yet undiscovered. But they are every one of them known to Universal Mind, for it was Universal Mind that first imaged them there. And as part of Universal Mind, they can be known to you.

How else did the Prophets of old foretell, thousands of years ago, the airplane, the cannon, the radio? What was the genius that enabled Ezekiel to argue from his potter's wheel, his water wheel and the stroke of the lightning to an airplane, with its wheels within wheels, driven by electricity and guided by man? How are we to explain the descriptions of artillery in the Apocalypse and the astonishing declaration in the Gospels that the utterances of the chamber would be broadcast from the housetops?

"TO THE MANNER BORN"

Few of us have any idea of our mental powers. The old idea was that man must take this world as he found it. He had been born into a certain position in life, and to try to rise above his fellows was not only the height of bad taste, but sacrilegious as well. An All-wise Providence had decreed by birth the position a child should occupy in the web of organized society. For him to be discontented with his lot, for him to attempt to raise himself to a higher level, was tantamount to tempting Providence. The gates of Hell yawned wide for such scatterbrains, who were lucky if in this life they incurred nothing worse than the ribald scorn of their associates.

That is the system that produced aristocracy and feudalism. That is the system that feudalism and aristocracy strove to perpetuate.

The new idea—the basis of all democracies—is that man is not bound by any system, that he need not accept the world as he finds it. He can remake the world to his own ideas. It is merely the raw material. He can make what he wills of it.

It is this new idea that is responsible for all our inventions, all our progress. Man is satisfied with nothing. He is constantly remaking his world. And now more than ever will this be true, for psychology teaches us that each one has within himself the power to become what he wills.

Learn to control your thought. Learn to image upon your mind only the things you want to see reflected there.

You will never improve yourself by dwelling upon the drawbacks of your neighbors. You will never attain perfect health and strength by thinking of weakness or disease. No man ever made a perfect score by watching his rival's target. You have to think strength, think health, think riches.

To paraphrase Pascal—"Our achievements today are but the sum of our thoughts of yesterday."

For thought is energy. Mental images, are concentrated energy. And energy concentrated on any definite purpose becomes power. To those who perceive the nature and transcendency of this force, all physical power sinks into insignificance.

What is imagination but a form of thought? Yet it is the instrument by which all the inventors and discoverers have opened the way to new worlds. Those who grasp this force, be their state ever so humble, their natural gifts ever so insignificant, become our leading men. They are our governors and supreme law-givers, the guides of the drifting host which follows them as by an irrevocable decree. To quote Glenn Clark in the *Atlantic Monthly,* "Whatever we have of civilization is their work, theirs alone. If progress was made they made it. If spiritual facts were discerned, they discerned them. If justice and order were put in place of insolence and chaos, they wrought the change. Never is progress achieved by the masses. Creation ever remains the task of the individual."

Our railroads, our telephones, our automobiles, our libraries, our newspapers, our thousands of other conveniences, comforts and necessities are due to the creative genius of but two percent of our population.

And the same two percent own a great percentage of the wealth of the country.

The question arises, Who are they? What are they? The sons of the rich? No—few of them had any early advantages. Many of them have never seen the inside of a college. It was grim necessity that drove them, and somehow, some way, they found a method of drawing upon their Genie-of-the-Mind, and through that inner force they have reached success.

You don't need to stumble and grope. You can call upon your inner forces at will. There are three steps necessary:

First, to realize that you have the power;

Second, to know what you want.

Third, to center your thought upon it with singleness of purpose.

To accomplish these steps takes only a fuller understanding of the Power-that-is-within-you.

But what is this power? Where should you go to locate it? Is it a thing, a place, an object? Has it bounds, form or material shape? No! Then how shall you go about finding it?

If you have begun to *realize* that there is a power within you, if you have begun to arouse in your conscious mind the ambition and desire to use this power—you have started in the pathway of Wisdom. If you are willing to go forward, to endure the mental discipline of mastering this method, nothing in the world can hinder you or keep you from overcoming every obstacle.

Begin at once, today, to use what you have learned. All growth comes from practice. All the forces of life are active—peace—joy—power. The unused talent decays. Open the door—

"Behold I stand at the door and knock; if ANY MAN hear my voice and open the door, I will come in to him, and will sup with him and he with me."

So let us make use of this dynamo, which is *you.* What is going to start it working? Your *Faith,* the faith that is begotten of understanding. Faith is the impulsion, the propulsion of this power within. Faith is the confidence, the assurance, the enforcing truth, the knowing that the right idea of life will bring you into the reality of existence and the manifestation of All power.

All cause is in Mind—and Mind is everywhere. All the knowledge there is, all the wisdom there is, all the power there is, is all about you—no matter where you may be. Your Mind is part of it. You have access to it. If you fail to avail yourself of it, you have no one to blame but yourself. For as the drop of water in the ocean shares in all the properties of the rest of the ocean water, so you share in that all-power, all-wisdom of Mind. If you have been sick and ailing, if poverty and hardship have been your lot, don't blame it on "fate." Blame yourself. "Yours is the earth and everything that's in it." But you must *take* it. The power is there—but *you* must *use* it. It is round about you like the air you breathe. You don't expect others to do your breathing for you. Neither can you expect them to use your Mind for you. Universal Intelligence is not only the mind of the Creator of the universe, but it is also the mind of MAN, *your* intelligence, *your* mind, "Let this mind be in you, which was also in Christ Jesus!"

So start today by KNOWING that you can *do* anything you wish to do, *have* anything you wish to have, *be* anything you wish to be. The rest will follow.

"Ye shall ask what ye will and it shall be done unto you."

CHAPTER IV

DESIRE—THE FIRST LAW OF GAIN

If you had a fairy wishing ring, what one thing would you wish for? Wealth? Honor? Fame? Love? What one thing do you desire above everything else in life?

Whatever it is, you can have it. Whatever you desire wholeheartedly, with singleness of purpose—you can have. But the first and all-important essential is to know what this one thing is. Before you can win your heart's desire, you must get clearly fixed in your mind's eye what it is that you want.

It may sound paradoxical, but few people do know what they want. Most of them struggle along in a vague sort of way, hoping—like Micawber—for something to turn up. They are so taken up with the struggle that they have forgotten—if they ever knew—what it is they are struggling for. They are like a drowning man—they use up many times the energy it would take to get them somewhere, but they fritter it away in aimless struggles—without thought, without direction, exhausting themselves, while getting nowhere.

You have to know what you want before you stand much chance of getting it. You have an unfailing "Messenger to Garcia" in that Genie-of-Your-Mind—but YOU must formulate the message. Aladdin would have stood a poor chance of getting anything from his Genie if he had not had clearly in mind the things he wanted the Genie to get.

In the realm of mind, the realm in which is all practical power, you can possess what you want at once. You have but to claim it, visualize it, believe in it, to bring it into actuality. It is yours for the taking. For the Genie-of-Your-Mind can give you power over circumstances, health, happiness and prosperity. And all you need to put it to work is an earnest, intense desire.

Sounds too good to be true? Well, let us go back for a moment to the start. You are infected with that "divine dissatisfaction with things as they are" which has been responsible for all the great accomplishments of this world—else you would not have gotten thus far in this book. Your heart is hungering for something better. "Blessed are they which do hunger and thirst after righteousness (right-wiseness) for they shall be filled." You are tired of the worry and grind, tired of the deadly dull routine and daily tasks that lead nowhere. Tired of all the petty little ills and ailments that have come to seem the lot of man here on earth.

Always there is something within you urging you on to bigger things, giving you no peace, no rest, no chance to be lazy. It is the same "something" that drove Columbus across the ocean; that drove Hannibal across the Alps; that drove Edison onward and upward from a train boy to the inventive wizard of the century; that drove Henry Ford from a poor mechanic at forty to probably the richest man in the world at sixty.

This "something" within you keeps telling you that you can do anything you want to do, be anything you want to be, have anything you want to have—and you have a sneaking suspicion that it may be right.

That "something" within you is your Higher Self, your part of Universal Mind, your Genie-of-the-Brain. Men call it ambition, and "Lucky is the man," wrote Arthur Brisbane, "whom the Demon of Ambition harnesses and drives through life. This wonderful little coachman is the champion driver of all the world and of all history.

"Lucky you, if he is *your* driver.

"He will keep you going until you do something worth while—working, running and moving ahead.

"And that is how a real man ought to be driven.

"This is the little Demon that works in men's brains, that makes the blood tingle at the thought of achievement and that makes the face flush and grow white at the thought of failure.

"Every one of us has this Demon for a driver, IN YOUTH AT LEAST.

"Unfortunately the majority of us he gives up as very poor, hopeless things, not worth driving, by the time we reach twenty-five or thirty.

"How many men look back to their teens, when they were harnessed to the wagon of life with Ambition for a driver? When they could not wait for the years to pass and for opportunity to come?

"It is the duty of ambition to drive, and it is your duty to *keep Ambition alive and driving.*

"If you are doing nothing, if there is no driving, no hurrying, no working, *you may count upon it that there will be no results. Nothing much worth while in the years to come.*

"Those that are destined to be the big men twenty years from now, when the majority of us will be nobodies, *are those whom this demon is driving relentlessly, remorselessly, through the hot weather and the cold weather, through early hours and late hours.*

"Lucky YOU if you are in harness and driven by the Demon of Ambition."

Suppose you *have* had disappointments, disillusionments along the way. Suppose the fine point of your ambition has become blunted. Remember, there is no obstacle that there is not some way around, or over, or through—and if you will depend less upon the 10 percent of your abilities that reside in your conscious mind, and leave more to the 90 percent that constitute your subconscious and superconscious, you can overcome all obstacles. Remember this—there is no condition so hopeless, no life so far gone, that mind cannot redeem it.

Every untoward condition is merely *a lack* of something. Darkness, you know, is not real. It is merely a lack of light. Turn on the light and the darkness will be seen to be nothing. It vanishes instantly. In the same way poverty is simply a lack of necessary supply. Find the avenue of supply and your poverty vanishes. Sickness is merely the absence of health. If you are in perfect health, sickness cannot hurt you. Doctors and nurses go about at will among the sick without fear—and suffer as a rule far less from sickness than does the average man or woman.

So there is nothing you have to *overcome*. You merely have to *acquire* something. And always Mind can show you the way. You can obtain from Mind anything you want, if you will learn how to do it. "I think we can rest assured that one can do and be practically what he desires to be," says Farnsworth in "Practical Psychology." And psychologists all over the world have put the same thought in a thousand different ways.

"It is not will, but desire," says Charles W. Mears, "that rules the world." "But," you will say, "I have had plenty of desires all my life. I've always wanted to be rich. How do you account for the difference between my wealth and position and power and that of the rich men all around me?"

THE MAGIC SECRET

The answer is simply that you have never focused your desires into one great dominating desire. You have a host of mild desires. You mildly wish you were rich, you wish you had a position of responsibility and influence, you wish you could travel at will. The wishes are so many and varied that they conflict with each other and you get nowhere in particular. You lack one *intense* desire, to the accomplishment of which you are willing to subordinate everything else.

Do you know how Napoleon so frequently won battles in the face of a numerically superior foe? By concentrating his men at the actual *point of contact!* His artillery was often greatly outnumbered, but it accomplished far more than the enemy's because instead of scattering his fire, he *concentrated it all on the point of attack!*

The time you put in aimlessly dreaming and wishing would accomplish marvels if it were concentrated on one definite object. If you have ever taken a magnifying glass and let the sun's rays play through it on some object, you know that as long as the rays are scattered they accomplish nothing. But focus them on one tiny spot and see how quickly they start something.

It is the same way with your mind. You have to concentrate *on one idea at a time.*

"But how can I learn to concentrate?" many people ask. Concentration is not a thing to be learned. It is merely a thing to do. You concentrate whenever you become sufficiently interested in anything. Get so interested in a ball game that you jump up and down on your hat, slap a man you have never seen before on the back, embrace your nearest neighbor—*that* is concentration. Become so absorbed in a thrilling play or movie that you no longer realize the orchestra is playing or there are people around you—*that* is concentration.

And that is all concentration ever is—getting so interested in some one thing that you pay no attention to anything else that is going on around you.

If you want a thing badly enough, you need have no worry about your ability to concentrate on it. Your thoughts will just naturally center on it like bees on honey.

In his experiments at Duke University, Dr. J. B. Rhine has shown that the mind can definitely influence inanimate objects, but only when there is intense interest or desire.

When the subject's interest was distracted, when he failed to concentrate his attention, he had no power over the object. It was only as he gave his entire attention to it, concentrated his every energy upon it, that he got successful results.

Dr. Rhine has proved through physical experiments what most of us have always believed—that there is a Power over and above the merely physical power of the mind or body, that through intense concentration or desire we can link up with that Power, and that once we do, nothing is impossible to us.

Man is no longer at the mercy of blind chance or Fate. He can control his own destiny. Science is at last proving what Religion has taught from the beginning—that God gave men *dominion,* and that we have only to understand and use this dominion to become the Masters of our Fate, the Captains of our Souls.

So hold in your mind the things you most desire. Affirm them. Believe them to be existing facts. Let me quote again the words of the Master, because there is nothing more important to remember in this whole book. "Therefore I say unto you, what things soever ye desire when ye pray, *believe that ye receive them* and ye shall have them."

And again I say, the most important part is the *"believe that ye receive them."* Your subconscious mind is exceedingly amenable to suggestion. If you can truly believe that you *have* received something, you impress that belief upon your subconscious mind, which in turn passes it along to the superconscious. Being a part of Universal Mind, sharing that Universal Mind's all-power, it has only to put the Creative Force all about it into the mold of your thought and bring the object into being. "The Father that is within me, He doeth the works." Your mind will respond to your desire in the exact proportion in which you believe. "As thy faith is, so be it unto thee."

The people who live in beautiful homes, who have plenty to spend, who travel about in yachts and fine cars, are for the most part people who started out to accomplish *some one definite thing.* They had one clear goal in mind, and everything they did centered on that goal.

Most men just jog along in a rut, going through the same old routine day after day, eking out a bare livelihood, with no definite desire other than the vague hope that fortune will some day drop in their lap. Fortune doesn't often play such pranks. And a rut, you know, differs from a grave only in depth. A life such as that is no better than the animals live. Work all day for money to buy bread, to give you strength to work all the next day to buy more bread. There is nothing to it but the daily search for food and sustenance. No time for aught but worry and struggle. No hope of anything but the surcease of sorrow in death.

You can *have* anything you want—if you want it badly enough. You can *be* anything you want to be, *have* anything you desire, *accomplish* anything you set out to accomplish—if you will hold to that desire with singleness of purpose; if you will understand and BELIEVE in your own powers to accomplish.

What is it that you wish in life? Is it health? In the chapter on health we shall show you that you can be radiantly well—without drugs, without tedious exercises. It matters not if you are crippled or bedridden or infirm. Your body rebuilds itself largely every eleven months. You can start now rebuilding along perfect lines.

Is it wealth you wish? In the chapter on success we shall show you how you can increase your income, how you can forge rapidly ahead in your chosen business or profession.

Is it happiness you ask for? Follow the rules herein laid down and you will change your whole outlook on life. Doubts and uncertainty will vanish, to be followed by calm assurance and abiding peace. You will possess the things your heart desires. You will have love and companionship. You will win to contentment and happiness.

But desire must be impressed upon the subconscious before it can be accomplished. Merely conscious desire seldom gets you anything. It is like the day dreams that pass through your mind. Your desire must be visualized, must be persisted in, must be concentrated upon, must be impressed upon your subconscious mind before it can reach the superconscious or *Creative Mind.* Don't bother about the means for accomplishing your desire—you can safely leave these to our superconscious mind. If you can visualize the thing you want, if you can impress upon your subconscious mind the *belief that you have it,* you can safely leave to your Higher Self the finding of the means of getting it. Trust the Universal Mind to show the way. The mind that provided everything in such profusion must joy *in* seeing us take advantage of that profusion. "For herein is the Father glorified—that ye bear much fruit."

You do not have to wait until tomorrow, or next year, or the next world, for happiness. You do not have to wait to be saved. "The Kingdom of Heaven is within you." That does not mean that it is up in the heavens or on some star or in the next world. It means *here* and *now!* All the possibilities of happiness are always here and always available. At the open door of every man's life there lies this pearl of great price—the understanding of man's dominion over the earth. With that understanding and conviction you can do everything which lies before you to do and you can do it to the satisfaction of everyone and the well-being of yourself. God and good are synonymous. And God—good—is absent only to those who believe He is absent.

Find your desire, impress it upon your thought, and you have opened the door for opportunity. And remember, in this new heaven and new earth which we are trying to show you, *the door of opportunity is never closed.* As a matter of fact, you constantly have *all that you will take.* So keep yourself in a state of receptivity. It is your business to receive abundantly and perpetually. The law of opportunity enforces its continuance and availability. "Every good gift and every perfect gift is from above and cometh down from the Father of light, with whom is *no variableness, neither shadow of turning.*"

Infinite Mind saith to every man, "Come ye to the open fountain." The understanding of the law of life will remedy every discord, giving "Beauty for ashes, the oil of joy for mourning, the garment of praise for the spirit of heaviness."

Believe that you share in that goodness and bounty. Act the part you wish to play in this life. Act healthy, act prosperous, act happy. Make such a showing with what you have that you will carry the conviction to your subconscious mind that all good and perfect gifts ARE yours. Register health, prosperity and happiness on your inner mind and some fine morning soon you will wake to find that *you are* healthy, prosperous and happy, that you *have* your dearest wish in life.

"THE SOUL'S SINCERE DESIRE"

Do you know what prayer is? Just an earnest desire that we take to God—to Universal Mind—for fulfillment. As Montgomery puts it—"Prayer is the soul's *sincere desire,* uttered or unexpressed." It is our Heart's Desire. At least, the only prayer that is worth anything is the prayer that asks for our real desires. That kind of prayer is heard. That kind of prayer is answered.

Mere lip prayers get you nowhere. It doesn't matter what your lips may say. The thing that counts is what your heart desires, what your mind images on your subconscious thought, and through it on your part of Universal Mind. "Thou, when thou prayest, be not as the hypocrites are; for they love to pray standing in the synagogue and at the corners of the streets, that they may be seen of men. Verily I say unto you, they have their reward."

What was it these hypocrites that Jesus speaks of really wanted? "To be seen of men." And their prayers were answered. Their sincere desire was granted. They were seen of men. "They have their reward." But as for what their lips were saying, neither God nor they paid any attention to it.

"Thou, when thou prayest, enter into thy closet, and when thou hast shut the door, pray to thy Father which is in secret, and thy Father which seeth in secret, shall reward thee openly." Go where you can be alone, where you can concentrate your thoughts on your one innermost sincere desire, where you can impress that desire upon your subconscious mind without distraction, and so reach the Universal Mind (the Father of all things).

But even sincere desire is not enough by itself. There must be BELIEF, too, "What things soever ye desire, when ye pray, believe that ye receive them and ye shall have them." You must realize God's ability to give you every good thing. You must believe in his readiness to do it. Model your thoughts after the Psalmists of old. They first asked for that which they wanted, then killed all doubts and fears by affirming God's power and His willingness to grant their prayers. Read any of the Psalms and you will see what I mean. So when you pray, ask for the things that you want. Then affirm God's readiness and His Power to grant your prayer, and THANK Him for having done so.

Glenn Clark, in "The Soul's Sincere Desire," gives some wonderfully helpful suggestions along these lines. To quote him:

"For money troubles, realize: There is no want in Heaven, and affirm:

> Our Heavenly Father, we know that thy Love is as infinite as the sky is infinite, and Thy Ways of manifesting that love are as unaccountable as the stars of the heavens.
>
> Thy Power is greater than man's horizon, and Thy Ways of manifesting that Power are more numerous than the sands of the sea.
>
> As Thou keepest the stars in their courses, so shalt Thou guide our steps in perfect harmony, without clash or discord of any kind, if we keep our trust in Thee. For we know Thou wilt keep him in perfect peace whose mind is stayed on Thee, because he trusteth in Thee. We know that, if we acknowledge Thee in all our ways, Thou wilt direct our paths. For Thou art the God of Love, Giver of every good and

> perfect gift, and there is none beside Thee. Thou art omnipotent, omniscient, and omnipresent, in all, through all, and over all, the only God. And Thine is the Kingdom, and the Power, and the Glory, forever, Amen.

"For aid in thinking or writing, realize: There is no lack of ideas, and affirm:

> Thy wisdom is greater than all hidden treasures, and yet as instantly available for our needs as the very ground beneath our feet.

"For happiness: There is no unhappiness in Heaven, so affirm:

> Thy joy is brighter than the sun at noonday and Thy Ways of expressing that Joy as countless as the sunbeams that shine upon our path.

This is the kind of prayer the Psalmists of old had recourse to in their hours of trouble—this is the kind of prayer that will bring you every good and perfect gift.

Make no mistake about this—*prayer is effective.* It *can* do anything. It doesn't matter how trivial your desires may be—if it is RIGHT for you to have them, it is RIGHT for you to pray for them.

According to a United Press dispatch some time ago:

"Prayer belongs to the football field as much as to the pulpit, and a praying team stands a good chance of 'getting there,' Tim Lowry, Northwestern University football star, told a large church audience here.

" 'Just before the Indiana-Northwestern game last year,' Tim said, "we worried a great deal about the outcome. Then we saw that bunch of big husky Indiana players coming toward us and we knew something had to be done quick.

" 'Fellows,' I said, 'I believe in prayer and we better pray.' We did and won a great victory.

"When the next game came, every fellow prayed again.

"You don't need to think that churches have a copyright on prayer."

In "Prayer As a Force," A. Maude Royden compares the man who trusts his desires to prayer with the swimmer who trusts himself to the water:

"Let me give you a very simple figure which I think may perhaps convey my meaning. If you are trying to swim you must believe that the sea is going to keep you afloat. You must give yourself to the sea. There is the ocean and there are you in it, and I say to you, 'According to your faith you will be able to swim!' I know perfectly well that it is literally according to your faith. A person who has just enough confidence in the sea and in himself to give one little hop from the ground will certainly find that the water will lift him but not very much; he will come down again. Persons who have enough confidence really to start swimming but no more, will not swim very far, because their confidence is so very small and they swim with such rapid strokes, and they hold their breath to such an extent, that by and by they collapse; they swim five or six, or twelve or fourteen strokes, but they do not get very far, through lack of confidence.

"Persons who know with assurance that the sea will carry them if they do certain things, will swim quite calmly, serenely, happily, and will not mind if the water goes right over them. 'Oh,' you say, 'that person is doing the whole thing!' *He can't do it without the sea!* You might hypnotize people into faith; you might say, 'You are now in the ocean; swim off the edge of this precipice.' You might make them do it, they might have implicit faith in you, you might hypnotize them into thinking they were swimming; but if they swam off the edge of the cliff they would fall. You can't swim without the sea! I might say to you, 'It lies with you whether you swim or not, according to your faith be it unto you'; but if the sea is not there you can't swim. That is exactly what I feel about God. 'According to your faith be it unto you.' Yes, certainly, if you try to swim in that ocean which is the love of God your faith will be rewarded, and according to your faith it will be to you. In exact proportion to your faith you will find the answer, like a scientific law. There is not one atom of faith you put in God that will not receive its answer."

But remember: you would not plant a valuable seed in

your garden, and then, a day or a week later, go out and dig it up to see if it were sprouting. On the contrary, you would nourish it each morning with water. It is the same with your prayers. Don't plant the seed of your desire in your subconscious mind and then go out the next morning and tear it up with doubts and fears. Nourish it by holding in thought the thing you desire, by believing in it, visualizing it, SEEING it as an accomplished fact.

If you ask for our own formula for successful prayer, we would say—

First. Center your thoughts on the thing that you want. Visualize it. Make a mental image of it—in fact, make an actual picture of it if you can. You are planting the seed of Desire. But don't be content with that. Planting alone will not make a seed of corn grow. It has to be warmed by sunshine, nurtured by rain. So with the seed of your Desire.

It must be warmed by Faith, nurtured by constant Belief. So—

Second. Read the 91st and the 23rd Psalms, just as a reminder of God's power and His readiness to help you in all your needs.

Third. Don't forget to be thankful, not merely for past favors, *but for the granting of this favor you are now asking!* To be able to thank God for it sincerely, in advance of its actual material manifestation, is the finest evidence of belief.

Fourth. BELIEVE! See it as an accomplished fact. When the thought of it occurs to you, and doubts and fears creep in, say to yourself—"God is attending to that," and KNOW THAT HE IS!

It is this sincere conviction, registered upon your subconscious mind, and through it upon your part of Universal Mind, that brings the answer to your prayers. Once convince your subconscious mind that you HAVE the thing you want, and you can forget it and go on to your next problem. Mind will attend to the bringing of it into being.

CHAPTER V

ALADDIN & COMPANY

But the feeble hands and helpless,
Groping blindly in the darkness,
Touch God's right hand in that darkness,
And are lifted up and strengthened.

—LONGFELLOW

It is not always the man who struggles hardest who gets on in the world. It is the direction as well as the energy of struggle that counts in making progress. To get ahead—you must swim with the tide. Men prosper and succeed who work in accord with natural forces. A given amount of effort with these forces carries a man faster and farther than much more effort used against the current. Those who work blindly, regardless of these forces, make life difficult for themselves and rarely prosper.

It has been estimated by wise observers that on the average something like 60 percent of the factors producing success or failure lie outside a man's conscious efforts—

separate from his daily round of details. To the extent that he cooperates with the wisdom and power of Universal Mind he is successful, well and happy. To the extent that he fails to cooperate, he is unsuccessful, sick and miserable.

All down the ages some have been enabled to "taste and see that the Lord is good." Prophets and Seers being blessed with the loving kindness of God, have proclaimed a God of universal goodness, saying: "The earth is full of the goodness of the Lord"; "Thou wilt show me the path of life; in Thy presence is fullness of joy."

Now we know that this Infinite Good is not more available to one than it is to all. We *know* that the only limit to it is in our capacity to receive. If you had a problem in mathematics to work out, you would hardly gather together the necessary figures and leave them to arrange themselves in their proper sequence. You would know that while the method for solving every problem has been figured out, *you* have to *work* it. The principles are there, but *you* have to *apply* them.

The first essential is to understand the principle—to learn how it works—how to use it. The second is to APPLY that understanding to the problem in hand.

In the same way, the Principle of Infinite Energy, of Vital Force, is ever available. But that Energy, that Force, is static. It is up to you to make it dynamic. You must understand the law. You must *apply* your understanding in order to solve your problems of poverty, discord, disease.

Science shows that it is possible to accomplish any good thing. But distrust of your ability to reach the goal desired often holds you back and failure is the inevitable result.

Only by understanding that there is but one power—and that this power is Mind, not circumstances or environment—is it possible to bring your real abilities to the surface and put them to work.

Few deny that intelligence governs the universe. It matters not whether you call this intelligence Universal Mind or Providence or God or merely Nature. All admit Its directing power. All admit that It is a force for good, for progress. But few realize that our own minds are a part of this Universal Mind in just the same way that the rays of the sun are part of the sun.

If we work in harmony with It, we can draw upon Universal Mind for all power, all intelligence, in the same way that the sun's rays draw upon their source for the heat and light they bring the earth.

It is not enough to *know* that you have this power. You must put it into *practice*—not once, or twice, but *every hour and every day.* Don't be discouraged if it seems at times not to work. When you first studied arithmetic, your problems did not always work out correctly, did they? Yet you did not on that account doubt the principle of mathematics. You knew that the fault was with your methods, not with the principle. It is the same in this. The power is there. Correctly used, it can do anything.

All will agree that the Mind which first brought the Life

Principle to this earth—which imaged the earth itself and the trees and the plants and the animals—is all-powerful. All will agree that to solve any problem, to meet any need, Mind has but to *realize* the need and it will be met. What most of us do not understand or realize is that we ourselves, being part of Universal Mind, have this same power. Just as the drop of water from the ocean has all the properties of the great bulk of the water in the ocean. Just as the spark of electricity has all the properties of the thunderbolt. And having that power, we have only to realize it and use it to get from life any good we may desire.

In the beginning all was void—space—nothingness. How did Universal Mind construct the planets, the firmaments, the earth and all things on and in it from this formless void? *By first making a mental image on which to build.*

That is what you, too, must do. You control your destiny, your fortune, your happiness to the exact extent to which you can think them out, VISUALIZE them, SEE them, BELIEVE in them, and allow no vagrant thought of fear or worry to mar their completion and beauty. The quality of your thought is the measure of your power. Clear, forceful thought has the power of attracting to itself everything it may need for the fruition of those thoughts. As W. D. Wattles put it in his "Science of Getting Rich":

"There is a thinking stuff from which all things are made and which, in its original state, permeates, penetrates, and fills the interspaces of the universe. A thought in this substance produces the thing that is imagined by the thought. Man can form things in his thought, and, by impressing his thought upon formless substance, can cause the thing he thinks about to be created."

The connecting link between your conscious mind and the Universal is thought, and every thought that is in harmony with progress and good, every thought that is freighted with the right idea, can penetrate to Universal Mind. And penetrating to it, it comes back with the power of Universal Mind to accomplish it. You don't need to originate the ways and means. The Universal Mind knows how to bring about any necessary results. There is but one right way to solve any given problem. When your human judgment is unable to decide what that one right way is, turn to Universal Mind for guidance. You need never fear the outcome, for if you heed its advice you cannot go wrong.

Always remember—your mind is but a conductor—good or poor as you make it—for the power of Universal Mind. And thought is the connecting energy. Use that conductor, and you will improve its conductivity. Demand much, and you will receive the more. The Universal is not a niggard in any of its gifts. "Ask and ye shall receive, seek and ye shall find, knock and it shall be opened unto you."

That is the law of life. And the destiny of man lies not in poverty and hardship, but in living up to his high estate in unity with Universal Mind, with the power that governs the universe.

To look upon poverty and sickness as sent by God and therefore inevitable, is the way of the weakling. God never sent us anything but good. What is more, He has never yet failed to give to those who would use them the means to overcome any condition not of His making. Sickness and poverty are not of His making. They are not evidences of virtue, *but of weakness.* God gave us everything in abundance, and he expects us to manifest that abundance. If you had a son you loved very much, and you surrounded him with good things which he had only to exert himself in order to reach, you wouldn't like it if he showed himself to the world half-starved, ill-kempt and clothed in rags, merely because he was unwilling to exert himself enough to reach for the good things you had provided. No more, in my humble opinion, does God.

Man's principal business in life, as I see it, is to establish a contact with Universal Mind. It is to acquire an understanding of this power that is in him. "With all thy getting, get understanding," said Solomon.

Happy is the man that findeth wisdom,
And the man that getteth understanding.
For the gaining of it is better than the gaining of silver.
And the profit thereof than fine gold.
She is more precious than rubies:
And none of the things thou canst desire are to be
compared unto her.
Length of days is in her right hand:
In her left hand are riches and honor.
Her ways are ways of pleasantness,

And all her paths are peace.
She is a tree of life to them that lay hold upon her.
And happy is every one that retaineth her.

—PROVERBS

When you become conscious, even to a limited degree, of your one-ness with Universal Mind, your ability to call upon It at will for anything you may need, it makes a different man of you. Gone are the fears, gone are the worries. You know that your success, your health, your happiness will be measured only by the degree to which you can impress the fruition of your desires upon mind.

The toil and worry, the wearisome grind and the back-breaking work, will go in the future as in the past to those who will not use their minds. The less they use them, the more they will sweat. And the more they work only from the neck down, the less they will be paid and the more hopeless their lot will become. *It is Mind that rules the world.*

But to use your mind to the best advantage does not mean to toil along with the mere conscious part of it. It means hitching up your conscious mind with the Man Inside You, with the little "Mental Brownies," as Robert Louis Stevenson called them, and then working together for a definite end.

"My Brownies! God bless them!" said Stevenson, "Who do one-half of my work for me when I am fast asleep, and in all human likelihood do the rest for me as well when I am wide awake and foolishly suppose that I do it myself. I had long been wanting to write a book on man's double being. For two days I went about racking my brains for a plot of any sort, and on the second night I dreamt the scene in Dr. Jekyll and Mr. Hyde at the window; and a scene, afterward split in two, in which Hyde, pursued, took the powder and underwent the change in the presence of his pursuer."

Many another famous writer has spoken in similar strain, and every man who has problems to solve has had like experiences. You know how, after you have studied a problem from all angles, it sometimes seems worse jumbled than when you started on it. Leave it then for a while—forget it—and when you go back to it, you find your thoughts clarified, the line of reasoning worked out, your problem solved for you. It is your little "Mental Brownies" who have done the work for you!

The flash of genius does not originate in your own brain. Through intense concentration you establish a circuit through your subconscious mind with the Universal, and it is from It that the inspiration comes. All genius, all progress, is from the same source. It lies with you merely to learn how to establish this circuit at will so that you can call upon It at need. It can be done.

"In the Inner Consciousness of each of us," quotes Dumont in "The Master Mind," "there are forces which act much the same as would countless tiny mental brownies or helpers who are anxious and willing to assist us in our mental work, if we will but have confidence and trust in them.

This is a psychological truth expressed in the terms of the old fairy tales. The process of calling into service these Inner Consciousness helpers is similar to that which we constantly employ to recall some forgotten fact or name. We find that we cannot recollect some desired fact, date, or name, and instead of racking our brains with an increased effort, we (if we have learned the secret) pass on the matter to the Inner Consciousness with a silent command, 'Recollect this name for me,' and then go on with our ordinary work. After a few minutes—or it may be hours—all of a sudden, pop! will come the missing name or fact before us—flashed from the planes of the Inner Consciousness, by the help of the kindly workers or 'brownies' of those planes. The experience is so common that we have ceased to wonder at it, and yet it is a wonderful manifestation of the Inner Consciousness' workings of the mind. Stop and think a moment, and you will see that the missing word does not present itself accidentally, or 'just because.' There are mental processes at work for your benefit, and when they have worked out the problem for you they gleefully push it up from their plane on to the plane of the outer consciousness where you may use it.

"We know of no better way of illustrating the matter than by this fanciful figure of the 'mental brownies,' in connection with the illustration of the 'subconscious storehouse.' If you would learn to take advantage of the work of these Subconscious Brownies, we advise you to form a mental picture of the Subconscious Storehouse in which is stored all sorts of knowledge that you have placed there during your lifetime, as well as the impressions that you have acquired by race inheritance—racial memory, in fact. The information stored away has often been placed in the storage rooms without any regard for systematic storing, or arrangement, and when you wish to find something that has been stored away there a long time ago, the exact place being forgotten, you are compelled to call to your assistance the little brownies of the mind, which perform faithfully your mental command, 'Recollect this for me!' These brownies are the same little chaps that you charge with the task of waking you at four o'clock tomorrow morning when you wish to catch an early train—and they obey you well in this work of the mental alarm clock. These same little chaps will also flash into your consciousness the report, 'I have an engagement at two o'clock with Jones'—when looking at your watch you will see that it is just a quarter before the hour of two, the time of your engagement.

"Well then, if you will examine carefully into a subject which you wish to master, and will pass along the results of your observations to these Subconscious Brownies, you will find that they will work the raw materials of thought into shape for you in a comparatively short time. They will analyze, systematize, collate, and arrange in consecutive order the various details of information which you have passed on to them, and will add thereto the articles of similar information that they will find stored away in the recesses of your memory. In this way they will group together various scattered bits of knowledge that you have forgotten. And, right here, let us say to you that you never absolutely forget anything that you have placed in your mind. You may be unable to recollect certain things, but they are not lost—sometime later some associative connection will be made with some other fact, and lo! the missing idea will be found fitted nicely into its place in the larger idea—the work of our little brownies. Remember Thompson's statement: 'In view of having to wait for the results of these unconscious processes, I have proved the habit of getting together material in advance, and then leaving the mass to digest itself until I am ready to write about it.' This subconscious 'digestion' is really the work of our little mental brownies.

"There are many ways of setting the brownies to work. Nearly everyone has had some experience, more or less, in the matter, although often it is produced almost unconsciously, and without purpose and intent. Perhaps the best way for the average person—or rather the majority of persons—to get the desired results is for one to get as clear an idea of what one really wants to know—as clear an idea or mental image of the question you wish answered. Then after rolling it around in your mind—mentally chewing it, as it were—giving it a high degree of voluntary attention, you can pass it on to your Subconscious Mentality with the mental command: *'Attend to this for me—work out the answer!'* or some similar order, This command may be given silently, or else spoken aloud—either will do. Speak to the Subconscious Mentality—or its little workers—just as you would speak to persons in your employ, kindly but firmly.

Talk to the little workers, and firmly command them to do your work. And then forget all about the matter—throw it off your conscious mind, and attend to your other tasks. Then in due time will come your answer—flashed into your consciousness—perhaps not until the very minute that you must decide upon the matter, or need the information. You may give your brownies orders to report at such and such a time—just as you do when you tell them to awaken you at a certain time in the morning so as to catch the early train, or just as they remind you of the hour of your appointment, if you have them all well trained."

Have you ever read the story by Richard Harding Davis of "The Man Who Could Not Lose?" In it the hero is intensely interested in racing. He has studied records and "dope" sheets until he knows the history of every horse backward and forward.

The day before the big race he is reclining in an easy chair, thinking of the morrow's race, and he drops off to sleep with that thought on his mind. Naturally, his subconscious mind takes it up, with the result that he dreams the exact outcome of the race.

That was mere fiction, of course, but if races were run solely on the speed and stamina of the horses, it would be possible to work out the results in just that way. Unfortunately, other factors frequently enter into every betting game.

But the idea behind Davis' story is entirely right. The way to contact your subconscious mind, the way to get the help of the "Man Inside You" in working out any problem is:

First, fill your mind with every bit of information regarding that problem that you can lay your hands on.

Second, pick out a chair or lounge or bed where you can recline in perfect comfort, where you can forget your body entirely.

Third, let your mind dwell upon the problem for a moment, not worrying, not fretting, but placidly, and then turn it over to the "Man Inside You." Say to him—"This is your problem. You can do anything. You know the answer to everything. Work this out for me!" And utterly relax. Drop off to sleep, if you can. At least, drop into one of those half-sleepy, half-wakeful reveries that keep other thoughts from obtruding upon your consciousness. Do as Aladdin did—summon your Genie, give him your orders, then forget the matter, secure in the knowledge that he will attend to it for you. When you waken, *you will have the answer!*

For whatever thought, whatever problem you can get across to your subconscious mind at the moment of dropping off to sleep, that "Man Inside You," that Genie-of-Your-Mind will work out for you.

In "The Workshop of the Unconscious," published in "The American Mercury" some time ago, Professor Brand Blanshard of Yale University gave the five steps necessary to set the subconscious to work on a definite problem:

"1. Specify your problem consciously. Coin it at the beginning into a perfectly definite question. Remember that thinking is not musing, or wool-gathering, or dreaming, or daydreaming, or 'inviting one's soul'; it is the attempt to find a suggestion that will settle a particular point, and if there is no point to settle, thought is left without guidance.

"2. Mobilize at the outset the resources you already have. Carry the making of conscious suggestions as far as you can; that will start the unconscious ball rolling with a vigorous push.

"3. Take time. The unconscious dislikes being hurried; it will not be bullied. If you attempt to bully it, it will probably go on strike. . . . Sleep on a decision for a single night—and it will be a better decision. And the more time the unconscious can get, the better it likes it.

"4. Seize the intimations of the unconscious when they come. They may come at any time and in any volume. . . . Stop what you are doing abruptly. Listen quietly but intently to such voices as you can hear; if the time is ripe, you will find that they come in increasing volume and perhaps that in one pregnant half-hour everything essential in your speech or article is there before you.

"5. Don't confuse unconscious thinking with worry. Both, to be sure, are forms of brooding. But in fact they are mortal enemies. Worry is half-conscious fear, and fear freezes the very springs of thought and action. . . . Creative work is impossible to minds preoccupied and distraught. It is pleasant to think that genius blows where it lists and will make its way through any circumstances, but there is little truth in the notion. . . . No mind can create while it is divided against itself. For that reason it is well, at times, to give up conscious effort and let the unconscious have its way with us."

Of course, not everyone can succeed in getting his thoughts across to the subconscious at the first or the second attempt. It requires understanding and faith, just as the working out of problems in mathematics requires an understanding of and faith in the principles of mathematics. But keep on trying, and you WILL do it. And when you do, *the results are sure.*

If it is something that you want, VISUALIZE it first in your mind's eye, see it in every possible detail, see yourself going through every move it will be necessary for you to go through when your wish comes into being. Build up a complete story, step by step, just as though you were acting it all out. Get from it every ounce of pleasure and satisfaction that you can. Be *thankful* for this gift that has come to you. It helps if you make a "Treasure Map" of the thing you want. Cut out pictures from magazines showing objects as nearly like those you desire as you can find. Paste these pictures on a sheet of paper and all around them write affirmations to the effect that you HAVE the things you want, verses from the Bible promising us everything of good, etc. Then relax; go to sleep if you can; give the "Man Inside You" a chance to work out the consummation of your wish without interference.

When you waken, hold it all pleasurably in thought again for a few moments. Don't let doubts and fears creep in, but go ahead, confidently, knowing that your wish is working itself out. Know this, believe it—and if there is nothing harmful in it, IT WILL WORK OUT!

But remember that your subconscious must be convinced of the reality of your belief that you HAVE the thing you ask for, so it is important that you DO something to convince it. If you have prayed for a home, go out and buy some furnishing for it, even if it be only some kitchenware from the 5 and 10 cent store. Or get some boards and start making shelves for your closets. If you have asked for money, start GIVING some to charity, as you would if you had plenty. ACT THE PART! As Emerson put it—"Do the thing, and you shall have the reward."

Somewhere in Universal Mind there exists the correct solution of every problem. It matters not how stupendous and complicated, or how simple a problem may appear to be. There always exists the right solution in Universal Mind. And because this solution does exist, there also exists the ability to ascertain and to prove what that solution is. You can know, and you can do, every right thing. Whatever it is necessary for you to know, whatever it is necessary for you to do, you can know and you can do, if you will but seek the help of Universal Mind and be governed by its suggestions.

Try this method every night for a little while, and the problem does not exist that you cannot solve.

CHAPTER VI

SEE YOURSELF DOING IT

You say big corporations scheme
To keep a fellow down;
They drive him, shame him, starve him, too,
If he so much as frown.
God knows I hold no brief for them;
Still, come with me to-day
And watch those fat directors meet,
For this is what they say:
"In all our force not one to take
The new work that we plan!
In all the thousand men we've hired
Where shall we find a man?"

—ST. CLAIR ADAMS*

*From "It Can Be Done." George Sully & Company.

You've often heard it said that a man is worth two dollars a day from the neck down. How much he is worth from the neck up depends upon how much he is able to SEE.

"Without vision the people perish" did not refer to good eyesight. It was the eyes of the mind that counted in days of old just as they do today. Without them you are just so much power "on the hoof," to be driven as a horse or an ox is driven. And you are worth only a little more than they.

But given vision—imagination—the ability to visualize conditions and things a month or a year ahead; given the eyes of the mind—there is no limit to your value or to your capabilities.

The locomotive, the steamboat, the automobile, the airplane—all existed complete in the imagination of some man before ever they became facts. The wealthy men, the big men, the successful men, visioned their successes in their minds' eyes before ever they won them from the world.

From the beginning of time, nothing has ever taken on material shape without first being visualized in mind. The only difference between the sculptor and the mason is in the mental image behind their work. Rodin employed masons to hew his block of marble into the general shape of the figure he was about to form. *That was mere mechanical labor.* Then Rodin took it in hand and from that rough hewn piece of stone there sprang the wondrous figure of "The Thinker." *That was art!*

The difference was all in the imagination behind the hands that wielded mallet and chisel. After Rodin had formed his masterpiece, ordinary workmen copied it by the thousands. Rodin's work brought fabulous sums. The copies brought day wages. Conceiving ideas—*creating something—is* what pays, in sculpture as in all else. Mere handwork is worth only hand wages.

"The imagination," says Glenn Clark in "The Soul's Sincere Desire," "is of all qualities in man the most Godlike—that which associates him most closely with God. The first mention we read of man in the Bible is where he is spoken of as an 'image.' 'Let us make man in our image, after our likeness.' The only place where an image can be conceived is in the imagination. Thus man, the highest creation of God, was a creation of God's imagination.

"The source and center of all man's creative power—the power that above all others lifts him above the level of brute creation, and that gives him dominion, is his power of making images, or the power of the imagination. There are some who have always thought that the imagination was something which makes-believe that which is not. This is fancy—not imagination. Fancy would convert that which is real into pretense and sham; imagination enables one to see through the appearance of a thing to what it really *is.*"

There is a very real law of cause and effect which makes the dream of the dreamer come true. It is the law of visualization—the law that calls into being in this outer material world everything that is real in the inner world. Imagination pictures the thing you desire. VISION idealizes it. It reaches beyond the thing that is, into the conception of what can be. Imagination gives you the picture. Vision gives you the impulse to make the picture your own.

Make your mental image clear enough, picture it vividly in every detail, BELIEVE in it, and the Genie-of-Your-Mind" will speedily bring it into being as an everyday reality.

That law holds true of everything in life. There is nothing you can rightfully desire that cannot be brought into being through visualization.

Suppose there is a position you want—the general managership of your company. See yourself—just as you are now—sitting in the general manager's chair. See your name on his door. See yourself handling his affairs as you would handle them. Get that picture impressed upon your subconscious mind. See it! *Believe it!* The Genie-of-Your-Mind will find the way to make it come true.

The keynote of successful visualization is this: See things as you would have them be instead of as they are. Close your eyes and make clear mental pictures. Make them look and act just as they would in real life. In short, day dream—but day dream with a purpose. Better still, get those pictures down on paper using, if you need to, pictures of similar things cut from magazines. Concentrate on one idea at a time to the exclusion of all others, and continue to concentrate on that one idea until it has been accomplished.

Do you want an automobile? A home? A factory? They can all be won in the same way. They are all in their essence ideas of mind, and if you will but build them up in your own mind first, stone by stone, complete in every detail, you will find that the Genie-of-Your-Mind can build them up similarly in the material world.

"The building of a transcontinental railroad from a mental picture," says C. W. Chamberlain in "The Uncommon Sense of Applied Psychology," "gives the average individual an idea that it is a big job. The fact of the matter is, the achievement, as well as the perfect mental picture, is made up of millions of little jobs, each fitting in its proper place and helping to make up the whole.

"A skyscraper is built from individual bricks, the laying of each brick being a single job which must be completed before the next brick can be laid."

It is the same with any work, any study. To quote Professor James:

"As we become permanent drunkards by so many separate drinks, so we become saints in the moral, and authorities and experts in the practical and scientific spheres, by so many separate acts and hours of working. Let no youth have any anxiety about the upshot of his education whatever the line of it may be. If he keep faithfully busy each hour of the working day he may safely leave the final result to itself. He can with perfect certainty count on waking some fine morning, to find himself one of the competent ones of his generation, in whatever pursuit he may have singled out. . . . Young people should know this truth in advance. The ignorance of it has probably engendered more discouragement and faintheartedness in youths embarking on arduous careers than all other causes taken together."

Remember that the only limit to your capabilities is the one you place upon them. There is no law of limitation. The only law is of supply. Through your subconscious mind you can draw upon universal supply for anything you wish. The ideas of Universal Mind are as countless as the sands on the seashore. Use them. And use them lavishly, just as they are given. There is a little poem by Jessie B. Rittenhouse* that so well describes the limitations that most of us put upon ourselves that I quote it here:

I bargained with Life for a penny,
And Life would pay no more,
However I begged at evening
When I counted my scanty store.

For Life is a just employer;
He gives you what you ask,
But once you have set the wages,
Why, you must bear the task.

*From "The Door of Dreams." Houghton, Mifflin & Co., Boston.

I worked for a menial's hire,
Only to learn, dismayed,
That any wage I had asked of Life,
Life would have paid.

Aim high! If you miss the moon, you may hit a star. Everyone admits that this world and all the vast firmament must have been thought into shape from the formless void by some Universal Mind. That same Universal Mind rules today, and it has given to each form of life power to attract to itself whatever it needs for its perfect growth. The tree, the plant, the animal—each one finds its need.

You are an intelligent, reasoning creature. Your mind is part of Universal Mind. And you have power to *say* what you require for perfect growth. Don't be a niggard with yourself. Don't sell yourself for a penny. Whatever price you set upon yourself, life will give. So aim high. Demand much! Make a clear, distinct mental image of what it is you want. Hold it in your thought. Visualize it, see it, *believe in it!* The ways and means of satisfying that desire will follow. For supply always comes on the heels of demand.

It is by doing this that you take your fate out of the hands of chance. It is in this way that you control the experiences you are to have in life. But be sure to visualize *only what you want.* The law works both ways. If you visualize your worries and your fears, you will make them real. Control your thought and you control circumstances. Conditions will be what you make them.

Most of us are like factories where two-thirds of the machines are idle, where the workmen move around in a listless, dispirited sort of way, doing only the tenth part of what they could do if the head of the plant were watching and directing them. Instead of that, he is off idly dreaming or waiting for something to turn up. What he needs is someone to point out to him his listless workmen and idle machines, and show him how to put each one to working full time and overtime.

And that is what YOU need, too. You are working at only a tenth of *your* capacity. You are doing only a tenth of what *you* are capable of. The time you spend idly wishing or worrying can be used in so directing your subconscious mind that it will bring you anything of good you may desire.

Philip of Macedon, Alexander's father, perfected the "phalanx"—a triangular formation which enabled him to center the whole weight of his attack on one point in the opposing line. It drove through everything opposed to it. In that day and age it was invincible. And the idea is just as invincible today.

Keep the one thought in mind, SEE it being carried out step by step, and you can knit any group of workers into one homogeneous whole, all centered on the one idea. You can accomplish any one thing. You can put across any definite idea. Keep that mental picture ever in mind and you will make it as invincible as was Alexander's phalanx of old.

It is not the guns or armament
Or the money they can pay,
It's the close cooperation
That makes them win the day.
It is not the individual
Or the army as a whole
But the everlasting team work
of every bloomin' soul.

—J. MASON KNOX

The error of the ages is the tendency mankind has always shown to limit the power of Mind, or its willingness to help in time of need.

"Know ye not," said Paul, "that ye are the temples of the Living God?"

No—most of us do not know it. Or at least, if we do, we are like the Indian family out on the Cherokee reservation. Oil had been found on their land and money poured in upon them. More money than they had ever known was in the world. Someone persuaded them to build a great house, to have it beautifully furnished, richly decorated. The house when finished was one of the show places of that locality. But the Indians, while very proud of their showy house, continued to *live in their old sod shack!*

So it is with many of us. We may know that we are "temples of the Living God." We may even be proud of that fact. But we never take advantage of it to dwell in that temple, to proclaim our dominion over things and conditions. We never avail ourselves of the power that is ours.

The great Prophets of old had the forward look. Theirs was the era of hope and expectation. They looked for the time when the revelation should come that was to make men "sons of God." "They shall obtain joy and gladness, and sorrow and sighing shall flee away."

Jesus came to fulfill that revelation. "Ask and ye shall receive, that your joy may be full."

The world has turned in vain to matter and materialistic philosophy for deliverance from its woes. In the future the only march of actual progress will be in the mental realm, and this progress will not be in the way of human speculation and theorizing, but in the *actual demonstration* of the Universal, Infinite Mind.

The world stands today within the vestibule of the vast realm of divine intelligence, wherein is found the transcendent, practical power of Mind over all things.

CHAPTER VII

"AS A MAN THINKETH"

Our remedies oft in ourselves do lie
Which we ascribe to heaven."

—Shakespeare

In our great-grandfather's day, when witches were believed to fly by night and cast their spell upon all unlucky enough to cross them, men thought that the power of sickness or health, of good fortune or ill, resided outside themselves.

We laugh today at such benighted superstition. But even in this day and age there are few who realize that the things they *see* are but *effects.* Fewer still who have any idea of the *causes* by which those effects are brought about.

Every human experience is an effect. You laugh, you weep, you joy, you sorrow, you suffer or you are happy. Each of these is an effect, the cause of which can be easily traced.

But all the experiences of life are not so easily traceable to their primary causes. We save money for our old age—a sudden emergency in our affairs comes up or a relative has a financial crisis; and all our savings are swallowed up. We stay at home on a holiday to avoid risk of accident, and fall off a stepladder or down the stairs and break a limb. We drive slowly for fear of danger, and a speeding car comes from behind and knocks us into a ditch. A man goes over Niagara Falls in a barrel without harm, and then slips on a banana peel, breaks his leg, and dies of it.

What is the cause back of it all? If we can find it and control it, we can control the effect. We shall no longer then be the football of fate. We shall be able to rise above the conception of life in which matter is our master.

There is but one answer. The world without is a reflection of the world within. We image thoughts of disaster upon our subconscious minds and the Genie-of-Our-Mind finds ways of bringing them into effect—even though we stay at home, even though we take every possible precaution. The mental image is what counts, be it for good or ill. It is a devastating or a beneficent force, just as we choose to make it. To paraphrase Thackeray—"The world is a looking-glass, and gives back to every man the reflection of his own thought."

You see, matter is not *real* substance. Material science today shows that matter has no natural eternal existence. Dr. Willis R. Whitney, in an address before the American Chemical Society some years ago, discussing "Matter—Is There Anything in It?" stated that "the most we know about matter is that it is almost entirely *space*. It is as empty as the sky. It is almost as empty as a perfect vacuum, although it usually contains a lot of energy." Thought is the only force. Just as polarity controls the electron, gravitation the planets, tropism the plants and lower animals—just so thought controls the action and the environment of man. And thought is subject wholly to the control of mind. Its direction rests with us.

Walt Whitman had the right of it when he said—"Nothing external to me has any power over me."

The happenings that occur in the material world are in themselves neither cheerful nor sorrowful, just as outside of the eye that observes them colors are neither green nor red. It is our thoughts that make them so. And we can color those thoughts according to our own fancy. We can make the world without but a reflection of the world within. We can make matter a force subject entirely to the control of our mind. For matter is merely our view of what Universal Mind sees rightly.

We cannot change the past experience, but we can determine what the new ones shall be like. We can make the coming day just what we want it to be. We can *be* tomorrow what *we think* today. For thoughts are causes and the conditions are the effects.

What is the reason for most failures in life? The fact that they first thought failure. They allowed competition, hard times, fear and worry to undermine their confidence. Instead of working aggressively ahead, spending money to make more money, they stopped every possible outlay, tried to "play safe," but expected others to continue spending with them. War is not the only place where "the best defensive is a strong offensive."

The law of compensation is always at work. Man is not at the caprice of fate. He is his own fate. "As a man thinketh in his heart, so is he." We are our own past thoughts, with the things that these thoughts have attracted to us added on.

The successful man has no time to think of failure. He is too busy thinking up new ways to succeed. You can't pour water into a vessel already full.

All about you is energy—electronic energy, exactly like that which makes up the solid objects you possess. The only difference is that the loose energy round about is unappropriated. It is still virgin gold—undiscovered, unclaimed. You can think it into anything you wish—into gold or dross, into health or sickness, into strength or weakness, into success or failure. Which shall it be? "There is nothing either good or bad," said Shakespeare, "but thinking makes it so." The understanding of that law will enable you to control every other law that exists. In it is to be found the panacea for all ills, the satisfaction of all want, all desire. It is Creative Mind's own provision for man's freedom.

Have you ever read Basil King's "Conquest of Fear"? If you haven't, do so by all means. Here is the way he visions the future:

"Taking Him (Jesus) as our standard we shall work out, I venture to think, to the following points of progress:

"*a.* The control of matter in furnishing ourselves with food and drink by means more direct than at present employed, as He turned water into wine and fed the multitudes with the loaves and fishes,

"*b.* The control of matter by putting away from ourselves, by methods more sure and less roundabout than those of today, sickness, blindness, infirmity, and deformity.

"*c.* The control of matter by regulating our atmospheric conditions as He stilled the tempest.

"*d.* The control of matter by restoring to this phase of existence those who have passed out of it before their time, or who can ill be spared from it, as He 'raised' three young people from 'the dead' and Peter and Paul followed His example.

"*e.* The control of matter in putting it off and on at will, as He in His death and resurrection.

"*f.* The control of matter in passing altogether out of it, as He in what we call His Ascension into Heaven."

Mortals are healthy or unhealthy, happy or unhappy, strong or weak, alive or dead, in the proportion that they think thoughts of health or illness, strength or weakness. Your body, like all other material things, manifests only what your mind entertains in belief. In a general way you have often noticed this yourself. A man with an ugly disposition (which is a mental state) will have harsh, unlovely features. One with a gentle disposition will have a smiling and serene countenance. All the other organs of the human body are equally responsive to thought. Who has not seen the face become red with rage or white with fear? Who has not known of people who became desperately ill following an outburst of temper? Physicians declare that just as fear, irritability and hate distort the features, they likewise distort the heart, stomach and liver.

Experiments conducted on a cat shortly after a meal showed that when it was purring contentedly, its digestive organs functioned perfectly. But when a dog was brought into the room and the cat drew back in fear and anger, the X-ray showed that its digestive organs were so contorted as to be almost tied up in a knot!

Each of us makes his own world—and he makes it through mind. It is a commonplace fact that no two people see the same thing alike. "A primrose by a river's brim, a yellow primrose was to him, and it was nothing more."

Thoughts are the causes. Conditions are merely effects. We can mold ourselves and our surroundings by resolutely directing our thoughts toward the goal we have in mind.

Ordinary animal life is very definitely controlled by temperature, by climate, by seasonal conditions. Man alone can adjust himself to any reasonable temperature or condition. Man alone has been able to free himself to a great extent from the control of natural forces through his understanding of the relation of cause and effect. And now man is beginning to get a glimpse of the final freedom that shall be his from all material causes when he shall acquire the complete understanding that mind is the only cause and that effects are what he sees.

"We moderns are unaccustomed," says one talented writer, "to the mastery over our own inner thoughts and feelings. That a man should be a prey to any thought that chances to take possession of his mind, is commonly among us assumed as unavoidable. It may be a matter of regret that he should be kept awake all night from anxiety as to the issue of a lawsuit on the morrow, but that he should have the power of determining whether he be kept awake or not seems an extravagant demand. The image of an impending calamity is no doubt odious, but its very odiousness (we say) makes it haunt the mind all the more pertinaciously, and it is useless to expel it. Yet this is an absurd position for man, the heir of all the ages, to be in: hagridden by the flimsy creatures of his own brain. If a pebble in our boot torments us, we expel it. We take off the boot and shake it out. And once the matter is fairly understood, it is just as easy to expel an intruding and obnoxious thought from the mind. About this there ought to be no mistake, no two opinions. The thing is obvious, clear and unmistakable. It should be as easy to expel an obnoxious thought from the mind as to shake a stone out of your shoe; and until a man can do that, it is just nonsense to talk about his ascendancy over nature, and all the rest of it. He is a mere slave, and a prey to the bat-winged phantoms that flit through the corridors of his own brain. Yet the weary and careworn faces that we meet by thousands, even among the affluent classes of civilization, testify only too clearly how seldom this mastery is obtained. How rare indeed to find a *man!* How common rather to discover a *creature* hounded on by tyrant thoughts (or cares, or desires), cowering, wincing under the lash.

"It is one of the prominent doctrines of some of the oriental schools of practical psychology that the power of expelling thoughts, or if need be, killing them dead on the spot, *must be* attained. Naturally the art requires practice, but like other arts, when once acquired there is no mystery or difficulty about it. It is worth practice. It may be fairly said that life only begins when this art has been acquired. For obviously when, instead of being ruled by individual thoughts, the whole flock of them in their immense multitude and variety and capacity is ours to direct and dispatch and employ where we list, life becomes a thing so vast and grand, compared to what it was before, that its former condition may well appear almost antenatal. If you can kill a thought dead, for the time being, you can do anything else with it that you please. And therefore it is that this power is so valuable. And it not only frees a man from mental torment (which is nine-tenths at least of all the torment of life), but it gives him a concentrated power of handling mental work absolutely unknown to him before. The two are co-relative to each other."

There is no intelligence in matter—whether it be stone or iron, wood or flesh. Matter is Vital Force crystallized into the pattern we have given it. Mind is the only intelligence. It alone is eternal. It alone is supreme in the universe.

When we reach that understanding, we will no longer have cause for fear, because we will realize that all Vital Force is good. It is only our patterns that are at fault. When the results turn out badly, we have only to discard them and change the pattern—go back to the perfect one that is in Universal Mind. Remember the old fairy story of how the Sun was listening to a lot of earthly creatures talking of a very dark place they had found? A place of Stygian blackness. Each told how terrifically dark it had seemed. The Sun went and looked for it. He went to the exact spot they had described. He searched everywhere. But he could find not even a tiny dark spot. And he came back and told the earth-creatures he did not believe there *was* any dark place.

When the sun of understanding shines on all the dark spots in our lives, we will realize that there is no cause, no creator, no power, except good; evil is not an entity—it is merely the *absence of good*. And there can be no ill effects without an evil cause. Since there is no evil cause, only good can have reality or power. There is no beginning or end to good. From it there can be nothing but blessing for the whole race. In it is found no trouble. If God (or Good—the two are synonymous) is the only cause, then the only effect must be like the cause. "All things were made by Him; and without Him was not anything made that was made."

Don't be content with passively reading this. Use it! Practice it! Exercise is far more necessary to mental development than it is to physical. Practice the "daily dozen" of right thinking. Stretch your mind to realize how infinitely far it can reach out, what boundless vision it can have. Breathe out all the old thoughts of sickness, discouragement, failure, worry and fear. Breathe in deep, long breaths (thoughts) of unlimited health and strength, unlimited happiness and success. Claim the perfect pattern and then pour all your Vital Force, all your faith and hope and desire, into it.

Practice looking forward—always looking forward to something better—better health, finer physique, greater happiness, bigger success. Take these mental breathing exercises every day, pouring your Vital Force into these new patterns, and see how quickly the good effects will be apparent to all. See how readily you can tune in on wave lengths of health and happiness and prosperity. Your mental radio is always open, every waking hour. Keep it attuned to happy thoughts, to good instead of evil. For whatever type of thought you entertain, whatever wave length you tune in on, that is the pattern your Vital Force will take, for good or bad. So be sure to exhale all the thoughts of fear and worry and disease and lack that have been troubling you, be sure to tune them OUT on your mental radio and inhale and entertain only those you want to see realized.

CHAPTER VIII

THE LAW OF SUPPLY

They do me wrong who say I come no more
When once I knock and fail to find you in;
For every day I stand outside your door,
And bid you wake, and rise to fight and win.

Wail not for precious chances passed away,
Weep not for golden ages on the wane!
Each night I burn the records of the day—
At sunrise every soul is born again!

—WALTER MALONE*

Have you ever run a race, or worked at utmost capacity for a protracted period, or swum a great distance? Remember how, soon after starting, you began to feel tired? Remember how, before you had gone any great distance, you thought you had reached your limit? But remember, too, how, when you kept going, you got

*Courtesy of Mrs. Ella Malone Watson.

your second wind, your tiredness vanished, your muscles throbbed with energy, you felt literally charged with speed and endurance?

Stored in every human being are great reserves of energy of which the average individual knows nothing. Most people are like a man who drives a car in low gear, not knowing that by the simple shift of a lever he can set it in high and not merely speed up the car, but do it with far less expenditure of power.

The law of the universe is the law of supply. You see it on every hand. Nature is lavish in everything she does.

Look at the heavens at night. There are millions of stars there—millions of worlds—millions of suns among them. Surely there is no lack of wealth or profusion in the Mind that could image all of these; no place for limitation there! Look at the vegetation in the country round about you. Nature supplies all that the shrubs or trees may need for their growth and sustenance! Look at the lower forms of animal life—the birds and the wild animals, the reptiles and the insects, the fish in the sea. Nature supplies them bountifully with everything they need. They have but to help themselves to what she holds out to them with such lavish hand. Look at all the natural resources of the world—coal and iron and oil and metals. There is enough for everyone. We hear a lot about the exhaustion of our resources of coal and oil, but there is available coal enough to last mankind for thousands of years. There are vast oil fields practically untouched, probably others bigger still yet to be discovered, and when all these are exhausted, the extraction of oil from shales will keep the world supplied for countless more years.

There is abundance for everyone. But just as you must strain and labor to reach the resources of your "second wind," just so you must strive before you can make manifest the law of supply in nature.

THE WORLD BELONGS TO YOU

It is your estate. It owes you not merely a living, but everything of good you may desire. You must *demand* these things of it, though. You must fear naught, dread naught, stop at naught. You must have the faith of a Columbus, crossing an unknown sea, holding a mutinous crew to the task long after they had ceased to believe in themselves or in him—*and giving to the world a new hemisphere.* You must have the faith, of a Washington—defeated, discredited, almost wholly deserted by his followers, yet holding steadfast in spite of all—*and giving to America a new liberty.* You must *dominate*—not cringe. You must make the application of the law of supply.

"Consider the lilies how they grow." The flowers, the birds, all of creation, are incessantly active. The trees and flowers in their growth, the birds and wild creatures in building their nests and finding sustenance, are always working—*but never worrying.* "Your Father knoweth that ye have need of these things." "And all these things shall be added unto you."

If all would agree to give up worrying—to be industrious, but never anxious about the outcome—it would mean the beginning of a new era in human progress, an age of liberty, of freedom from bondage. Jesus set forth the universal law of supply when he said—"Therefore I say unto you, be not anxious for the morrow, what ye shall eat, or wherewithal ye shall be clothed—but seek first the kingdom of God, *and all those things shall be added unto you.*"

What is this "Kingdom of God"?

Jesus tells us—"The Kingdom of God is within you." It is the "Father within you" to which He so frequently referred. It is Mind—your part of Universal Mind. "Seek first the Kingdom of God." Seek first an understanding of this Power within you—learn to contact it—to use it—"and all those things shall be added unto you."

All riches have their origin in Mind. Wealth is in ideas—not money. Money is merely the material medium of exchange for ideas. The paper money in your pockets is in itself worth no more than so many pieces of paper. It is the idea behind it that gives it value. Factory buildings, machinery, materials, are in themselves worthless without a manufacturing or a selling idea behind them. How often you see a factory fall to pieces, the machinery rust away, after the idea behind them gave out. Factories, machines, are simply the tools of trade. It is the idea behind them that makes them go.

So don't go out seeking wealth. Look within you for ideas! "The Kingdom of God is within you." Use it—*purposefully!* Use it to THINK constructively. Don't say you are *thinking* when all you are doing is exercising your faculty of memory. As Dumont says in "The Master Mind"—"They are simply allowing the stream of memory to flow through their field of consciousness, while the Ego stands on the banks and idly watches the passing waters of memory flow by. They call this 'thinking,' while in reality there is no process of Thought under way."

They are like the old mountaineer sitting in the shade alongside his cabin. Asked what he did to pass the long hours away, he said—"Waal, sometimes I set and think; and sometimes I just set."

Dumont goes on to say, in quoting another writer: "When I use the word 'thinking,' I mean *thinking with a purpose, with an end in view, thinking to solve a problem*. I mean the kind of thinking that is forced on us when we are deciding on a course to pursue, on a life work to take up perhaps; the kind of thinking that was forced upon us in our younger days when we had to find a solution to a problem in mathematics; or when we tackled psychology in college. I do not mean 'thinking' in snatches, or holding petty opinions on this subject and on that. I mean thought on significant questions which lie outside the bounds of your narrow personal welfare. This is the kind of thinking which is now so rare—so sadly needed!"

The Kingdom of God is the Kingdom of Thought, of Achievement, of Health, of Happiness and Prosperity. "I came that ye might have life and have it more abundantly."

But you have to *seek* it. You have to do more than ponder. You have to *think*—to think constructively—to seek how you may discover new worlds, new methods, new needs. The greatest discoveries, you know, have arisen out of things which everybody had *seen,* but only one man had NOTICED. The biggest fortunes have been made out of the opportunities which many men *had,* but only one man GRASPED.

Why is it that so many millions of men and women go through life in poverty and misery, in sickness and despair? Why? Primarily because they make a reality of poverty through their fear of it. They visualize poverty, misery and disease, and thus bring them into being. And secondly, they cannot demonstrate the law of supply for the same reason that so many millions cannot solve the first problem in algebra. The solution is simple—but they have never been shown the method. They do not understand the law.

The essence of this law is that you must *think* abundance, *see* abundance, *feel* abundance, *believe* abundance. Let no thought of limitation enter your mind. There is no lawful desire of yours for which, as far as mind is concerned, there is not abundant satisfaction. And if you can visualize it in mind, you can realize it in your daily world.

"Blessed is the man whose delight is in the *law* of the Lord: And he shall be like a tree planted by the rivers of water, that bringeth forth his fruit in his season: his leaf also shall not wither; and whatsoever he doeth shall prosper."

Don't worry. Don't doubt. Don't dig up the seeds of prosperity and success to see whether they have sprouted. Have faith! Nourish your seeds with renewed desire. Keep before your mind's eye the picture of the thing you want. BELIEVE IN IT! No matter if you seem to be in the clutch of misfortune, no matter if the future looks black and dreary—FORGET YOUR FEARS! Realize that the future is of your own making. There is no power that can keep you down but yourself. Set your goal. Forget the obstacles between. Forget the difficulties in the way. Keep only the goal before your mind's eye—*and you'll win it!*

Judge Troward, in his Edinburgh Lectures on Mental Science, shows the way:

"The initial step, then, consists in determining to picture the Universal Mind as the ideal of all we could wish it to be, both to ourselves and to others, together with the endeavor to reproduce this ideal, however imperfectly, in our own life; and this step having been taken, we can then cheerfully look upon it as our ever-present Friend, providing all good, guarding from all danger, and guiding us with all counsel. Similarly if we think of it as a great power devoted to supplying all our needs, we shall impress this character also upon it, and by the law of subjective mind, it will proceed to enact the part of that special providence which we have credited it with being; and if, beyond general care of our concerns, we would draw to ourselves some particular benefit, the same rule holds good of impressing our desire upon the universal subjective mind. And thus the deepest problems of philosophy bring us back to the old statement of the law: 'Ask and ye shall receive; seek and ye shall find; knock and it shall be opened unto you.' This is the summing-up of the natural law of the relation between us and the Divine Mind. It is thus no vain boast that mental science can enable us to make our lives what we will. And to this law there is no limit. What it can do for us today it can do tomorrow, and through, all that procession of tomorrows that loses itself in the dim vistas of eternity. *Belief in limitation is the one and only thing that causes limitation,* because we thus impress limitation upon the creative principle; and in proportion as we lay that belief aside, our boundaries will expand, and increasing life and more abundant blessing will be ours."

You are not working for some firm merely for the pittance they pay you. You are part of the great scheme of things. And what you do has its bearing on the ultimate result. That being the case, you are working for Universal Mind, and Universal Mind is the most generous paymaster there is. Just remember that you can look to it for all good things. Supply is *where* you are and *what* you need.

Do you want a situation? Close your eyes and realize that somewhere is the position for which you of all people are best fitted, and which is best fitted to your ability. The position where you can do the utmost of good, and where life, in turn, offers the most to you. Realize that Universal Mind knows exactly where this position is, and that through your subconscious mind you, too, can know it. Realize that this is YOUR position, that it NEEDS you, that it belongs to you, that it is right for you to have it, that you are entitled to it. Hold this thought in mind every night for just a moment, then go to sleep knowing that your subconscious mind HAS the necessary information as to where this position is and how to get in touch with it. Mind you—not WILL have, but HAS. The earnest realization of this will bring that position to you, and you to it, as surely as the morrow will bring the sun. Make the law of supply operative and you find that the things you seek are seeking you.

Get firmly fixed in your own mind the definite conviction that you can do anything you greatly want to do. There is no such thing as lack of opportunity. There is no such thing as only one opportunity. You are subject to a law of boundless and perpetual opportunity, and you can enforce that law in your behalf just as widely as you need. Opportunity is infinite and ever present.

Berton Braley has it well expressed in his poem on "Opportunity"*:

For the best verse hasn't been rhymed yet,
The best house hasn't been planned,
The highest peak hasn't been climbed yet,
The mightiest rivers aren't spanned.
Don't worry and fret, faint hearted,
The chances have just begun,
For the Best jobs haven't been started,
The Best work hasn't been done.

*From "A Banjo at Armageddon." George H. Doran Company.

Nothing stands in the way of a will which wants—an intelligence which knows. The great thing is to start. "Begin your work," says Ausonius. "To begin is to complete the first half. The second half remains. Begin again and the work is done." It matters not how small or unimportant your task may seem to be. It may loom bigger in Universal Mind than that of your neighbor, whose position is so much greater in the eyes of the world. Do it well—and Universal Mind will work with you.

But don't feel limited to any one job or any one line of work. Man was given dominion over all the earth. "And God said, Let us make man in our image, after our likeness: and let them have dominion over the fish of the sea, and over the fowl of the air, and over the cattle, and over all the earth, and over every creeping thing that creepeth upon the earth."

All of energy, all of power, all that can exercise any influence over your life, is in your hands through the power of thought. God—good—is the only power there is. Your mind is part of His mind. He is "the Father that is within you that doeth the works."

So don't put any limit upon His power by trying to limit your capabilities. You are not in bondage to anything. All your hopes and dreams can come true. Were you not given dominion over all the earth? And can anyone else take this dominion from you?

All the mysterious psychic powers about which you hear so much today are perfectly natural. Professor Rhine of Duke University has demonstrated them in all manner of subjects. I have them. You have them. They only await the time when they shall be allowed to assert their vigor and prove themselves your faithful servitors.

"Be not afraid!" Claim your inheritance. The Universal Mind that supplies all wisdom and power is *your* mind. And to the extent that you are governed by your understanding of its infinite law of supply you will be able to demonstrate plenty. "According to your faith, be it unto you,"

"Analyze most of the great American fortunes of the past generation," says *Advertising and Selling Fortnightly,* "and you will find that they were founded on great faiths. One man's faith was in oil, another's in land, another's in minerals.

"The fortunes that are being built today are just as surely being built on great faiths, but there is this difference: the emphasis of the faith has been shifted. Today it takes faith in a product or an opportunity, as it always did, but it takes faith in the public, in addition. Those who have the greatest faith in the public—the kind of faith possessed by Henry Ford and H. J. Heinz—*and make that faith articulate*—build the biggest fortunes."

"WANTED"

There is one question that bothers many a man. Should he stick to the job he has, or cast about at once for a better one. The answer depends entirely upon what you are striving for. The first thing is to set your goal. What is it you want? A profession? A political appointment? An important executive position? A business of your own?

Every position should yield you three things:

1. Reasonable pay for the present.
2. Knowledge, training, or experience that will be worth money to you in the future.
3. Prestige or acquaintances that will be of assistance to you in attaining your goal.

Judge every opening by those three standards. But don't overlook chances for valuable training, merely because the pay is small. Though it is a pretty safe rule that the concern with up-to-the-minute methods that it would profit you to learn, also pays up-to-the-minute salaries.

Hold each job long enough to get from it every speck of information there is in it. Hold it long enough to learn the job ahead. Then if there seems no likelihood of a vacancy soon in that job ahead, find one that corresponds to it somewhere else.

Progress! Keep going ahead! Don't be satisfied merely because your salary is being boosted occasionally. Learn something every day. When you reach the point in your work that you are no longer adding to your store of knowledge or abilities, you are going backward, and it's time for you to move. Move upward in the organization you are with if you can—but MOVE!

Your actual salary is of slight importance compared with

the knowledge and ability you add to your mind. Given a full storehouse there, the salary or the riches will speedily follow. But the biggest salary won't do you much good for long unless you have the knowledge inside you to back it up.

It is like a girl picking her husband. She can pick one with a lot of money and no brains, or she can pick one with no money but a lot of ability. In the former case, she will have a high time for a little while, ending in a divorce court or in her having a worthless young "rounder" on her hands and no money to pay the bills. In the other, the start will be hard, but she is likely to end up with a happy home she has helped to build, an earnest, hard-working husband who has "arrived"—*and happiness.*

Money ought to be a consideration in marriage—but never *the* consideration. Of course it is an easy matter to pick a man with neither money nor brains. But when it is a choice of money *or* brains—take the brains every time. Possessions are of slight importance compared to mind. Given the inquiring, alert type of mind—you can get any amount of possessions. But the possessions without the mind are nothing. Nine times out of ten the best thing that can happen to any young couple is to have to start with little or nothing and work out their salvation together.

What is it *you* want most from life? Is it riches?

Picture yourself with all the riches you could use, with all the abundance that Nature holds out with such lavish hand everywhere. What would you do with it?

Daydream for a while. Believe that you *have* that abundance *now*. Practice being rich in your own mind. See yourself driving that expensive car you have always longed for, living in the sort of house you have often pictured, well-dressed, surrounded by everything to make life worth while. Picture yourself spending this money that is yours, lavishly, without a worry as to where more is coming from, knowing that there is no limit to the riches of Mind. Picture yourself doing all those things you would like to do, living the life you would like to live, providing for your loved ones as you would like to see them provided for. *See* all this in your mind's eye. *Believe* it to be true for the moment. *Know* that it will all be true in the not-very-distant future. Get from it all the pleasure and enjoyment you can.

It is the *first step* in making your dreams come true. You are creating the model in mind. And if you don't allow fear or worry to tear it down, Mind will re-create that model for you in your everyday life.

"All that the Father hath is yours," said Jesus. And a single glance at the heavens and the earth will show you that He has all riches in abundance. Reach out mentally and appropriate to yourself some of these good gifts. You have to do it mentally before you can enjoy it physically. "'Tis mind that makes the body rich," as Shakespeare tells us.

See the things you want as *already yours*. Know that they will come to you at need. Then LET them come. Don't fret and worry about them. Don't think about your LACK of them. Think of them as YOURS, as *belonging* to you, as already in your possession.

Look upon money as water that runs the mill of your mind. You are constantly grinding out ideas that the world needs. Your thoughts, your plans, are necessary to the great scheme of things. Money provides the power. But *it* needs YOU, it needs your ideas, before it can be of any use to the world. The Falls of Niagara would be of no use without the power plants that line the banks. The Falls need these plants to turn their power to account. In the same way, money needs your ideas to become of use to the world.

So instead of thinking that you need money, realize that money needs YOU. Money is just so much wasted energy without work to do. Your ideas provide the outlet for it, the means by which money can do things. Develop your ideas, secure in the knowledge that money is always looking for such an outlet. When the ideas are perfected, money will gravitate your way without conscious effort on your part, if only you don't dam up the channels with doubts and fears.

"First have something good—then advertise!" said Horace Greeley. First have something that the world needs, even if it be only faithful, interested service—then open up your channels of desire, and dollars will flow to you.

And remember that the more you have to offer—the more of riches will flow to you. Dollars are of no value except as they are used.

You have seen the rich attacked time and again in newspapers and magazines. You have read numberless articles and editorials against them. You have heard agitators declaim against them by the hour. But did you ever hear one of them say a single word against the richest man of them all—Henry Ford? I did not. And why? Because Henry Ford's idea of money was that it was something to be *used*—something to provide more jobs, something to bring more comfort, more enjoyment, into an increasingly greater number of lives.

That is why money flowed to him so freely. That is why he got so much out of life. And that is how you, too, can get in touch with Infinite Supply. Realize that it is not money you have to seek, but a way to *use* money for the world's advantage. *Find the need!* Look at everything with the question—How could that be improved? To what new uses could this be put? Then set about supplying that need, in the absolute confidence that when you have found the way, money will flow freely to and through you. Do your part—and you can confidently look to Universal Mind to provide the means.

Get firmly in mind the definite conviction that YOU CAN DO ANYTHING RIGHT THAT YOU MAY WISH TO DO. Then set your goal and let everything you do, all your work, all your study, all your associations, be a step toward that goal. To quote Berton Braley* again—

*From "Things As They Are." George H. Doran Company.

If you want a thing bad enough
To go out and fight for it,
Work day and night for it,
Give up your time and your peace and your sleep for it,
If only desire of it
Makes you quite mad enough
Never to tire of it,
Makes you hold all other things tawdry and cheap for it,
If life seems all empty and useless without it
And all that you scheme and you dream is about it,
If gladly you'll sweat for it,
Fret for it,
Plan for it,
Lose all your terror of God or man for it,
If you'll simply go after that thing that you want,
With all your capacity,
Strength and sagacity,
Faith, hope and confidence, stern pertinacity,
If neither cold poverty, famished and gaunt,
Nor sickness nor pain
Of body or brain
Can turn you away from the thing that you want,
If dogged and grim you besiege and beset it,
You'll get it!

CHAPTER IX

THE FORMULA OF SUCCESS

One ship drives east, and another drives west,
With the self-same winds that blow.
'Tis the set of the sails, and not the gales
Which tells us the way they go.

Like the waves of the sea are the ways of fate
As we voyage along thru life.
'Tis the set of the soul which decides its goal
And not the calm or the strife.

—Ella Wheeler Wilcox

What is the eternal question which stands up and looks you and every sincere man squarely in the eye every morning?

"How can I better my condition?" That is the real life question which confronts you, and will haunt you every day till you solve it.

Read this chapter carefully and I think you will find the answer to this important life question which you and every man must solve if he expects ever to have more each Monday morning, after pay day, than he had the week before.

To begin with, all wealth depends upon a clear understanding of the fact that mind—thought—is the only creator. The great business of life is thinking. Control your thoughts and you control circumstance.

Just as the first law of gain is desire, so the formula of success is FAITH. Believe that you have it—see it as an existent fact—and anything you can rightly wish for is yours. Faith is "the substance of things hoped for, the evidence of things not seen."

It is now a good many years since Professor Henry made his famous experiment with a charged magnet, which revolutionized the electrical practice of his age.

First he took an ordinary magnet of large size, suspended it from a rafter, and with it lifted a few hundred pounds of iron.

Then he wrapped the magnet with wire and charged it with the current from a small battery. Instead of only a few hundred, *the now highly charged magnet lifted three thousand pounds!*

Your magnet is your subconscious mind. Impelled by strong desire, it can bring you a reasonable amount of the good things of life, But charge it with a strong current of faith, of belief in its power, *and there is no limit to the good things it will bring to you.*

You have seen men, inwardly no more capable than

yourself, accomplish the seemingly impossible. You have seen others, after years of hopeless struggle, suddenly win their most cherished dreams. And you have probably wondered, "What is the power that gives new life to their dying ambitions, that supplies new impetus to their jaded desires, that gives them a new start on the road to success?"

That power is belief—*faith.* Someone, something, gave them a new belief in themselves, a new faith in their power to win—and they leaped ahead and wrested success from seemingly certain defeat.

Do you remember the picture Harold Lloyd was in some years ago, showing a country boy who was afraid of his shadow? Every boy in the countryside bedeviled him. Until one day his grandmother gave him a talisman that she assured him his grandfather had carried through the Civil War and which, so she said, had the property of making its owner invincible. Nothing could hurt him, she told him, while he wore this talisman. Nothing could stand up against him. He believed her. And the next time the bully of the town started to cuff him around, he wiped up the earth with him. And that was only the start. Before the year was out he had made a reputation as the most daring soul in the community.

Then, when his grandmother felt that he was thoroughly cured, she told him the truth—that the "talisman" was merely a piece of old junk she had picked up by the roadside—that she knew all he needed was *faith in himself,* belief that he could do these things.

THE TALISMAN OF NAPOLEON

Stories like that are common. It is such a well-established truth that you can do only what you think you can, that the theme is a favorite one with authors. I remember reading a story years ago of an artist—a mediocre sort of artist—who was visiting the field of Waterloo and happened upon a curious lump of metal half buried in the dirt, which so attracted him that he picked it up and put it in his pocket. Soon thereafter he noticed a sudden increase in confidence, an absolute faith in himself, not only as to his own chosen line of work, but in his ability to handle any situation that might present itself. He painted a great picture—just to show that he *could* do it. Not content with that, he visioned an empire with Mexico as its basis, actually led a revolt that carried all before it—until one day he lost his talisman. *And immediately his bubble burst.*

I instance this just to illustrate the point that it is *your own belief in yourself* that counts. It is the consciousness of dominant power within you that makes all things attainable. *You can do anything you think you can.* This knowledge is literally the gift of the gods, for through it you can solve every human problem. It should make of you an incurable optimist. It is the open door to welfare. *Keep it open*—by expecting to gain everything that is right.

You are entitled to every good thing. Therefore expect nothing but good. Defeat does not *need* to follow victory.

You don't have to "knock wood" every time you congratulate yourself that things have been going well with you. Victory should follow victory—and it will if you "let this mind be in you which was also in Christ Jesus." It is the mind that means health and life and boundless opportunity and recompense. No limitation rests upon you. So don't let any enter your life. Remember that Mind will do every good thing for you. It will remove mountains for you.

"Bring ye all the tithes into the storehouse, and prove me now herewith, saith the Lord of hosts, if I will not open you the windows of heaven, and pour you out a blessing, that there shall not be room enough to receive it."

Bring all your thoughts, your desires, your aims, your talents, into the Storehouse—the Consciousness of Good, the Law of Infinite supply—and prove these blessings. There is every reason to know that you are entitled to adequate provision. Everything that is involved in supply is a thing of thought. Now reach out, stretch your mind, try to comprehend *unlimited thought, unlimited supply,*

Do not think that supply must come through one or two channels. It is not for you to dictate to Universal Mind the means through which It shall send Its gifts to you. There are millions of channels through which It can reach you. Your part is to impress upon Mind your need, your earnest desire, your boundless belief in the resources and the willingness of Universal Mind to help you. Plant the seed of desire. Nourish it with a clear visualization of the ripened fruit. Water it with sincere faith. But leave the means to Universal Mind.

Open up your mind. Clear out the channels of thought. Keep yourself in a state of receptivity. Gain a mental attitude in which you are constantly *expecting good.* You have the: fundamental right to all good, you know. "According to your faith, be it unto you."

The trouble with most of us is that we are mentally lazy. It is so much easier to go along with the crowd than to break trail for ourselves. But the great discoverers, the great inventors, the great geniuses in all lines have been men who dared to break with tradition, who defied precedent, who believed that there is no limit to what Mind can do—and who stuck to that belief until their goal was won, in spite of all the sneers and ridicule of the wiseacres and the "It-can't-be-done"rs.

Not only that, but they were never satisfied with achieving just one success, They knew that the first success is like the first olive out of the bottle. All the others come the more easily for it. They realized that they were a part of the Creative Intelligence of the Universe, and that the part shares all the properties of the whole. That realization gave them the faith to strive for any right thing, the knowledge that the only limit upon their capabilities was the limit of their desires. Knowing that, they couldn't be satisfied with any ordinary success. They had to keep on and on and on.

Edison didn't sit down and fold his hands when he gave us the talking machine. Or the electric light. These great achievements merely opened the way to new fields of accomplishment.

Open the channels between your mind and Universal Mind, and there is no limit to the riches that will come pouring in. Concentrate your thoughts on the particular thing you are most interested in, and ideas in abundance will come flooding down, opening a dozen ways of winning the goal you are striving for.

Don't let one success—no matter how great—satisfy you. The Law of Creation, you know, is the Law of Growth. You can't stand still. You must go forward—or be passed by. Complacency—self-satisfaction—is the greatest enemy of achievement. You must keep looking forward. Like Alexander, you must be constantly seeking new worlds to conquer. Depend upon it, the power will come to meet the need. There is no such thing as failing powers, if we look to Mind for our source of supply. The only failure of mind comes from worry and fear—or from disuse.

William James, the famous psychologist, taught that "The more mind does, the more it can do." For ideas release energy. You can *do* more and better work than you have ever done. You can *know* more than you know now. You know from your own experience that under proper mental conditions of joy or enthusiasm, you can do three or four times the work without fatigue that you can ordinarily. Tiredness is more boredom than actual physical fatigue. You can work almost indefinitely when the work is a pleasure.

You have seen sickly persons, frail persons, who couldn't do an hour's light work without exhaustion, suddenly buckle down when heavy responsibilities were thrown upon them, and grow strong and rugged under the load. Crises not only draw upon the reserve power you have, but they help to create new power.

"IT COULDN'T BE DONE"

It may be that you have been deluded by the thought of incompetence. It may be that you have been told so often that you cannot do certain things that you've come to believe you can't. Remember that success or failure is merely a state of mind. Believe you cannot do a thing—and you can't. Know that you *can* do it—and you *will.* You must *see yourself doing it.*

If you think you are beaten, you are;
If you think you dare not, you don't;
If you'd like to win, but you think you can't,
It's almost a cinch, you won't;
If you think you'll lose, you've lost,
For out in the world you'll find
Success begins with a fellow's will—
It's all in the state of mind.

Full many a race is lost
Ere even a race is run,
And many a coward fails
Ere even his work's begun.
Think big, and your deeds will grow,
Think small and you fall behind,
Think that you can, and you will;
It's all in the state of mind.

If you think you are outclassed, you are;
You've got to think high to rise;
You've got to be sure of yourself before
You can ever win a prize.
Life's battle doesn't always go
To the stronger or faster man;
But sooner or later, the man who wins
Is the fellow who thinks he can.

There is a vast difference between a proper understanding of one's own ability and a determination to make the best of it—and offensive egotism. It is absolutely necessary for every man to believe in himself, before he can make the most of himself. All of us have something to sell. It may be our goods, it may be our abilities, it may be our services. You have to believe in yourself to make your buyer take stock in you at par and accrued interest. You have to feel the same personal solicitude over a customer lost, as a revivalist over a backslider, and hold special services to bring him back into the fold. You have to get up every morning with determination, if you are going to go to bed that night with satisfaction.

There is mighty sound sense in the saying that all the world loves a booster. The one and only thing you have to win success with is MIND. For your mind to function at its highest capacity, you have to be charged with good cheer and optimism. No one ever did a good piece of work while in a negative frame of mind. Your best work is always done when you are feeling happy and optimistic.

And a happy disposition is the *result*—not the *cause*—of happy, cheery thinking. Health and prosperity are the *results* primarily of optimistic thoughts. *You* make the pattern. If the impress you have left on the world about you seems faint and weak, don't blame fate—blame your pattern! You will never cultivate a brave, courageous demeanor by thinking cowardly thoughts. You cannot gather figs from thistles. You will never make your dreams come true by choking them with doubts and fears. You must put foundations under your air castles, foundations of UNDERSTANDING and BELIEF. Your chances of success in any undertaking can always be measured by your BELIEF in yourself.

Are your surroundings discouraging? Do you feel that if you were in another's place success would be easier? Just bear in mind that your real environment is within you. All the factors of success or failure are in your inner world. *You* make your own inner world—and through it your outer world. You can choose the material from which to build. If you have not chosen wisely in the past, you can choose again now the material you want to rebuild it. The richness of life is within you. No one has failed so long as he can begin again.

Start right in and *do* all those things you feel you have it in you to do. Ask permission of no man. Concentrating your thought upon any proper undertaking will make its achievement possible. Your belief that you *can* do the thing gives your thought forces their power. Fortune waits upon you. Seize her boldly, hold her—and she is yours. She belongs rightfully to you. But if you cringe to her, if you go up to her doubtfully, timidly, she will pass you by in scorn. For she is a fickle jade who must be mastered, who loves boldness, who admires confidence.

A Roman boasted that it was sufficient for him to strike the ground with his foot and legions would spring up. And his very boldness cowed his opponents. It is the same with your mind. Take the first step, and your mind will mobilize all its forces to your aid. But the first essential is that you *begin.* Once the battle is started, all that is within and without you will come to your assistance, if you attack in earnest and meet each obstacle with resolution. But *you* have to start things.

"The Lord helps them that help themselves" is a truth as old as man. It is, in fact, plain common sense. Your superconscious mind has all power, but your conscious mind is the watchman at the gate. *It* has to open the door. *It* has to press the spring that releases the infinite energy. No failure is possible in the accomplishment of any right object you may have in life, if you but understand your power and will perseveringly try to use it in the proper way.

The men who have made their mark in this world all had one trait in common—*they believed in themselves!* "But," you may say, "how can I believe in myself when I have never yet done anything worth while, when everything I put my hand to seems to fail?" You can't, of course. That is, you couldn't if you had to depend upon your conscious mind alone. But just remember what one far greater than you said—"I can of mine own self do nothing. The Father that is within me—He doeth the works."

That same "Father" is within you. And it is by knowing that He *is* in you, and that through Him you can do anything that is right, that you can acquire the belief in yourself which is so necessary. Certainly the Mind that imaged the heavens and the earth and all that they contain has all wisdom, all power, all abundance. With this Mind to call upon, you know there is no problem too difficult for you to undertake. The *knowing* of this is the first step, *Faith.* But St. James tells us—"Faith without works is dead," so go on to the next step. Decide on the one thing you want most from life. No matter what it may be. There is no limit, you know, to Mind. Visualize this thing that you want. See it, feel it, BELIEVE in it. Make your mental blueprint, and *begin to build!*

Suppose people DO laugh at your idea. Suppose Reason does say—"It can't be done!" People laughed at Galileo. They laughed at Henry Ford. Reason contended for countless ages that the earth was flat. Reason said—or so numerous automotive engineers argued—that the original Ford motor wouldn't run. But the earth *is* round—and many of those millions of Model T Fords are still running.

Let us start right now putting into practice some of these truths that you have learned. What do you want most of life right now? Take that one desire, concentrate on it, impress it upon your subconscious mind, and through it upon the superconscious.

Psychologists have discovered that the best time to make suggestions to your subconscious mind is just before going to sleep, when the senses are quiet and the body is relaxed, So let us take your desire and suggest it to your subconscious mind tonight. The two prerequisites are the earnest DESIRE, and an intelligent, understanding BELIEF. Someone has said, you know, that education is three-fourths encouragement, and the encouragement is the suggestion that the thing can be done.

You know that you can have what you want, if you want it badly enough and can believe in it earnestly enough. So tonight, just before you drop off to sleep, concentrate your thought on this thing that you most desire from life. BELIEVE that you have it. SEE YOURSELF possessing it. FEEL yourself using it.

Do that every night until you ACTUALLY DO BELIEVE that you have the thing you want. When you reach that point, *YOU WILL HAVE IT!*

Even better than making such suggestions to yourself is to put them on a record and have them played to you while you are asleep. That is the most successful method yet discovered. We have been told that the Army used this method with great success during the war in teaching languages. Certainly it would be the quickest way to learn any difficult subject.

CHAPTER X

"THIS FREEDOM"

Ye shall know the truth
And the truth shall make you free.

I have heard that quotation ever since I was a little child. Most of us have. But to me it was never anything much but a quotation—until some years ago. It is only since then that I have begun to get an inkling of the real meaning of it—an understanding of the comfort back of it. Perhaps to you, too, it has been no more than a sonorous phrase. If so, you will be interested in what I have since gotten from it.

To begin with, what is the "truth" that is so often referred to in all our religious teaching? The truth about what? And what is it going to free us from?

The truth as I see it now is the underlying reality in everything we meet in life. There is, for instance, one right way to solve any given problem in mathematics. That one right way is the truth as far as that problem is concerned. To know it is to free yourself from all doubt and vain imagining and error. It is to free yourself from any trouble that might arise through solving the problem incorrectly.

In the same way, there is but one BEST way of solving every situation that confronts you. That BEST way is the truth. To know it is to make you free from all worry or trouble in connection with that situation. For if it is met in the RIGHT way, only good can come of it.

Then there is your body. There is only one RIGHT idea of every organism in your body. One CORRECT method of functioning for each of them. And Universal Mind holds that RIGHT idea, that CORRECT method. The functioning of your body, the rebuilding of each cell and tissue, is the work of your subconscious mind. If you will constantly hold before it the thought that its model is perfection, that weakness or sickness or deformity is merely ABSENCE of perfection—not a reality in itself—in short, if you will realize the *Truth* concerning your body, your subconscious mind will speedily make you free and keep you free from every ill.

It matters not what is troubling you today. If you will KNOW that whatever it may seem to be is merely the absence of the true idea, if you will realize that the only thing that counts is the truth that Universal Mind knows about your body, you can make that truth manifest.

Affirm the good, the true—and the evil will vanish. It is like turning on the light—the darkness immediately disappears. For there is no actual substance in darkness—it is merely absence of light. Nor is there any substance in sickness or evil—it is merely the absence of health or good.

That is the truth that was the mentality of Jesus—what Paul describes as "the mind which was also in Christ Jesus."

Jesus declared that "we should know the truth, and the truth would make us free." That truth was the power which He exercised. He had so perfect an understanding of truth that it gave Him absolute dominion over evil, enabled Him to heal diseases of every nature, even to raise the dead. The power that He exercised then was not confined to His time, nor limited to His own immediate followers. "Lo, I am with you always," He said, "even unto the end of the world." And He is just as available to us now as He was to His own disciples 1900 years ago.

"I have given you power to tread serpents and scorpions under foot and to trample on all the power of the enemy; and in no case shall anything do you harm."

That gift was never meant to be confined to His own disciples or to any other one group. God has never dealt in special or temporary gifts. He gives to *all*—to all who will accept—to all who have an understanding heart.

All sickness, all poverty, all sorrow, is the result of the incorrect use of some gift of God, which in itself is inherently good. It is just as though we took the numbers that were given us to work out a problem, and put them in the wrong places. The result would be incorrect, inharmonious. We would not be expressing the truth. The moment we rearrange those numbers properly, we get the correct answer—harmony—the *truth!* There was nothing wrong with the principle of mathematics before—the fault was all with us, with our incorrect arrangement of the figures.

What is true of the principle of mathematics is true of every principle. The principle is changeless, undying. It is only our expression of the principle that changes as our understanding of it becomes more thorough. Lightning held only terror for man until he made of electricity his servant. Steam was only so much waste until man learned to harness it. Fire and water are the most destructive forces known—until properly used, then they are man's greatest helpers. There is nothing wrong with any gift of God—once we find the way to use it. The truth is always there if we can find the principle behind it. The figures in mathematics are never bad. It is merely our incorrect arrangement of them.

The great need is an open mind and the desire for understanding. How far in the science of mathematics would you get if you approached the study of it with the preconceived notion that two plus two makes five, and nothing you heard to the contrary was going to change that belief? "Except ye turn, and become as little children, ye shall not enter into the kingdom of heaven." You must drop all your preconceived ideas, all your prejudices. You must never say—"Oh, that sounds like so-and-so. I don't want any of it." Just remember that any great movement must have at least a grain of truth back of it, else it could never grow to any size. Seek that grain of truth. Be open-minded. Keep your eyes and ears open for the truth. If you can do this, you will find that new wordings, different interpretations, are but the outer shell. You can still see the Truth beneath.

THE ONLY POWER

He who is looking for wisdom, power, or permanent success, will find it only within. Mind is the only cause. Your body is healthy or sick according to the images of thought you impress upon your subconscious mind. If you will hold thoughts of health instead of sickness, if you will banish all thoughts of disease and decay, you can build up a perfect body.

You believe that disease is necessary, that you have to expect a certain amount of it. You hear of it every day, and subconsciously at least you are constantly in fear of it. And through that very fear you create it, when if you would spend that same amount of time thinking and believing in the necessity of HEALTH, you would never need to know disease.

Disease is not sent by God. It is not a visitation of Providence. If it were, what would be the use of doctoring it? You couldn't fight against the power of God!

God never sent us anything but good. He never gave us disease. When we allow disease to take hold of us, it is because we have lost touch with God—lost the perfect model of us that He holds in mind. And what we have to strive for is to get back the belief in that perfect model—to forget the diseased image we are holding in our thought.

Remember the story of Alexander and his famous horse, Bucephalus? No one could ride the horse because it was afraid of its shadow, but Alexander faced it toward the sun—and rode it without trouble. Face toward the sun and the shadows will fall behind you, too. Face toward the perfect image of every organ, and the shadows of disease will never touch you.

There is no germ in a draft capable of giving you a cold. There is no bacteria in exposure to the weather that can give you a fever or pneumonia. It is you that gives them to yourself. The draft doesn't reason this out. Neither does your body. They are both of them merely phases of matter. They are not intelligent. It is your conscious mind that has been educated to think that a cold must follow exposure to a draft. This it is that suggests it to your subconscious mind and brings the cold into being.

Before you decide again that you have a cold, ask yourself, Who is it that is taking this cold? It cannot be my nose, for it has no intelligence. It does only what my subconscious mind directs. And anyway, how could my nose know that a draft of air has been playing on the back of my neck? If it wasn't my nose that decided it, what was it? The only thing it can have been is my mind. Well, if mind can tell me to have a cold, surely it can stop that cold, too. So let's reverse the process, and instead of holding before the subconscious mind images of colds and fevers, think only of health and life and strength. Instead of trying to think back to discover how we "caught" cold, and thus strengthening the conviction that we have one, let us deny its existence and so knock the props out from under the creative faculties that are originating the cold. Let us hold before our subconscious mind only the perfect idea of nose and head and throat that is in Universal Mind. Let us make it use the Truth for its pattern, instead of the illusory ideas of conscious mind.

Farnsworth in his "Practical Psychology" tells of a physician who has lived on a very restricted diet for years while at home. But about once a year he comes to New York for a week. While here, he eats anything and everything that his fancy dictates, and never suffers the least inconvenience. As soon as he gets home he has to return to his diet. Unless he sticks to his diet, he expects to be *ill—and he is ill.* "As a man thinketh, so is he." What one expects to get he is apt to get, especially where health is concerned. For matter has no sensation of its own. The conscious mind is what produces pain, is what feels, acts or impedes action.

Functional disorders are caused by certain suggestions getting into the subconsciousness and remaining there. They are not due to physical, but to mental causes—due to wrong thinking. The basis of all functional disorders is in the mind, though the manifestation be dyspepsia, melancholia, palpitation of the heart, or any one of a hundred others. There is nothing organically wrong with the body.

It is your mental image that is out of adjustment. Change the one and you cure the other.

There is but one right idea in Universal Mind for every organism in your body—this right idea is perfect and undying—and you have only to hold it before your subconscious mind with faith and desire to see it realized in your body. *This is the truth that makes you free.*

CHAPTER XI

THE LAW OF ATTRACTION

For life is the mirror of king and slave.
'Tis just what you are and do;
Then give to the world the best you have,
And the best will come back to you.

—MADELINE BRIDGES

The old adage that "He profits most who serves best" is no mere altruism.

Look around you. What businesses are going ahead? What men are making the big successes? Are they the ones who grab the passing dollar, careless of what they offer in return? Or are they those who are striving always to give a little greater value, a little more work than they are paid for?

When scales are balanced evenly, a trifle of extra weight thrown into either side overbalances the other as effectively as a ton.

In the same way, a little better value, a little extra effort, makes the man or the business stand out from the great mass of mediocrity like a tall man among pygmies, and brings results out of all proportion to the additional effort involved.

It pays—not merely altruistically, but in good, hard, round dollars—to give a little more value than seems necessary, to work a bit harder than you are paid for. It's that extra ounce of value that counts.

For the law of attraction is service. We receive in proportion as we give out. In fact, we usually receive in far greater proportion. "Cast thy bread upon the waters and it will return to you an hundred-fold."

Back of everything is the immutable law of the Universe—that what you are is but the effect. Your thoughts are the causes. The only way you can change the effect is by first changing the cause.

People live in poverty and want because they are so wrapped up in their sufferings that they give out thoughts only of lack and sorrow. They expect want. They open the door of their mind only to hardship and sickness and poverty. True—they hope for something better—but their hopes are so drowned by their fears that they never have a chance.

You cannot receive good while expecting evil. You cannot demonstrate plenty while looking for poverty. "Blessed is he that expecteth much, for verily his soul shall be filled." Solomon outlined the law when he said:

There is that scattereth, and increaseth yet more;
And there is that withholdeth more than is meet, but it
tendeth only to want.
The liberal soul shall be made fat;
And he that watereth shall be watered also himself.

The Universal Mind expresses itself largely through the individual. It is continually seeking an outlet. It is like a vast reservoir of water, constantly replenished by mountain springs. Cut a channel to it and the water will flow in ever-increasing volume. In the same way, if you once open up a channel of service by which the Universal Mind can express itself through you, its gifts will flow in ever-increasing volume and YOU will be enriched in the process.

This is the idea through which great bankers are made. A foreign country needs millions for development. Its people are hard-working, but lack the necessary implements to make their work productive. How are they to find the money?

They go to a banker—put their problem up to him. He has not the money himself, but he knows how and where to raise it. He sells the promise to pay of the foreign country (their bonds, in other words) to people who have money to invest. His is merely a service. But it is such an invaluable service that both sides are glad to pay him liberally for it.

In the same way, by opening up a channel between universal supply and human needs—by doing your neighbors or your friends or your customers service—you are bound to profit yourself. And the wider you open your channel—the greater service you give or the better values you offer—the more things are bound to flow through your channel, the more you are going to profit thereby.

But you must *use* your talent if you want to profit from it. It matters not how small your service—using it will make it greater. You don't have to retire to a cell and pray. That is a selfish method—selfish concern for your own soul to the exclusion of all others. Mere self-denial or asceticism as such does no one good. You must DO something, USE the talents God has given you to make the world better for your having been in it.

Remember the parable of the talents. You know what happened to the man who went off and hid his talent, whereas those who made use of theirs were given charge over many things.

That parable, it has always seemed to me, expresses the whole law of life. The only right is to *use* all the forces of good. The only wrong is to *neglect* or to abuse them.

"Thou shalt love the Lord thy God. This is the first and the greatest Commandment." Thou shalt show thy love by using to the best possible advantage the good things (the "talents" of the parable) that He has placed in your hands. "And the second is like unto it. Thou shalt love thy neighbor as thyself." Thou shalt not abuse the good things that have been provided you in such prodigality, by using them against your neighbor. Instead, thou shalt treat him (love him) as you would be treated by him. Thou shalt use the good about you for the advantage of all. Thou shalt *serve!*

If you are a banker, you must use the money you have in order to make more money. If you are a merchant, you must sell the goods you have in order to buy more goods. If you are a doctor, you must help the patient you have in order to get more practice. If you are a clerk, you must do your work a little better than those around you if you want to earn more money than they. And if you want more of the universal supply, you must use that which you have in such a way as to make yourself of greater service to those around you.

"Whosoever shall be great among you," said Jesus, "shall be your minister, and whosoever of you will be the chiefest, shall be servant of all." In other words, if you would be great, you must serve. And he who serves most shall be greatest of all.

If you want to make more money, instead of seeking it for yourself, see how you can make more for others. In the process you will inevitably make more for yourself, too. We get as we give—but we must give first.

It matters not where you start—you may be a day laborer. But still you can give—give a bit more of energy, of work, of thought, than you are paid for. "Whosoever shall compel thee to go a mile," said Jesus, "go with him twain." Try to put a little extra skill into your work. Use your mind to find some better way of doing whatever task may be set for you. It won't be long before you are out of the common labor class.

There is no kind of work that cannot be bettered by thought. There is no method that cannot be improved by thought. So give generously of your thought to your work. Think every minute you are at it—"Isn't there some way in which this could be done easier, quicker, better?" Read in your spare time everything that relates to your own work or to the job ahead of you. In these days of magazines and books and libraries, few are the occupations that are not thoroughly covered in some good work.

Remember in Lorimer's "Letters of a Self-Made Merchant to His Son," the young fellow that old Gorgan Graham hired against his better judgment and put in the "barrel gang" just to get rid of him quickly? Before the month was out the young fellow had thought himself out of that job by persuading the boss to get a machine that did the work at half the cost and with a third of the gang. Graham just had to raise his pay and put him higher up. But he wouldn't stay put. No matter what the job, he always found some way it could be done better and with fewer people. Until he reached the top of the ladder.

There are plenty of men like that in actual life. They won't stay down. They are as full of bounce as a cat with a small boy and a dog after it. Thrown to the dog from an upper window, it is using the time of falling to get set for the next jump. By the time the dog leaps for where it hit, the cat is up the tree across the street.

The true spirit of business is the spirit of that plucky old Danish sea captain, Peter Tordenskjold. Attacked by a

Swedish frigate, after all his crew but one had been killed and his supply of cannon balls was exhausted, Peter boldly kept up the fight, firing pewter dinner-plates and mugs from his one remaining gun.

One of the pewter mugs hit the Swedish captain and killed him, and Peter sailed off triumphant!

Look around YOU now. How can YOU give greater value for what you get? How can you SERVE better? How can you make more money for your employers or save more for your customers? Keep that thought ever in the forefront of your mind and *you'll never need to worry about making more for yourself!*

A BLANK CHECK

There was an article by Gardner Hunting in an old issue of "Christian Business," that was so good that I reprint it here entire:

"All my life I have known in a vague way that getting money is the result of earning it; but I have never had a perfect vision of that truth till recently. Summed up now, the result of all my experience, pleasant and unpleasant, is that a man gets back exactly what he gives out, only multiplied.

"If I give to anybody service of a kind that he wants, I shall get back the benefit myself. If I give more service, I shall get more benefit. If I give a great deal more, I shall get a great deal more. But I shall get back more than I give. Exactly as when I plant a bushel of potatoes, I get back thirty or forty bushels, and more in proportion to the attention I give the growing crop. If I give more to my employer than he expects of me, he will give me a raise—and on no other condition. What is more, his giving me a raise does not depend on his fair-mindedness—he has to give it to me or lose me, because if he does not appreciate me somebody else will.

"But this is only part of it. If I give help to the man whose desk is next to mine, it will come back to me multiplied, even if he apparently is a rival. What I give to him, I give to the firm, and the firm will value it, because it is teamwork in the organization that the firm primarily wants, not brilliant individual performance. If I have an enemy in the organization, the same rule holds; if I give him, with the purpose of helping him, something that will genuinely help him, I am giving service to the organization. Great corporations appreciate the peace-maker, for a prime requisite in their success is harmony among employees. If my boss is unappreciative, the same rule holds; if I give him more, in advance of appreciation, he cannot withhold his appreciation and keep his own job.

"The more you think about this law, the deeper you will see it goes. It literally hands you a blank check, signed by the Maker of Universal Law, and leaves you to fill in the amount—and the kind—of payment you want! Mediocre successes are those that obey this law a little way—that fill in the check with a small amount—but that stop short of big vision in it. If every employee would only get the idea of this law firmly fixed in him as a principle, not subject to wavering with fluctuating moods, the success of the organization would be miraculous. One of my fears is apt to be that, by promoting the other fellow's success, I am sidetracking my own; but the exact opposite is the truth.

"Suppose every employee would look at his own case as an exact parallel to that of his firm. What does his firm give for the money it gets from the public? Service! Service in advance! The better the service that is given out, the more money comes back. What does the firm do to bring public attention to its service? It advertises; that is part of the service. Now, suppose that I, as an employee, begin giving my service to the firm in advance of all hoped for payment. Suppose I advertise my service. How do I do either? I cannot do anything constructive in that firm's office or store or plant or premises that is not service, from filing a letter correctly to mending the fence or pleasing a customer; from looking up a word for the stenographer, to encouraging her to look it up herself; demonstrating a machine to a customer or encouraging him to demonstrate it himself; from helping my immediate apparent rival to get a raise, to selling the whole season's output. As for advertising myself, I begin advertising myself the moment I walk into the office or the store or the shop in the morning; I cannot help it. Everybody who looks at me sees my advertisement. Everybody around me has my advertisement before his eyes all day long. So has the boss—my immediate chief and the head of the firm, no matter where they are. And if I live up to my advertising, nobody can stop me from selling my goods—my services! The more a man knocks me, the more he advertises me; because he calls attention to me; and if I am delivering something better than he says I am, the interested parties—my employers—will see it, and will not be otherwise influenced by what he says.

"More than that, I must give to every human being I come in contact with, from my wife to the bootblack who shines my shoes; from my brother to my sworn foe. Sometimes people will tell you to smile; but the smile I give has got to be a real smile that lives up to its advertising. If I go around grinning like a Cheshire cat, the Cheshire cat grin will be what I get back—multiplied! If I give the real thing, I'll get back the real thing—multiplied! If any body objects that this is a selfish view to take, I answer him that any law of salvation from anything by anybody that has ever been offered for any purpose, is a selfish view to take. The only unselfishness that has ever been truly taught is that of giving a lesser thing in hope of receiving a greater.

"Now, why am I so sure of this law? How can you be sure? I have watched it work; it works everywhere. You have only to try it, and keep on trying it and it will prove true for you. It is not true because I say so, nor because anybody else says so; it is just true. Theosophists call it the law of Karma; humanitarians call it the law of Service; business men call it the law of common sense; Jesus Christ called it the law of Love. It rules whether I know it or not, whether I believe it or not, whether I defy it or not. I *can't* break it! Jesus of Nazareth, without reference to any religious idea you may have about Him, without consideration as to whether He was or was not divine, was the greatest business Man that ever lived, and he said: 'Give and ye shall receive—good measure, pressed down, shaken together, running over!' And this happens to be so—not because He said it—but because it is the Truth, which we all, whether we admit it or not, worship *as* God. No man can honestly say that he does not put the truth supreme.

"It is the truth—the principle of giving and receiving—only there are few men who go the limit on it. But going the limit is the way to unlimited returns!

"What shall I give? What I have, of course. Suppose you believe in this idea—and suppose you should start giving it out, the idea itself, tactfully, wisely, and living it yourself in your organization. How long do you think it will be before you are a power in that organization, recognized as such and getting pay as such? It is more valuable than all cleverness and special information you can possibly possess without it. What you have, give—to everybody. If you have an idea, do not save it for your own use only; give it. It is the best thing you have to give and therefore the thing best to give—and therefore the thing that will bring the best back to you. I believe that if a man would follow this principle, even to his trade-secrets, he would profit steadily more and more; and more certainly than he will by holding on to anything for himself. He would never have to worry about his own affairs—because he would be working on fundamental law. Law never fails—and it will be easy for you to discover what is or is not law. And if law is worth using part of the time, it is worth using all the time.

"Look around you first, with an eye to seeing the truth, and then put the thing to the test. Through both methods of investigation you will find a blank check waiting for you to fill in with 'whatsoever you desire,' and a new way to pray and to get what you pray for."

CHAPTER XII

THE THREE REQUISITES

Waste no tears
Upon the blotted record of lost years,
But turn the leaf, and smile, oh smile, to see
The fair white pages that remain for thee.

Prate not of thy repentance. But believe
The spark divine dwells in thee: let it grow.
That which the upreaching spirit can achieve
The grand and all creative forces know;
They will assist and strengthen as the light
Lifts up the acorn to the oak-tree's height.
Thou has but to resolve, and lo! God's whole
Great universe shall fortify thy soul.

—Ella Wheeler Wilcox

Sometime today or tomorrow or next month, in practically every commercial office and manufacturing plant in the United States, an important executive will sit back in his chair and study a list of names on a sheet of white paper before him.

Your name may be on it.

A position of responsibility is open and he is face to face with the old, old problem—"Where can I find the man?"

The faces, the words, the work, the impressions of various men will pass through his mind in quick review. What is the first question he will ask concerning each?

"Which man is strongest on initiative, which one can best assume responsibility?"

Other things being equal, THAT is the man who will get the job. For the first requisite in business as in social life is confidence in yourself—*knowledge of your power.* Given that, the second is easy—initiative or *the courage to start things.* Lots of men have ideas, but few have the confidence in themselves or the courage to start anything.

With belief and initiative, the third requisite follows almost as a matter of course—*the faith to go ahead* and do things in the face of all obstacles.

"Oh, God," said Leonardo da Vinci, "you sell us everything for the price of an effort."

Certainly no one had a better chance to know than he. An illegitimate son, brought up in the family of his father, the misfortune of his birth made him the source of constant derision. He had to do something to lift himself far above the crowd. And he did. "For the price of an effort" he became the greatest artist in Italy—probably the greatest in the world—in a day when Italy was famous for her artists. Kings and princes felt honored at being associated with this illegitimate boy. He made the name he had no right to, famous for his work alone.

"Work out your own salvation," said Paul. And the first requisite in working it out is a knowledge of your power. "Every man of us has all the centuries in him."—Morley. All the ages behind you have bequeathed you stores of abilities which you are allowing to lie latent. Those abilities are stored up in your superconscious mind. Call upon them. Use them. As Whittier put it—

All the good the past has had
Remains to make our own time glad.

Are you an artist? The cunning of a Leonardo, the skill of a Rembrandt, the vision of a Reynolds, is behind those fingers of yours. Use the Genie-of-Your-Mind to call upon them.

Are you a surgeon, a lawyer, a minister, an engineer, a business man? Keep before your mind's eye the biggest men who have ever done the things you now are doing. Use them as your model. And not as your model simply, but as your inspiration. Start in where they left off. Call upon the innermost recesses of your superconscious mind, for their skill, their judgment, their initiative. Realize that you have it in you to be as great as they. Realize that all that they did, all that they learned, all the skill they acquired is stored safely away in Universal Mind and that through your superconscious mind *you have ready access to it.*

The mind in you is the same mind that animated all the great conquerors of the past, all the great inventors, all the great artists, statesmen, leaders, business men. What they have done is but a tithe of what still remains to do—of what men in your day and your children's day will do. You can have a part in it. Stored away within you is every power that any man or woman ever possessed. It awaits only your call.

In "Thoughts on Business," we read: "It is a great day in a man's life when he truly begins to discover himself. The latent capacities of every man are greater than he realizes, and he may find them if he diligently seeks for them. A man may own a tract of land for many years without knowing its value. He may think of it as merely a pasture. But one day he discovers evidences of coal and finds a rich vein beneath his land. While mining and prospecting for coal he discovers deposits of granite. In boring for water he strikes oil. Later he discovers a vein of copper ore, and after that silver and gold. These things were there all the time—even when he thought of his land merely as a pasture. But they have a value only when they are discovered and utilized.

"Not every pasture contains deposits of silver and gold,

neither oil nor granite, nor even coal. But beneath the surface of every man there must be, in the nature of things, a latent capacity greater than has yet been discovered. And one discovery must lead to another until the man finds the deep wealth of his own possibilities. History is full of the acts of men who discovered somewhat of their own capacity; but history has yet to record the man who fully discovered all that he might have been."

Everything that has been done, thought, gained, or been is in Universal Mind. And you are a part of Universal Mind. You have access to it. You can call upon it for all you need in the same way you can go to your files or to a library for information. If you can realize this fact, you will find in it the key to the control of every circumstance, the solution of every problem, the satisfaction of every right desire.

But to use that key, you must bear in mind the three requisites of faith in your powers, initiative, and courage to start. "Who would stand before a blackboard," says Mary B. Eddy in "Science and Health," "and pray the principle of mathematics to solve the problem? The rule is already established, and it is our task to work out the solution." In the same way, all knowledge you can need is in Universal Mind, but it is up to *you* to tap that mind.

And without the three requisites you will never do it.

Never let discouragement hold you back. Discouragement is the most dangerous feeling there is, because it is the most insidious. Generally looked upon as harmless, it is for that very reason the more sinister. For failure and success are oftentimes separated by only the distance of that one word—Discouragement.

There is an old-time fable that the devil once held a sale and offered all the tools of his trade to anyone who would pay their price. They were spread out on the table, each one labeled—hatred, malice, envy, despair, sickness, sensuality—all the weapons that everyone knows so well.

But off on one side, apart from the rest, lay a harmless-looking, wedge-shaped instrument marked "Discouragement." It was old and worn looking, but it was priced far above all the rest. When asked the reason why, the devil replied:

"Because I can use this one so much more easily than the others. No one knows that it belongs to me, so with it I can open doors that are tight bolted against the others. Once I get inside I can use any tool that suits me best."

No one ever knows how small is the margin between failure and success. Ask the Fords, the Edisons, ask any successful man and he will tell you how narrow is the chasm that separates failure from success, how surely it can be bridged by perseverance and faith.

Cultivate confidence in yourself. Cultivate the feeling that you ARE succeeding. Know that you have unlimited power to do every right thing. Know that with Universal Mind to draw upon, no position is too difficult, and no problem too hard. "He that believeth on me, the works that I do shall he do also; and greater works than these shall he do." When you put limitations upon yourself, when you doubt your ability to meet any situation, you are placing a limit upon Universal Mind, for "The Father that is within me, He doeth the works."

With that knowledge of your power, with that confidence in the unlimited resources of Universal Mind, it is easy enough to show initiative, it is easy enough to find the courage to start things.

You have a right to dominion over all things—over your body, your environment, your business, your health. Develop these three requisites and you will gain that dominion.

Remember that you are a part of Universal Mind, and that the part shares every property of the whole. Remember that, as the spark of electricity is to the thunderbolt, so is your mind to Universal Mind. Whatever of good you may desire of life, whatever qualification, whatever position, you have only to work for it whole-heartedly, confidently, with singleness of purpose—*and you can get it.*

CHAPTER XIII

THAT OLD WITCH—BAD LUCK

How do you tackle your work each day?
Are you scared of the job you find?
Do you grapple the task that comes your way
With a confident, easy mind?
Do you stand right up to the work ahead
Or fearfully pause to view it?
Do you start to toil with a sense of dread
Or feel that you're going to do it?

What is the thought that is in your mind?
Is fear ever running through it?
If so, just tackle the next you find
By thinking you're going to do it.

—EDGAR A. GUEST*

*From "A Heap o' Livin'." The Reilly & Lee Co.

Has that old witch—bad luck—ever camped on your doorstep? Have ill health, misfortune and worry ever seemed to dog your footsteps?

If so, you will be interested in knowing that YOU were the procuring cause of all that trouble. For fear is merely creative thought in negative form.

Remember back in 1929 how fine the business outlook seemed, how everything looked rosy and life flowed along like a song? We had crops worth ten billions of dollars. We had splendid utilities, great railways, almost unlimited factory capacity. Everyone was busy. The government had a billion dollars in actual money. The banks were sound. The people were well employed. Wages were good. Prosperity was general. *Then something happened.* A wave of fear swept over the country. The prosperity could not last. People wouldn't pay such high prices. There was too much inflation. What was the result?

As Job put it in the long ago, "The thing that I greatly feared has come upon me."

The prosperity vanished almost over night. Failures became general. Millions were thrown out of work. And all because of panic, fear.

'Tis true that readjustments were necessary. 'Tis true that prices were too high, that inventories were too big, that values generally were inflated. But it wasn't necessary to burst the balloon to let out the gas. There are orderly natural processes of readjustment that bring things to their proper level with the least harm to anyone.

But fear—panic—knows no reason. It brings into being overnight the things that it fears. It is the greatest torment of humanity. It is about all there is to Hell. *Fear is, in short, the Devil.* It causes most of the sin, disaster, disease and misery of the world. It is the only thing you can put into business which will not draw dividends in either fun or dollars. If you guess right, you don't get any satisfaction out of it.

The cause of much sickness is fear. You image some disease in your thought, and your body proceeds to build upon this model that you hold before it. You have seen how fear makes the face pallid, how it first stops the beating of the heart, then sets it going at trip-hammer pace. Fear changes the secretions. Fear halts the digestion. Fear puts lines and wrinkles into the face. Fear turns the hair gray.

Mind controls every function of the human body. If the thought you hold before your subconscious mind is the fear of disease, of colds or catarrh, of fever or indigestion, those are the images your subconscious mind will work out in your body. For your body itself is merely so much matter—an aggregation of protons and electrons, just as the table in front of you is an aggregation of these same buttons of force, but with a different density and rate of motion. Take away your mind, and your body is just as inert, just as lifeless, just as senseless, as the table. Every function of your body, from the beating of your heart to the secretions in your glands, is controlled by mind. The digestion of your food is just as much a function of your mind as the moving of your finger.

Your body is like clay in the hands of a potter. Your mind can make of it what it will. The clay has nothing to say about what form it shall take. Neither have your head, your heart, your lungs, your digestive organs anything to say about how conditions shall affect them. They do not decide whether they shall be dizzy or diseased or lame. It is mind that makes this decision. They merely conform to it AFTER mind has decided it. Matter has undergone almost any and every condition without harm, when properly sustained by mind. And what it has done once, it can do again.

When you understand that your muscles, your nerves, your bones have no feeling or intelligence of their own, when you learn that they react to conditions only as mind directs that they shall react, you will never again think or speak of any organ as imperfect, as weak or ailing. You will never again complain of tired bodies, aching muscles, or frayed nerves. On the contrary, you will hold steadfast to thoughts of exhaustless strength, of superabundant vitality, knowing that, as Shakespeare said—"There is nothing, either good or bad, but thinking makes it so."

Never fear disaster, for the fear of it is an invitation to disaster to come upon you. Fear being vivid, easily impresses itself upon the subconscious mind. And by so impressing itself, it brings into being the thing that is feared. It is the Frankenstein monster that we all create at times, and which, created, turns to rend its creator. Fear that something you greatly prize will be lost and the fear you feel will create the very means whereby you will lose it.

Fear is the Devil. It is the ravening lion roaming the earth seeking whom it may devour. The only safety from it is to deny it. The only refuge is in the knowledge that it has no power other than the power you give to it.

HE WHOM A DREAM HATH POSSESSED

You fear debt. So your mind concentrates upon it and brings about greater debts. You fear loss. And by visualizing that loss you bring it about.

The only remedy for fear is to know that evil has no power—that it is a nonentity—merely a lack of something. You fear ill health, when if you would concentrate that same amount of thought upon good health you would insure the very condition you fear to lose. Farnsworth in his "Practical Psychology" tells of a man who had conceived the idea when a boy that the eating of cherries and milk together had made him sick. He was very fond of both, but always had to be careful not to eat them together, for whenever he did he had been ill. Mr. Farnsworth explained to him that there was no reason for such illness, because all milk sours anyway just as soon as it reaches the stomach. As a matter of fact it cannot be digested until it does sour. He then treated the man mentally for this wrong association of ideas, and after the one treatment the man was never troubled in this way again, though he had been suffering from it for forty-five years.

If you had delirium tremens, and thought you saw pink elephants and green alligators and yellow snakes all about you, it would be a foolish physician that would try to cure you of snakes. Or that would prescribe glasses to improve your eyesight, when he knew that the animals round about you were merely distorted visions of your mind.

The Bible contains one continuous entreaty to cast out fear. From beginning to end, the admonition "Fear not" is insistent; Fear is the primary cause of all bodily impairment. Jesus understood this and He knew that it could be abolished. Hence His frequent admonition—"Fear not, be not afraid."

Struggle there is. And struggle there will always be. But struggle is merely wrestling with trial. We need difficulties to overcome. But there is nothing to be afraid of. Everything is an effect of mind. Your thought forces, concentrated upon anything, will bring that thing into manifestation. Therefore concentrate them only upon good things, only upon those conditions you wish to see manifested. *Think* health, power, abundance, happiness. Drive all thoughts of poverty and disease, of fear and worry, as far from your mind as you drive filth from your homes. For fear and worry are the filth of the mind that causes all trouble, that brings about all disease. Banish them! Banish from among your associates any man with a negative outlook on life. Shun him as you would the plague. Can you imagine a knocker winning anything? He is doomed before he starts. Don't let him pull you down with him. "Fret not thyself," says the Psalmist, "else shalt thou be moved to do evil."

That wise old Psalmist might have been writing for us today. For there is no surer way of doing the wrong thing in business or in social life than to fret yourself, to worry, to fume, to want action of some kind, regardless of what it may be. Remember the Lord's admonition to the Israelites, *"Be still*—and know that I am God."

Have you ever stood on the shore of a calm, peaceful lake and watched the reflections in it? The trees, the mountains, the clouds, the sky, all were mirrored there—just as perfectly, as beautifully, as the objects themselves. But try to get such a reflection from the ocean! It cannot be done, because the ocean is always restless, always stirred up by winds or waves or tides.

So it is with your mind. You cannot reflect the richness and plenty of Universal Mind, you cannot mirror peace and health and happiness, if you are constantly worried, continually stirred by waves of fear, winds of anger, tides of toil and striving. You must relax at times. You must give mind a chance. You must realize that, when you have done your best, you can confidently lean back and leave the outcome to Universal Mind.

Just as wrong thinking produces disease in the body, so it also brings about discordant conditions in the realm of commerce. Experience teaches that we need to be protected more from our fears and wrong thoughts, than from so-called evil influences external to ourselves. We need not suffer for another man's wrong, for another's greed, dishonesty, avarice or selfish ambition. But if we hug to ourselves the fear that we do have to so suffer, take it into our thought, allow it to disturb us, then we sentence ourselves. We are free to reject every suggestion of discord, and to be governed harmoniously, in spite of what anything or anybody may try to do to us.

Do you know why experienced army officers would rather have soldiers of 18 or 20 than mature men of 30 or 40? Not because they can march farther. They can't! Not because they can carry more. They can't! But because when they go to sleep at night, they really sleep. *They wipe the slate clean!* When they awaken in the morning, they are ready for a new day and a new world.

But an older man carries the nervous strain of one day over to the next. He worries! With the result that at the end of a couple of months' hard campaigning, the older man is a nervous wreck.

And that is the trouble with most men in business. *They never wipe the slate clean! They worry!* And they carry each day's worries over to the next, with the result that some day the burden becomes more than they can carry.

THE BARS OF FATE

Fear results from a belief that there are really two powers in this world—Good and Evil. Like light and darkness. When the fact is that Evil is no more real than darkness. True, we lose contact with Good at times. We let the clouds of fear and worry come between us and the sunlight of Good and then all seems dark. But the sun is still shining on the other side of those clouds, and when we drive them away, we again see its light.

Realizing this, realizing that Good is ever available if we will but turn to it confidently in our need, what is there to fear? "Fear not, little flock," said Jesus, "for it is the Father's good pleasure to give you the kingdom." And again—"Son, thou art ever with me, and all that I have is thine."

If this means anything, it means that the Father is ever available to all of us, that we have but to call upon Him in the right way and our needs will be met. It doesn't matter what those needs may be.

If Universal Mind is the Creator of all, and if everything in the Universe belongs to It, then your business, your work, isn't really yours—but the "Father's." And He is just as much interested in its success, as long as you are working in accordance with His plan, as you can be.

Everyone will admit that Universal Mind can do anything good. Everyone will admit that It can bring to a successful conclusion any undertaking It may be interested in. If Mind created your business, if It inspired your work, then It is interested in its successful conclusion.

Why not, then, call upon Mind when you have done all you know how to do and yet success seems beyond your efforts? Why not put your problem up to Mind, secure in the belief that It CAN and WILL give you any right thing you may desire? I know that many people hesitate to pray for material things, but if Universal Mind made them, they must have been made for some good purpose, and as long as you intend to use them for good, by all means ask for them.

If you can feel that your business, your work, is a good work, if you can be sure that it is advancing the great Scheme of Things by ever so little, you will never again fear debt or lack or limitation. For "The earth is the Lord's and the fullness thereof." Universal Mind is never going to lack for means to carry on Its work. When Jesus needed fish and bread, fish and bread were provided in such abundance that a whole multitude was fed. When He needed gold, the gold coin appeared in the fish's mouth. Where you are, Mind is, and where Mind is, there is all the power, all the supply of the universe.

You are like the owner of a power house that supplies electricity for light and heat and power to the homes and the factories around you. There is unlimited electricity everywhere about you, but you have to set your dynamo going to draw the electricity out of the air and into your power lines, before it can be put to practical account.

Just so, there are unlimited riches all about you, but you have to set the dynamo of your mind to work to bring them into such form as will make them of use to yourself and the world.

So don't worry about any present lack of money or other material things. Don't try to win from others what they have. Go where the money is! The material wealth that is in evidence is so small compared with the possible wealth available through the right use of mind, that it is negligible by comparison. The great rewards are for the pioneers. Look at Carnegie; at Woolworth; at Ford! Every year some new field of development is opened, some new world discovered. Steam, gas, electricity, telegraphy, wireless, the automobile, the airplane—each opens up possibilities of new worlds yet to come.

A hundred years ago, people probably felt that everything had been discovered that could be discovered, that everything was known that was likely ever to be known. One man quit the Patent Office in Washington back in the 1880's because as he put it—"everything had been invented that could be invented." Perhaps you feel that way about things now. Yet look at the tremendous strides mankind has taken in the past fifty years. And they are as nothing to what the future holds for us, once man has learned to harness the truly unlimited powers of his subconscious mind.

There are millions of dollars' worth of treasure under every square mile of the earth's surface. There are millions of ways in which this old world of ours can be made a better place to live. Set your mind to work locating some of this treasure, finding some of those ways. Don't wait for someone else to blaze the trail.

No one remembers who else was on the *Santa Maria,* but Columbus' name will be known forever! Carnegie is said to have made a hundred millionaires, but he alone became almost a *billionaire!*

Have you ever read Kipling's "Explorer"?

"There's no sense in going further—it's the edge of cultivation,"
So they said, and I believed it—broke my land and sowed my crop—
Built my barns and strung my fences in the little border station
Tucked away below the foothills where the trails run out and stop.

Till a voice, as bad as Conscience, rang interminable changes
On one everlasting Whisper day and night repeated—so:
"Something hidden. Go and find it. Go and look behind the Ranges—
Something lost behind the Ranges. Lost and waiting for you. Go!"

Your mind is part and parcel of Universal Mind. You have the wisdom of all the ages to draw upon. Use it! Use it to do your work in a way it was never done before. Use it to find new outlets for your business, new methods of reaching people, new and better ways of serving them. Use it to uncover new riches, to learn ways to make the world a better place to live in.

Concentrate your thought upon these things, knowing

that back of you is the vast reservoir of Universal Mind, that all these things are *already* known to It, and that you have but to make your contact for them to be known to you.

Optimism based on such a realization is never over-confidence. It is the joyous assurance of *absolute faith*. It is the assurance that made Wilson for a time the outstanding leader of the world. It is the assurance that heartened Lincoln during the black days of the Civil War. It is the assurance that carried Hannibal and Napoleon over the Alps, that left Alexander sighing for more worlds to conquer, that enabled Cortez and his little band to conquer a nation.

Grasp this idea of the availability of Universal Mind for your daily needs, and your vision will become enlarged, your capacity increased. You will realize that the only limits upon you are those you put upon yourself. There will be no such thing then as difficulties and opposition barring your way.

EXERCISE

You feed and nourish the body daily. But few people give any thought to nourishing that far more important part—the Mind. So let us try, each day, to set apart a few minutes time to give the Mind a repast.

To begin with, *relax!* Stretch out comfortably on a lounge or in an easy chair and let go of every muscle, loosen every bit of tension, forget every thought of fear or worry. Relax mentally and physically.

Few people know how to relax entirely. Most of us are

on a continual strain, and it is this strain that brings on physical disturbances—not any real work we may do. Here is a little exercise that will help you to thoroughly relax:

Recline comfortably on a lounge or bed. Stretch luxuriously first. Then when you are settled at your ease again, lift the right leg a foot or two. Let it drop limply. Repeat slowly twice. Do the same with the left leg. With the right arm. With the left arm. You will find then that all your muscles are relaxed. You can forget them and turn your thoughts to other things.

Try to realize the unlimited power that is yours. Think back to the dawn of time, when Mind first imaged from nothingness the heavens and the earth and all that in them is. Remember that, although your mind is to Universal Mind only as a drop of water to the ocean, this drop has all the properties of the great ocean; one in quality although not in quantity; your mind has all the creative power of Universal Mind.

"And God made man in His image, after His likeness." Certainly God never manifested anything but infinite abundance, infinite supply. If you are made in His image, there is no reason why you should ever lack for anything of good. You can manifest abundance, too.

Round about you is the same electronic energy from which Universal Mind formed the heavens and the earth. *Use it!* Consciously draw to you the Vital Force all about you. Take deep breaths of it. Then decide—What do you wish to form from it? What do you want most from life?

Hold that thing in your thought, visualize it, see yourself pouring Vital Force into it as into a mold. Make your model clear-cut and distinct.

1. Remember, the first thing necessary is a sincere desire, concentrating your thought on one thing with singleness of purpose.
2. The second is visualization—SEEING YOURSELF DOING IT—imaging the object in the same way that Universal Mind imaged all of creation.
3. Next is faith—BELIEVING that you HAVE this thing that you want. Seeing yourself in your mind's eye pouring your Vital Force into it, filling your thought-molds and making them realities.
4. The last is gratitude—gratitude for this thing that you have received, gratitude for the power that enabled you to create it, gratitude for all the gifts that Mind has laid at your feet in such profusion, gratitude for the illimitable supply of Vital Force, with which you can create anything of good.

Trust in the Lord . . . and verily thou shalt be fed.
Delight thyself also in the Lord, and He shall give thee the desires of thy heart.
Commit thy way unto the Lord, and He shall bring it to pass.

CHAPTER XIV

YOUR NEEDS ARE MET

Arise, O Soul, and gird thee up anew,
Though the black camel Death kneel at this gate;
No beggar thou that thou for alms shouldst sue:
Be the proud captain still of thine own fate.

—KENYON

You have heard the story of the old man who called his children to his bedside to give them a few parting words of advice. And this was the burden of it.

"My children," he said, "I have had a great deal of trouble in my life—a great deal of trouble—*but most of it never happened.*"

We are all of us like that old man. Our troubles weigh us down—in prospect—but we usually find that when the actual need arrives, Providence has devised some way of meeting them.

Dr. Jacques Loeb, a member of the Rockefeller Institute, conducted a series of tests with parasites found on plants, which show that even the lowest orders of creatures have the power to call upon Universal Supply for the resources to meet any unusual need.

"In order to obtain the material," reads the report of the tests, "potted rose bushes are brought into a room and placed in front of a closed window. If the plants are allowed to dry out, the aphides (parasites), previously wingless, change to winged insects. After the metamorphosis, the animals leave the plants, fly to the window and then creep upward on the glass.

"It is evident that these tiny insects found that the plants on which they had been thriving were dead, and that they could therefore secure nothing more to eat and drink from this source. The only method by which they could save themselves from starvation was to grow temporary wings and fly, which they did."

In short, when their source of sustenance was shut off and they had to find the means of migrating or perish, Universal Supply furnished the means for migration.

If Universal Mind can thus provide for the meanest of its creatures, is it not logical to suppose that It will do even more for us—the highest product of creation—if we will but call upon It, if we will but have a little faith? Viewed in the light of Mind's response to the need of those tiny parasites, does it seem so unbelievable that a sea should roll back while a people marched across it dry-shod? That a pillar of fire should lead them through the wilderness by night? That manna should fall from heaven, or water gush forth from a rock?

In moments of great peril, in times of extremity, when the brave soul has staked its all—those are the times when miracles are wrought, if we will but have faith.

That does not mean that you should rest supinely at your ease and let the Lord provide. When you have done all that is in you to do—when you have given of your best—don't worry or fret as to the outcome. Know that if more is needed, your need will be met. You can sit back with the confident assurance that having done your part, you can depend upon the Genie-of-Your-Mind to do the rest.

When the little state of Palestine was in danger of being overrun by Egypt on the one hand, or gobbled up by Assyria on the other, its people were frantically trying to decide which horn of the dilemma to embrace, with which enemy they should ally themselves to stave off the other. "With neither," the Prophet Isaiah told them, "in calmly resting your safety lieth; in quiet trust shall be your strength."

So it is with most of the great calamities that afflict us. If we would only "calmly rest, quietly trust," how much better off we should be. But no—we must fret and worry, and nine times out of ten do the wrong thing. And the more we worry and fret, the more likely we are to go wrong.

All of Universal Mind that is necessary to solve any given problem, to meet any need, is wherever that need may be. Supply is always *where* you are and *what* you need. It matters not whether it be sickness or trouble, poverty or danger, the remedy is there, waiting for your call. Go at your difficulty boldly, knowing that you have infinite resources behind you, and you will find these forces closing around you and coming to your aid. Remember, that to which you give your attention reveals itself.

It is like an author writing a book. For a long time he works in a kind of mental fog, but let him persevere, and there flashes suddenly a light that clarifies his ideas and shows him the way to shape them logically. At the moment of despair, you feel a source of unknown energy arising in your soul.

That does not mean that you will never have difficulties. Difficulties are good for you. They are the exercise of your mind. You are the stronger for having overcome them. But look upon them as mere exercise. As "stunts" that are given you in order that you may the better learn how to use your mind, how to draw upon Universal Supply. Like Jacob wrestling with the Angel, don't let them go until they have blessed you—until, in other words, you have learned something from having encountered them.

Remember this: No matter how great a catastrophe may befall mankind, no matter how general the loss, you and yours can be free from it. There is always a way of safety. There is always an "ark" by which the understanding few can be saved from the flood. The name of that ark is Understanding—understanding of your inner powers.

When the children of Israel were being led into the promised land, arid Joshua had given them their directions, they answered him: "All that thou commandest us we will do, and whithersoever thou sendest us, we will go. . . . Only the Lord thy God be with thee, as He was with Moses."

They came to the river Jordan, and it seemed an insurmountable barrier in their path, but Joshua commanded them to take the Ark of the Covenant, representing God's understanding with them, before them into the Jordan. They did it, and "the waters which came down from above stood and rose up upon an heap. . . . And the priests that bare the Ark of the Covenant of the Lord stood firm on dry ground in the midst of Jordan, and all the Israelites passed over on dry ground, until all the people were passed clean over Jordan."

THE ARK OF THE COVENANT

All through the Old Testament, when war and pestilence, fire and flood, were the common lot of mankind, there is constant assurance of safety for those who have this understanding, this "Covenant" with the Lord. "Because thou hast made the Lord which is my refuge—even the Most High—thy habitation, there shall no evil befall thee, neither shall any plague come nigh thy dwelling. For He shall give His angels charge over thee to keep thee in all thy ways."

That is His agreement with us—an agreement which gives us the superiority to circumstances which men have sought from time immemorial. All that is necessary on our side of the agreement is for us to remember the infinite powers that reside within us, to remember that our mind is part of Universal Mind and as such it can foresee, it can guard against and it can protect us from harm of any kind. We need not run away from trials or try to become stoical toward them. All we need is to bring our understanding to bear upon them—to know that no situation has ever yet arisen with which Universal Mind—and through it our own mind—was not fully competent to deal. To know that the right solution of every problem is in Universal Mind. That we have but to seek that solution and our trial is overcome.

"But where shall Wisdom be found? And where is the place of understanding? Acquaint now thyself with God, and be at peace."

If evil threatens us, if failure, sickness or accident seems imminent, we have only to decide that these evils do not come from Universal Mind, therefore they are unreal and have no power over us. They are simply the absence of the right condition which Universal Mind knows. Refuse, therefore, to see them, to acknowledge them—and seek through Mind for the right condition which shall nullify them.

If you will do this, you will find that you can appropriate from Mind whatever you require for your needs, *when* you require it. The greater your need, the more surely it will be met, if you can but realize this truth. "Fear not, little flock," said Jesus, "for it is your Father's good pleasure to give you the Kingdom."

Remember that your thought is all-powerful. That it is creative. That there is no limitation upon it of time or space.

And that it is ever-available. Look upon your Higher Self as your Guardian Angel, watching over you constantly, able and willing to guide, guard and direct you—if only you will put your dependence upon him.

Forget your worries. Forget your fears. In place of them, visualize the conditions you would like to see. Realize their availability. Declare to yourself that you already *have* all these things that you desire, that your needs *have* been met. Consciously draw to yourself all the Vital Force you need to fill in the mold of right conditions—breathe it in—then SEE yourself pouring that Vital Force into the conditions or objects you desire. Say to yourself: "How thankful I am that Mind has made all these good things available to me. I have everything that heart could desire to be grateful for."

Every time you do this, you are impressing the thought upon your subconscious mind, and through it upon the superconscious. And the moment you can convince your subconscious mind of the truth of it—*that moment* your superconscious mind will proceed to *make* it true. This is the way to put into practice the Master's advice—"Believe that ye RECEIVE it, and ye SHALL HAVE it."

There is no condition so hopeless, no cause so far gone, that this truth will not save it. Time and again patients given over by their doctors as doomed have made miraculous recoveries through the faith of some loved one.

"I hope that everyone who reads this Book may gain as much from their first reading as I did," wrote a happy subscriber from New York City. "I got such a clear understanding from that one reading that I was able to break the mental chain holding a friend to a hospital bed, and she left the hospital in three days, to the very great astonishment of the doctors handling the case."

In the same way, there are innumerable instances where threatened calamity has been warded off and good come instead. The great trouble with most of us is, we do not *believe.* We insist upon looking for trouble. We feel that the "rainy day" is bound to come, and we do our utmost to make it a surety by keeping it in our thoughts, preparing for it, fearing it. "Cowards die many times before their deaths; the valiant never taste of death but once." We cross our bridges a dozen times before we come to them. We doubt ourselves, we doubt our ability, we doubt everyone and everything around us. And our doubts sap our energy; kill our enthusiasm; rob us of success. We are like the old lady who "enjoys poor health." We always place that little word "but" after our wishes and desires, feeling deep down that there are some things too good to be true. We think there is a power apart from Good which can withhold blessings that should be ours. We doubt, because we cannot see the way by which our desires can be fulfilled. We put a limit upon the good that can come to us.

Your mind is part of Universal Mind. And Universal Mind has all supply. You are entitled to, and you can have, just as much of that supply as you are able to appropriate. To expect less is to get less, for it dwarfs your power of receiving. How did Universal Mind form the earth? By first making a mental mold, and then pouring the creative, Vital Force all about into it. That is the only way anything ever has been created. That is the only way YOU can create the conditions you desire.

It doesn't matter what your longings may be, provided they are right longings. If your little son has his heart set on a train and you feel perfectly able to get him a train, you are not going to hand him a picture book instead. It may be that the picture book would have greater educational value, but the love you have for your son is going to make you try to satisfy his longings as long as those longings are not harmful ones.

In the same way, Universal Mind will satisfy *your* longings, no matter how trivial they may seem, as long as they are not harmful ones. "Delight thyself also in the Lord, and He shall give thee the desires of thine heart."

If we would only try to realize that God is not some far-off Deity, not some stern Judge, but the beneficent force that we recognize as Nature—the life Principle that makes the flowers bud and the plants grow, that spreads abundance about us with lavish hand. If we could realize that He is the Universal Mind that holds all supply, that will give us the toy of our childhood or the needs of maturity, that all we need to obtain from Him our Heart's Desire is a right understanding of His availability—then we would lose all our fears, all our worries, all our sense of limitation.

For Universal Mind is an infinite, unlimited source of good. Not only the source of general good, but the specific good things you desire of life. To It there is no big or little problem. The removal of mountains is no more difficult than the feeding of a sparrow.

And to one—like the Master—with a perfect understanding, the "miracle" of raising Lazarus from the dead required no more effort than the turning of the water into wine. He knew that Universal Mind is all power—and there cannot be more than ALL. He knew that "To know God aright is life eternal." And Jesus knew God aright, so was able to demonstrate this knowledge of life eternal in overcoming sin, disease and death. For it is one and the same law that heals sin, sickness, poverty, heartaches, or death itself. That law is the right understanding of Divine Principle.

What does this ability to perform "miracles" consist of? What is the power or force by which we can prove this ability? Perhaps the simplest way is to begin with the realization that Universal Mind is man's working power.

THE SCIENCE OF THOUGHT

Can you stretch your mind a bit and try to comprehend this wonderful fact—that the ALL POWERFUL, ALL KNOWING, EVERLASTING CREATOR and Governor of the infinite universe, "Who hath measured the waters in the hollow of his hand, and meted out heaven with the span, and comprehended the dust of the earth in a measure, and weighed the mountains in scales, and the hills in a balance," is your working power? In proportion as we understand this fact, and make use of it, in that same proportion are we able to perform our miracles.

Your work is inspired to the extent that you realize the presence of Universal Mind in your work. When you rely entirely on your own conscious mind, your work suffers accordingly. "I can of mine own self do nothing; for the works which the Father hath given me to finish, the same works that I do bear witness of me." The miracles of Jesus bear witness of the complete recognition of God the Father as his working power.

And mind you, this inspiration, this working of Universal Mind with you, is available for all of your undertakings. Mind could not show Itself in one part of your life and withhold Itself from another, since It is all in all. Every rightly directed task, no matter how insignificant or menial it may appear to you, carries with it the inspiration of Universal Mind, since by the very nature of omnipotence, Its love and bestowals must be universal and impartial, "and whatsoever ye do, do it heartily as to the Lord."

Too many of us are like the maiden in the old Eastern legend. A Genie sent her into a field of grain, promising her a rare gift if she would pick for him the largest and ripest ear she could find, his gift to be in proportion to the size and perfection of the ear.

But he made this condition—she must pluck only one ear, and she must walk straight through the field without stopping, going back or wandering hither and thither.

Joyously she started. As she walked through the grain,

she saw many large ears, many perfect ones. She passed them by in scorn, thinking to find an extra-large, super-perfect one farther along. Presently, however, the soil became less fertile, the ears small and sparse. She couldn't pick one of these! Would now that she had been content with an ordinary-sized ear farther back. But it was too late for that. Surely they would grow better again farther on!

She walked on—and on—and always they became worse—till presently she found herself at the end of the field—*empty handed as when she set out!*

So it is with life. Every day has its worthwhile rewards for work well done. Every day offers its chance for happiness. But those rewards seem so small, those chances so petty, compared with the big things we see ahead. So we pass them by, never recognizing that the great position we look forward to, the shining prize we see in the distance, is just the sum of all the little tasks, the heaped up result of all the little prizes that we must win as we go along.

You are not commanded to pick out certain occupations as being more entitled to the Lord's consideration than others, but "Whatsoever ye do." Whether it be in the exalted and idealistic realms of poetry, music and art, whether in the cause of religion or philanthropy, whether in government, in business, in science, or simply in household cares, "whatsoever ye do" you are entitled to, and *have* all of inspiration at your beck and call. If you seem to have less than all, it is because you do not utilize your gift.

"Now he that planteth and he that watereth are one;

and every man shall receive his own reward according to his own labour. For we are labourers together with God."

How shall you take advantage of this Universal Supply? When next any need confronts you, when next you are in difficulties, close your eyes for a moment and realize that Universal Mind knows how that need can best be met, knows the solution of your difficulties. And that your superconscious mind, being part of the Universal Mind, can know this, too. So put your problem up to your own Higher Self with the sublime confidence that it will find the solution. Say aloud—"God goes before me and opens the way. Infinite Wisdom tells me just what to do." Then forget it for a while. When the time comes, the need will be met.

Dr. Winbigler corroborates the working out of this idea in the following:

"Suggestions lodged in the mind can effect a complete change, morally and physically. If mankind would become in spirit 'as a little child,' trusting in God implicitly, the greatest power would be utilized in the establishment of health and equilibrium, and the results would be untold in comfort, sanity, and blessing. For instance, here is one who is suffering from worry, fear, and the vexations of life. How can he get rid of these things and relieve this suffering? Let him go to a quiet room or place, twice a day, lie down and relax every muscle, assume complete indifference to those things which worry him and the functions of the body, and quietly accept what God, through this law of demand and supply, can give. In a few days he will find a great change in his feelings, and the sufferings will pass away and life will look bright and promising. Infinite wisdom has established that law; and its utilization by those who are worried and fearful will secure amazing results in a short time.

"The real reason for the change is found in the possibility of recovery by using the laws that God has placed within our reach, and thus securing the coveted health and power for all that we want and ought to do. The subliminal life is the connecting link between man and God, and by obeying His laws, one's life is put in contact with infinite resources and all that God is able and willing to give. Here is the secret of all the cures of disease, and the foundation for the possibility of a joyful existence, happiness and eternal life. Suggestion is the method of securing what God gives, and the mind is the agent through which these gifts are received. This is not a matter of theory, but a fact. If any one who is sick or who desires to be kept well will have stated periods of relaxation, openmindedness and faith, he can prove the beneficial and unvarying result of this method."

CHAPTER XV

THE MASTER OF YOUR FATE

A craven hung along the battle's edge,
And thought, "Had I a sword of keener steel—
That blue blade that the king's son bears,—but
this blunt thing—!"
And lowering crept away and left the field.
Then came the king's son, wounded, sore bestead
And weaponless, and saw the broken sword,
And ran and snatched it, and with battle-shout
Lifted afresh he hewed his enemy down,
And saved a great cause that heroic day.

—Edward Rowland Sill*

*From "Poems." Houghton Mifflin Co.

Where will *you* be at sixty-five? Five men in six at the age of sixty-five are living on charity. Just one in twenty is able to live without working at sixty-five.

That is what the American Bankers Association found when it took one hundred healthy men at twenty-five and traced them to sixty-five.

These hundred were healthy to start with. They all had the same chance for success. The difference lay in the way they used their MINDS. Ninety-five out of one hundred just do the tasks that are set them. They have no faith in themselves—no initiative—none of the courage that starts things. They are always directed or controlled by someone else.

At sixty-five, where will *you* be? Dependent or independent? Struggling for a living—accepting charity from someone else—or at the top of the heap?

"I am the Master of my fate."

Until you have learned that, you will never attain life's full success. Your fate is in your own hands. *You* have the making of it. What you are going to be six months or a year from now depends upon what you think today.

So make your choice now:

Are you going to bow down to matter as the only power? Are you going to look upon your environment as something that has been wished upon you and for which you are in no way responsible?

Or are you going to try to realize in your daily life that matter is merely an aggregation of protons and electrons subject entirely to the control of Mind, that your environment, your success, your happiness, are all of your own making, and that if you are not satisfied with conditions as they are, you have but to visualize them as you would have them be and put your creative power to work in order to change them?

The former is the easier way right now—the easy way that leads to the hell of poverty and fear and old age.

But the latter is the way that brings you to your Heart's Desire.

Merely because this Power of Universal Mind is invisible, is that any reason to doubt it? The greatest powers of Nature are invisible. Love is invisible, but what greater power is there in life? Joy is invisible, happiness, peace, contentment. Radio waves are invisible—yet you hear them. They are a product of the law governing sound waves. Law is invisible, yet you see the manifestation of different laws every day. To run a locomotive, you study the law of applying power, and you apply that law when you make the locomotive go.

These things are not the result of invention. The law has existed from the beginning. It merely waited for man to learn how to apply it. If man had known how to call upon Universal Mind to the right extent, he could have applied the law of sound waves, the law of steam, ages ago. Invention is merely a revelation and an unfoldment of Universal Wisdom.

That same Universal Wisdom knows millions of other laws of which man has not even a glimmering. You can call upon It. You can use that Wisdom as your own. By thinking of things as they might be instead of as they are, you will eventually find some great Need. And to find a need is the first step toward finding the supply to satisfy that need. You have to know what you are after, before you can send the Genie-of-your-Mind seeking it in Universal Mind.

THE ACRE OF DIAMONDS

You remember the story of the poor Boer farmer who struggled for years to glean a livelihood out of his rocky soil, only to give it up in despair and go off to seek his fortune elsewhere. Years later, coming back to his old farm, he found it swarming with machinery and life—more wealth being dug out of it every day than he had ever dreamed existed. It was the great Kimberley Diamond Mine!

Most of us are like that poor Boer farmer. We struggle along under our surface power, never dreaming of the giant power that could be ours if we would but dig a little deeper—rouse that great Inner Self who can give us more even than any acre of diamonds.

As Orison Swett Marden put it:

"The majority of failures in life are simply the victims of their mental defeats. Their conviction that they cannot succeed as others do robs them of that vigor and determination which self-confidence imparts, and they don't even half try to succeed.

"There is no philosophy by which a man can do a thing when he thinks he can't. The reason why millions of men are plodding along in mediocrity today, many of them barely making a living, when they have the ability to do something infinitely bigger, is because they lack confidence in themselves. They don't believe they can do the bigger thing that would lift them out of their rut of mediocrity and poverty; they are not winners mentally.

"The way always opens for the determined soul, the man of faith and courage.

"It is the victorious mental attitude, the consciousness of power, the sense of mastership, that does the big things in this world. If you haven't this attitude, if you lack self-confidence, begin now to cultivate it.

"A highly magnetized piece of steel will attract and lift a piece of unmagnetized steel ten times its own weight. Demagnetize that same piece of steel and it will be powerless to attract or lift even a feather's weight.

"Now, my friends, there is the same difference between the man who is highly magnetized by a sublime faith in himself, and the man who is demagnetized by his lack of faith, his doubts, his fears, that there is between the magnetized and the demagnetized pieces of steel. If two men of equal ability, one *magnetized by a divine self-confidence,* the other demagnetized by fear and doubt, are given similar tasks, one will succeed and the other will fail. The self-confidence of the one *multiplies his powers a hundredfold;* the lack of it subtracts a hundredfold from the power of the other."

Have you ever thought how much of your time is spent in choosing what you shall do, which task you will try, which way you shall go? Every day is a day of decision. We are constantly at crossroads, in our business dealings, our social relations, in our homes, there is always the necessity of a choice. How important then that we have faith in ourselves and in that Infinite intelligence within. "Commit thy works unto the Lord, and thy thoughts shall be established." "In all thy ways acknowledge him, and he shall direct thy paths."

In this ever-changing material age, with seemingly complex forces all about us, we sometimes cry out that we are driven by force of circumstances. Yet the fact remains that we do those things which we choose to do. For even though we may not wish to go a certain way, we allow ourselves to pursue it because it offers the least resistance.

To every man there openeth
A way, and ways, and a way.
And the high soul climbs the high way,
And the low soul gropes the low:
And in between, on the misty flats,
The rest drift to and fro.
But to every man there openeth
A high way and a low,

And every man decideth
The way his soul shall go.

—JOHN OXENHAM

Now, how about you? Are you taking active control of your own thought? Are you imaging upon your subconscious mind only such things as you want to see realized? Are you thinking healthy thoughts, happy thoughts, successful thoughts? "That to which I give my attention reveals itself." To what are you giving your attention?

The difference between the successful man and the unsuccessful one is not so much a matter of training or equipment. It is not a question of opportunity or luck. It is just in the way they each of them look at things.

The successful man sees an opportunity, seizes upon it, and moves upward another rung on the ladder of success. It never occurs to him that he may fail. He sees only the opportunity, he visions what he can do with it, and all the forces within and without him combine to help him win.

The unsuccessful man sees the same opportunity, he wishes that he could take advantage of it, but he is fearful that his ability or his money or his credit may not be equal to the task. He is like a timid bather, putting in one foot and then, drawing it swiftly back again—and while he hesitates some bolder spirit dashes in and beats him to the goal.

Nearly every man can look back—and not so far back either with most of us—and say, "If I had taken that chance, I would be much better off now."

You will never need to say it again, once you realize that the future is entirely within your own control. It is not subject to the whims of fortune or the capaciousness of luck. There is but one Universal Mind and that mind contains naught but good. In it are no images of Evil. From it comes no lack of supply. Its ideas are as numberless as the grains of sand on the seashore. And those ideas comprise all wealth, all power, all happiness.

You have only to image vividly enough on your subconscious mind the thing you wish, to draw from Universal Mind the necessary ideas to bring it into being. You have only to keep in mind the experiences you wish to meet, in order to control your own future.

When Frank A. Vanderlip, former President of the National City Bank, was a struggling youngster, he asked a successful friend what one thing he would urge a young man to do who was anxious to make his way in the world. "Look as though you have already succeeded," his friend told him. Shakespeare expresses the same thought in another way—"Assume a virtue if you have it not." Look the part. Dress the part. Act the part. Be successful in your own thought first. It won't be long before you will be successful before the world as well.

David V. Bush, in his book "Applied Psychology and Scientific Living," says:

"Man is like the wireless operator. Man is subject to miscellaneous wrong thought currents if his mind is not in tune with the Infinite, or if he is not keyed up to higher vibrations than those of negation.

"A man who thinks courageous thoughts sends these courageous thought waves through the universal ether until they lodge in the consciousness of someone who is tuned to the same courageous key. Think a strong thought, a courageous thought, a prosperity thought, and these thoughts will be received by someone who is strong, courageous and prosperous.

"It is just as easy to think in terms of abundance as to think in terms of poverty. If we think poverty thoughts we become the sending and receiving stations for poverty thoughts. We send out a 'poverty' mental wireless and it reaches the consciousness of some poverty-stricken 'receiver.' We get what we think.

"It is just as easy to think in terms of abundance, opulence and prosperity as it is to think in terms of lack, limitation and poverty.

"If a man will raise his rate of vibration by faith currents or hope currents, these vibrations go through the Universal Mind and lodge in the consciousness of people who are keyed to the same tune. Whatever you think is sometime, somewhere, received by a person who is tuned to your thought key.

"If a man is out of work and he thinks thoughts of success, prosperity, harmony, position and growth, just as surely as his thoughts are things—as Shakespeare says—someone will receive his vibrations of success, prosperity, harmony, position and growth.

"If we are going to be timid, selfish, penurious and picayunish in our thinking, these thought waves which we have started in the universal ether will go forth until they come to a mental receiving station of the same caliber. 'Birds of a feather flock together,' and minds of like thinking are attracted one to the other.

"If you need money, all you have to do is to send up your vibrations to a strong, courageous receiving station, and someone who can meet your needs will be attracted to you or you to him."

When you learn that you are entitled to win—in any right undertaking in which you may be engaged—*you will win*. When you learn that you have a right to a legitimate dominion over your own affairs, *you will have dominion over them*. The promise is that we can do all things through the Mind that was in Christ.

Universal Mind plays no favorites. No one human being has any more power than any other. It is simply that few of us use the power that is in our hands. The great men of the world are in no wise SUPER Beings. They are ordinary creatures like you and me, who have stumbled upon the way of drawing upon their subconscious mind—and through it upon the superconscious or Universal Mind. Speaking of Henry Ford's phenomenal success, his friend Thomas A. Edison said of him—"He draws upon his subconscious mind."

The secret of being what you have it in you to be is simply this: Decide now what it is you want of life, exactly what you wish your future to be. Plan it out in detail. Vision it from start to finish. See yourself as you are now, doing those things you have always wanted to do. Make them REAL in your mind's eye—feel them, live them, believe them, especially at the moment of going to sleep, when it is easiest to reach your subconscious mind—and you will soon be seeing them in real life.

It matters not whether you are young or old, rich or poor. The time to begin is NOW. It is never too late. Remember those lines of Appleton's:*

I knew his face the moment that he passed
Triumphant in the thoughtless, cruel throng—
I gently touched his arm—he smiled at me—
He was the Man that Once I Meant to Be!

Where I had failed, he'd won from life, Success;
Where I had stumbled, with sure feet he stood;
Alike—yet unalike—we faced the world,
And through the stress he found that life was good.
And I? The bitter wormwood in the glass,
The shadowed way along which failures pass!
Yet as I saw him thus, joy came to me—
He was the Man that Once I Meant to Be!

*From "The Quiet Courage." D. Appleton & Co.

We did not speak. But in his sapient eyes
I saw the spirit that had urged him on,
The courage that had held him through the fight

Had once been mine. I thought, "Can it be gone?"
He felt that unasked question—felt it so
His pale lips formed the one-word answer, "No!"

. . . . . .

Too late to win? No! Not too late for me—
He is the Man that Still I Mean to Be!

CHAPTER XVI

UNAPPROPRIATED MILLIONS

Somebody said that it couldn't be done,
But he with a chuckle replied
That "maybe it couldn't," but he would be one
Who wouldn't say so till he'd tried.
So he buckled right in with the trace of a grin
On his face. If he worried he hid it.
He started to sing as he tackled the tiling
That couldn't be done, and he did it.

—Edgar A. Guest*

The main difference between the mind of today and that of our great-great-grandfathers is that in their day conditions were comparatively static, whereas today they are dynamic. Civilization ran along for centuries with comparatively little change. Most people lived and died

*From "The Path to Home." The Reilly & Lee Co.

in the places where they were born. They followed their fathers' avocations. Seldom, indeed, did one of them break out of the class into which he had been born. Almost as seldom did they even *think* of trying to. No wonder, then, that civilization made little progress.

Today we are in the presence of continual change. Men are imbued with that divine unrest which is never satisfied with conditions as they are, which is always striving for improvement. And *thought* is the vital force behind all this change.

Your ability to think is your connecting link with Universal Mind, that enables you to draw upon It for inspiration, for energy, for power. Mind is the energy in *static* form. Thought is the energy in *dynamic* form.

And because life is dynamic—not static; because it is ever moving forward—not standing still; your success or failure depends entirely upon the *quality* of your thought.

For thought is creative energy. It brings into being the things that you think. Think the things you would see manifested, see them, *believe* them, and you can leave it to your superconscious mind to bring them into being.

Your mind is a marvelous storage battery of power on which you can draw for whatever things you need to make your life what you would have it be. It has within it all power, all resource, all energy—but YOU are the one that must use it. All that power is static unless you make it dynamic. In the moment of creative thinking your conscious mind becomes a Creator—it partakes of the power of Universal Mind. And there is nothing static about one who shares that All-power. The resistless Life Energy within him pushes him on to new growth, new aspirations. Just as the sap flowing through the branches of the trees pushes off the old dead leaves to make way for the new life, just so you must push away the old dead thoughts of poverty and lack and disease, before you can bring on the new life of health and happiness and unlimited supply.

This life is in all of us, constantly struggling for an outlet. Repress it—and you die. Doctors will tell you that the only reason people grow old is because their systems get clogged. The tiny pores in your arteries get stopped up. You don't throw off the old. You don't struggle hard enough, and the result is you fall an easy victim to failure and sickness and death.

Remember the story of Sinbad the Sailor, and the Old Man of the Sea? The Old Man's weight was as nothing when Sinbad first took him on his shoulders, but he clung there and clung there, slowly but surely sapping Sinbad's strength, and he would finally have killed him as he had killed so many others if Sinbad, by calling to his aid all his mental as well as his physical resources, had not succeeded in shaking him off.

Most of us have some Old Man of the Sea riding us, and because he clings tightly and refuses to be easily shaken off, we let him stay there, sapping our energies, using up our vitality, when to rid us of him it is only necessary to call to our aid ALL our resources, mental as well as physical, for one supreme effort.

When a storm arises, the hardy mariner doesn't turn off steam and drift helplessly before the wind. That might be the easy way, but that way danger lies. He turns on more steam and fights against the gale. And so should you. There is a something within you that thrives on difficulties. You prize that more which costs an effort to win. You need to blaze new trails, to encounter unusual hardships, in order to reach your hidden mental resources, just as the athlete needs to exert himself to the utmost to reach his "second wind."

Have you ever seen a turtle thrown on its back? For a while it threshes around wildly, reaching for something outside to take hold of that shall put it on its feet. Just as we humans always look for help outside ourselves first. But presently he draws all his forces within his shell, rests a bit to regain his strength, and then throws his whole force to one side—legs, head, tail, and all—*and over he goes!*

So it is with us. When we realize that the power to meet any emergency is within ourselves, when we stop looking outside for help and intelligently call upon Mind in our need, we shall find that we are tapping Infinite Resource. We shall find that we have but to center all those resources on the one thing we want most—to get anything from life that it has.

As Emerson put it, when we once find the way to get in touch with Universal Mind we are—

. . . owner of the sphere,
Of the seven stars and the solar year,
Of Caesar's hand and Plato's brain,
Of the Lord Christ's heart and Shakespeare's strain.

CHAPTER XVII

THE SECRET OF POWER

The great were once as you.
They whom men magnify today
Once groped and blundered on life's way
Were fearful of themselves, and thought
By magic was men's greatness wrought.
They feared to try what they could do;
Yet Fame hath crowned with her success
The selfsame gifts that you possess.

—EDGAR A. GUEST*

There lived until recently in one of the big Eastern cities a woman whose husband had died and left her nearly $100,000,000. She had unlimited power in her hands—yet she used none of it. She had unlimited wealth—yet she got no more from it than if it were in the thousands instead of millions. She knew nothing of her power, of her wealth. She was insane.

*Published by permission of The International Magazine Co. (*Cosmopolitan Magazine*).

You have just as great power in your hands—without this poor woman's excuse for not using it.

You have access to unlimited ideas, unlimited energy, unlimited wealth. The "Open, Sesame!" is through your subconscious and superconscious mind.

So long as you limit yourself to superficial conditions, so long as you are a mere "hewer of wood or carrier of water" for those around you who *do* use their minds, you are in no better position than the beasts of burden.

The secret of power lies in understanding the infinite resources of your own mind. When you begin to realize that the power to do anything, to be anything, to have anything, is within yourself, then *and then only* will you take your proper place in the world.

As Bruce Barton put it in "The Man Whom Nobody Knows"—

"Somewhere, at some unforgettable hour, the daring filled His (Jesus') heart. He knew that He was bigger than Nazareth."

Again in speaking of Abraham Lincoln, Barton said—"Inside himself he felt his power, but where and when would opportunity come?" And later in the book—

"But to every man of vision the clear voice speaks. Nothing splendid has ever been achieved except by those who dared believe that *something inside them was superior to circumstance.*"

No doubt Jesus' friends and neighbors all ridiculed the idea of any such power within Him. Just as most people today laugh at the thought of a power such as that within themselves.

So they go on with their daily grind, with the gaunt specters of sickness and need ever by their side, until death comes as a welcome relief. Are you going to be one of those? Or will you listen to that inner consciousness of power and find the "Kingdom of Heaven that is within you." For whatever you become conscious of, will be quickly brought forth into tangible form.

Don't judge your ability by what you have done in the past. Your work heretofore has been done with the help of your conscious mind alone. Add to that the infinite knowledge at the disposal of your superconscious mind, and what you have done is as nothing to what you will do in the future.

For knowledge does not apply itself. It is merely so much static energy. You must convert it into dynamic energy by the power of your thought. The difference between the $25-a-week clerk and the $25,000-a-year executive is solely one of thought. The clerk may have more brains than the executive—frequently *has* in actual weight of gray matter. He may even have a far better education. But he doesn't know how to apply his thought to get the greatest good from it.

If you have brains, *use* them. If you have skill, *apply* it. The world must profit by it, and therefore you.

We all have inspired moments when we see clearly how we may do great things, how we may accomplish wonderful undertakings. But we do not believe in them enough to make them come true. An imagination which begins and ends in daydreaming is weakening to character.

Make the daydreams come true. Make them so clear and distinct that they impress themselves upon your subconscious mind. There's nothing wrong with daydreaming, except that most of us stop there. We don't try to make the dreams come true. The great inventor, Tesla, "dreams" every new machine complete and perfect in every particular before ever he begins his model for it. Mozart "dreamed" each of his wonderful symphonies complete before ever he put a note on paper. But they didn't stop with the dreaming. They visualized those dreams, *and then brought them into actuality.*

We lose our capacity to have visions if we do not take steps to realize them.

Power implies service, so concentrate all your thought on making your visions of great deeds come true. Thinking is the current that runs the dynamo of power. To connect this current so that you can draw upon universal supply through your subconscious mind, is to become a Superman. Do this, and you will have found the key to the solution of every problem of life.

CHAPTER XVIII

THIS ONE THING I DO

How do you tackle your work each day?
Do you grapple the task that comes your way
With a confident, easy mind?
Do you start to toil with a sense of dread
Or feel that you're going to do it?

You can do as much as you think you can,
But you'll never accomplish more;
If you're afraid of yourself, young man,
There's little for you in store.
For failure comes from the inside first,
It's there, if we only knew it,
And you can win, though you face the worst,
If you feel that you're going to do it.

—EDGAR A. GUEST*

*From "A Heap o' Livin'." The Reilly & Lee Co.

How did the Salvation Army get so much favorable publicity out of the first World War? They were a comparatively small part of the "Services" that catered to the boys "over there," yet they carried off the lion's share of the glory. Do you know how they did it?

By concentrating on just one thing—DOUGHNUTS!

They served doughnuts to the boys—and they did it *well*. And that is the basis of all success in business—to focus on one thing and do that thing well. Better far to do one thing pre-eminently well than to dabble in forty.

Two thousand years ago, Porcius Marcus Cato became convinced, from a visit to the rich and flourishing city of Carthage, that Rome had in her a rival who must be destroyed. His countrymen laughed at him. He was practically alone in his belief. But he persisted. He concentrated all his thought, all his faculties, to that one end. At the end of every speech, somewhere in every talk, he centered his hearers, thought on what he was trying to put over by epitomizing his whole idea in a single sentence—"Carthage must be destroyed!" And *Carthage was destroyed*.

If one man's concentration on a single idea could destroy a great nation, what can you not do when you apply that same principle to the *building* of a business?

I remember when I was first learning horsemanship, my instructor impressed this fact upon me: "Remember that a horse is an animal of one idea. You can teach him only one thing at a time."

Looking back, I'd say the only thing wrong with his instruction was that he took in too little territory. He need not have confined himself to the horse. Most humans are the same way.

In fact, you can put ALL humans into that class if you want a thing done well. For you cannot divide your thought and do justice to any one of the different subjects you are thinking of. You must do one thing at a time. The greatest success rule I know in business—the one that should be printed over every man's desk, is—"This One Thing I Do." Take one piece of work at a time. Concentrate on it to the exclusion of all else. *Then finish it!* Don't half-do it, and leave it around to clutter up your desk and interfere with the next job. Dispose of it completely. Pass it along wherever it is to go. Be through with it *and forget it!* Then your mind will be clear to consider the next matter.

"The man who is perpetually hesitating which of two things he will do first," says William Wirt, "will do neither. The man who resolves, but suffers his resolution to be changed by the first counter-suggestion of a friend—who fluctuates from plan to plan and veers like a weather-cock to every point of the compass with every breath of caprice that blows—can never accomplish anything real or useful. It is only the man who first consults wisely, then resolves firmly, and then executes his purpose with inflexible perseverance, undismayed by those petty difficulties that daunt a weaker spirit, that can advance to eminence in any line."

Everything in the world, even a great business, can be resolved into atoms. And the basic principles behind the biggest business will be found to be the same as those behind the successful running of the corner newsstand. The whole practice of commerce is founded upon them. Any man can learn them, but only the alert and energetic can apply them. The trouble with most men is that they think they have done all that is required of them when they have earned their salary.

Why, that's only the beginning. Up to that point, you are working for someone else. From then on, you begin to work for yourself. Remember, you must *give* to *get*. And it is when you give that *extra* bit of time and attention and thought to your work that you begin to stand out above the crowd around you.

Norval Hawkins, for many years General Manager of Sales for the Ford Motor Company, wrote that "the greatest hunt in the Ford business right now is the MAN hunt." And big men in every industrial line echo his words. When it comes to a job that needs real ability, they are not looking for relatives or friends or men with "pull." They want a MAN—and they will pay any price for the right man.

Not only that, but they always have a weather eye open for promising material. And the thing they value most of all is INITIATIVE.

But don't try to improve the whole works at once.

Concentrate on one thing at a time. Pick some one department or some one process or some one thing and focus all your thought upon it. Bring to bear upon it the limitless resources of your subconscious mind. Then prepare a definite plan for the development of that department or the improvement of that process. Verify your facts carefully to make sure they are workable. *Then*—and not till then—present your plan.

In "Thoughts on Business," you read: "Men often think of a position as being just about so big and no bigger, when, as a matter of fact, a position is often what one makes it. A man was making about $1,500 a year out of a certain position and thought he was doing all that could be done to advance the business. The employer thought otherwise, and gave the place to another man who soon made the position worth $8,000 a year—at exactly the same commission.

"The difference was in the man—in other words, in what the two men thought about the work. One had a little conception of what the work should be, and the other had a big conception of it. One thought little thoughts, and the other thought big thoughts.

"The standards of two men may differ, not especially because one is naturally more capable than the other, but because one is familiar with big things and the other is not. The time was when the former worked in a smaller scope himself, but when he saw a wider view of what his work might be he rose to the occasion and became a bigger man. It is just as easy to think of a mountain as to think of a hill—

when you turn your mind to contemplate it. The mind is like a rubber band—you can stretch it to fit almost anything, but it draws in to a smaller scope when you let go.

"Make it your business to know what is the best that might be in your line of work, and stretch your mind to conceive it, and then devise some way to attain it.

"Big things are only little things put together. I was greatly impressed with this fact one morning as I stood watching the workmen erecting the steel framework for a tall office building. A shrill whistle rang out as a signal, a man over at the engine pulled a lever, a chain from the derrick was lowered, and the whistle rang out again. A man stooped down and fastened the chain around the center of a steel beam, stepped back and blew the whistle once more. Again the lever was moved at the engine, and the steel beam soared into the air up to the sixteenth story, where it was made fast by little bolts.

"The entire structure, great as it was, towering far above all the neighboring buildings, was made up of pieces of steel and stone and wood, put together according to a plan. The plan was first imagined, then penciled, then carefully drawn, and then followed by the workmen. It was all a combination of little things.

"It is encouraging to think of this when you are confronted by a big task. *Remember that it is only a group of little tasks, any of which you can easily do.* It is ignorance of this fact that makes men afraid to try."

One of the most essential requisites in the accomplishment of any important work is patience. Not the patience that sits and folds its hands and waits—Micawber like—for something to turn up. But the patience that never jeopardizes or upsets a plan by forcing it too soon. The man who possesses that kind of patience can always find plenty to do in the meantime.

Make your plan—then wait for the opportune moment to submit it. You'd be surprised to know how carefully big men go over suggestions from subordinates which show the least promise. One of the signs of a really big man, you know, is his eagerness to learn from everyone and anything. There is none of that "know it all" about him that characterized the general who was given a book containing the strategy by which Napoleon had for fifteen years kept all the armies of Europe at bay. "I've no time to read about bygone battles," he growled, thrusting the book away, "I have my own campaign to plan."

There is priceless wisdom to be found in books. As Carlyle put it—"All that mankind has done, thought, gained or been—it is lying in matchless preservation in the pages of books."

The truths which mankind has been laboriously learning through countless ages, at who knows what price off sweat and toil and starvation and blood—all are yours for the effort of reading them.

And in business, knowledge was never so priceless or so easily acquired. Books and magazines are filled with the hows and whys, the rights and wrongs of buying and selling, of manufacturing and shipping, of finance and management. They are within the reach of anyone with the desire to KNOW.

Nothing pays better interest than judicious reading. The man who invests in more knowledge of his business than he needs to hold his job, is acquiring capital with which to get a better job.

As old Gorgon Graham puts it in "The Letters of a Self-Made Merchant to His Son"—

"I ain't one of those who believe that a half knowledge of a subject is useless, but it has been my experience that when a fellow has that half knowledge, he finds it's the other half which would really come in handy.

"What you know is a club for yourself, and what you don't know is a meat-ax for the other fellow. That is why you want to be on the lookout all the time for information about the business and to nail a fact just as a sensible man nails a mosquito—the first time it settles near him."

The demands made upon men in business today are far greater than in any previous generation. To meet them, you have to use your talents to the utmost. You have to find in every situation that confronts you the best, the easiest and the quickest way of working it out. And the first essential in doing this is to plan your work ahead.

You'd be surprised at how much more work you can get through by carefully planning it, and then taking each bit in order and disposing of it before starting on the next.

Another thing—once started at work, don't let down.

Keep on going until it is time to quit. You know how much power it takes to start an auto that is standing motionless. But when you get it going, you can run along in high at a fraction of the expenditure of gas. It is the same way with your mind. We are all mentally lazy. We hate to start using our minds. Once started, though, it is easy to keep along on high, if only we won't let down. For the moment we let down, we have that starting to do all over again. You can accomplish ten times as much, with far less effort or fatigue, if you will keep right on steadily instead of starting and stopping, and starting and stopping again.

Volumes have been written about personal efficiency, and general efficiency, and every other kind of efficiency in business. But boiled down, it all comes to this:

1. Know what you want.
2. Analyze the thing you must do to get it.
3. Plan your work ahead.
4. Do one thing at a time.
5. Finish that one thing and send it on its way before starting the next.
6. Once started, KEEP GOING!

And when you come to some problem that "stumps" you, give your subconscious mind a chance.

Frederick Pierce, in "Our Unconscious Mind," gives an excellent method for solving business problems through the aid of the subconscious:

"Several years ago, I heard a successful executive tell a group of young men how he did his work, and included in the talk was the advice to prepare at the close of each day's business, a list of the ten most important things for the next day. To this I would add: Run them over in the mind just before going to sleep, not thoughtfully, or with elaboration of detail, but with the sure knowledge that the deeper centers of the mind are capable of viewing them constructively even though conscious attention is surrendered in sleep.

"Then, if there is a particular problem which seems difficult of solution, review its features lightly as a last game for the imaginative unconscious to play at during the night. Do not be discouraged if no immediate results are apparent. Remember that fiction, poetry, musical composition, inventions, innumerable ideas, spring from the unconscious, often in forms that give evidence of the highest constructive elaboration.

"Give your unconscious a chance. Give it the material, and stimulate it with keenly dwelt-on wishes along frank Ego Maximation lines. It is a habit which, if persisted in, will sooner or later present you with some very valuable ideas when you least expect them."

I remember reading of another man—a genius at certain kinds of work—who, whenever an especially difficult problem confronted him, "slept on it." He had learned the trick as a child. Unable to learn his lessons one evening, he had kept repeating the words to himself until he dozed in his chair, the book still in his hands. What was his surprise, on being awakened by his father a few minutes later, to find that he knew them perfectly! He tried it again and again on succeeding evenings, and almost invariably it worked. Now, whenever a problem comes up that he cannot solve, he simply stretches out on a lounge in his office, thoroughly relaxes, *and lets his subconscious mind solve the problem!*

CHAPTER XIX

THE MASTER MIND

One who never turned his back but marched breast
forward,
Never doubted clouds would break,
Never dreamed though right were worsted
Wrong would triumph,
Held we fall to rise, are baffled to fight better,
Sleep to wake.

—Browning

Among your friends there is one of those men who doesn't have much use for the word "can't."

You marvel at his capacity for work.

You admire him more the longer you know him.

You always respect him.

For he not only has made good, but he always will make good. He has found and appropriated to himself the "Talisman of Napoleon"—*absolute confidence in himself.*

The world loves a leader. All over the world, in every walk of life, people are eagerly seeking for some one to follow. They want some one else to do their thinking for them; they need some one to hearten them to action; they like to have some one else on whom to lay the blame when things go wrong; they want some one big enough to share the glory with them when success crowns his efforts.

But to instill confidence in them, that leader must have utter confidence in himself. A Caesar or a Napoleon who did not believe in himself would be inconceivable. It is that which makes men invincible—the Consciousness of their own Power. They put no limit upon their own capacities—therefore they have no limit. For Universal Mind sees all, knows all, and can do all, and we share in this absolute power to the exact extent to which we permit ourselves. Our mental attitude is the magnet that attracts from Universal Mind everything we may need to bring our desires into being. We make that magnet strong or weak as we have confidence in or doubt of our abilities. We draw to ourselves unlimited power or limit ourselves to humble positions according to our own beliefs.

A long time ago Emerson wrote: "There is one mind common to all individual men. Every man is an inlet to the same *and to all* of the same. He that is once admitted to the right of reason is made a freeman of the whole estate. What Plato has thought, he may think; what a saint has felt, he may feel; what at any time has befallen any man, he can understand. Who hath access to this Universal Mind, *is a party to all that is or can be done,* for this is the only and sovereign agent."

The great German physicist Nernst found that the longer an electric current was made to flow through a filament of oxide of magnesium, the greater became the conductivity of the filament.

In the same way, the more you call upon and use your subconscious mind, the greater becomes its conductivity in passing along to you the infinite resources of Universal Mind. The wisdom of a Solomon, the skill of a Michelangelo, the genius of an Edison, the daring of a Napoleon, *all* may be yours. It rests with you only to form the contact with Universal Mind in order to draw from it what you will.

Think of this power as something that you can connect with any time. It has the answer to all of your problems. It offers you freedom from fear, from worry, from sickness, from accident. No man and no thing can interfere with your use of this power or diminish your share of it. No one, that is, but yourself.

Don Carlos Musser expresses it well in "You Are":

"Because of the law of gravitation the apple falls to the ground. Because of the law of growth the acorn becomes a mighty oak. Because of the law of causation, a man is 'as he thinketh in his heart.' Nothing can happen without its adequate cause."

Success does not come to you by accident. It comes as the logical result of the operation of law. Mind, working through your brain and your body, makes your world. That it is not a better world and a bigger one, is due to your limited thoughts and beliefs. They dam back the flood of ideas that Mind is constantly striving to manifest through you. God never made a failure or a nobody. He offers to the highest and the lowest alike, all that is necessary to happiness and success. The difference is entirely in the extent to which each of us AVAILS himself of that generosity.

There is no reason why you should hesitate to aspire to any position, any honor, any goal, for the Mind within you is fully able to meet any need. It is no more difficult for it to handle a great problem than a small one. Mind is just as much present in your little everyday affairs as in those of a big business or a great nation. Don't set it doing trifling sums in arithmetic when it might just as well be solving problems of moment to yourself and the world.

Start something! Use your initiative. Give your mind something to work upon. The greatest of all success secrets is initiative. It is the one quality which more than any other has put men in high places.

Conceive something. Conceive it first in your own mind. Make the pattern there and your superconscious mind will draw upon the plastic substance or energy all about you to make that model real.

Drive yourself. Force yourself. It is the dreamer, the man with imagination, who has made the world move. Without him, we would still be in the Stone Age.

Galileo looked at the moon and dreamed of how he might reach it. The telescope was the fruition of that dream. Watt dreamed of what might be done with steam—and our great locomotives and engines of today are the result.

Franklin dreamed of harnessing the lightning—and today we have man-made thunderbolts.

Initiative, plus imagination, will take you anywhere. Imagination opens the eyes of the mind, and there is nothing good you can image there that is not possible of fulfillment in your daily life.

The connecting link between the human and the Divine, between the formed universe and formless energy, lies in your imaging faculty. It is, of all things human, the most God-like. It is our part of Divinity. Through it we share in the creative power of Universal Mind. Through it we can turn the most drab existence into a thing of life and beauty. It is the means by which we avail ourselves of all the good which Universal Mind is constantly offering to us in such profusion. It is the means by which we can reach any goal, win any prize.

What was it gave us the submarine, the airplane, wireless, electricity? Imagination. What was it that enabled man to build the Simplon Tunnel, the Panama Canal, the Golden Gate Bridge? Imagination. What is it that makes us successful and happy, or poor and friendless? Imagination—or the lack of it.

It was imagination that sent Spanish and English and French adventurers to this new world. It was imagination that urged the early settlers westward—ever westward. It was imagination that built our railroads, our towns, our great cities.

Parents foolishly try to discourage imagination in their

children, when all it needs is proper guidance. For imagination forms the world from which their future will take its shape. Restrain the one and you constrict the other. Develop the one in the right way, and there is no limit to the other. Uncontrolled, the imagination is like a rudderless ship. Or even, at times, like the lightning. But properly controlled, it is like the ship that carries riches from port to port. Or like the electric current, carrying unlimited power for industry and progress.

Do you want happiness? Do you want success? Do you want position, power, riches? *Image them!* How did God first make man? "In his image created He him." He "imaged" man in His Mind.

And that is the way everything has been made since time began. It was first imaged in Mind. That is the way everything you want must start—with a mental image.

So use your imagination! Picture in it your Heart's Desire. Image it—daydream it so vividly, so clearly, that you will actually BELIEVE you HAVE it. In the moment that you carry this conviction to your subconscious mind—in that moment your dream will become a reality. It may be a while before you realize it, but the important part is done. You have created the model. You can safely leave it to your Higher Self to do the rest.

When Jesus adjured His disciples—"Whatsoever ye desire, when ye pray, believe that ye RECEIVE it," He was not only telling them a great truth, but he was teaching what we moderns would call excellent psychology as well. For this "belief" is what acts upon the subconscious mind and through it upon the superconscious. It is through this "belief" that formless energy is compressed into material form.

Every man wants to get out of the rut, to grow, to develop into something better. Here is the open road—open to you whether you have schooling, training, position, wealth, or not. Remember this: Your subconscious mind knew more from the time you were a baby than is in all the books in all the colleges and libraries of the world.

So don't let lack of training, lack of education, hold you back. Your mind can meet every need—and will do so if you give it the chance. The Apostles were almost all poor men, uneducated men, yet they did a work that is unequalled in historical annals. Joan of Arc was a poor peasant girl, unable to read or write—*yet she saved France!* The pages of history are dotted with poor men, uneducated men, who thought great thoughts, who used their imaginations to master circumstances and became rulers of men. Most great dynasties started with some poor, obscure man. Napoleon came of a poor, humble family. He got his appointment to the Military Academy only through very hard work and the pulling of many political strings. Even as a Captain of Artillery he was so poverty-stricken that he was unable to buy his equipment when offered an appointment to India. Business today is full of successful men who have scarcely the rudiments of ordinary education. It was only after he had made his millions that Andrew Carnegie hired a tutor to give him the essentials of an education.

So it isn't training and it isn't education that makes you successful. These help, but the thing that really counts is that gift of the Gods—*Creative Imagination!*

You have that gift. *Use it!* Make every thought, every fact, that comes into your mind *pay you a profit.* Make it work and produce for you. Think of things—not as they are but as they MIGHT be. Make them real, live and interesting. Don't merely dream—but *CREATE!* Then use your imagination to make that CREATION of advantage to mankind—and, incidentally, yourself.

CHAPTER XX

WHAT DO YOU LACK?

I read the papers every day, and oft encounter tales which show there's hope for every jay who in life's battle fails. I've just been reading of a gent who joined the has-been ranks, at fifty years without a cent, or credit at the banks. But undismayed he buckled down, refusing to be beat, and captured fortune and renown; he's now on Easy Street. Men say that fellows down and out ne'er leave the rockly track, but facts will show, beyond a doubt, that has-beens do come back, I know, for I who write this rhyme, when forty-odd years old, was down and out, without a dime, my whiskers full of mold. By black disaster I was trounced until it jarred my spine; I was a failure so pronounced I didn't need a sign. And after I had soaked my coat, I said (at forty-three), "I'll see if I can catch the goat that has escaped from me." I labored hard; I strained my dome, to do my daily grind, until in triumph I came home, my billy-goat behind. And any man who still has health may with the winners stack, and have a chance at fame and wealth—for has-beens do come back.

—WALT MASON*

*From "Walt Mason—His Book." Barse & Hopkins.

Do you know why it is that the Communists are so opposed to religion?

Because religion, as it is commonly accepted, teaches man resignation to conditions as they are—teaches, in effect, that God created some men poor and some rich. That this unequal distribution is a perfectly natural thing. And that we must not rail against it because it will all be made right in the next world.

Napoleon, in his early Jacobin days, denounced religion for that very reason. But when he had won to power, when he planned to make himself Emperor, then he found he had need for that religion, and re-established the Church in France.

For, he reasoned, how can people be satisfied without religion? If one man is starving, near another who is making himself sick by eating too much, how can you expect to keep the starving one resigned to his fate unless you teach him it will all be made right in some indefinite future state?

Organized society could not exist, as he planned it, without some being rich and some poor, and to keep the poor satisfied, there must be an authority to declare—"God wills it thus. But just be patient. In the hereafter all this will be different. YOU will be the ones then to occupy the places of honor."

Religion, in other words—as it is ordinarily taught—*is a fine thing to keep the common people satisfied!*

But Christianity was never meant for a weapon to keep the rich wealthy and secure, the poor satisfied and in their proper place. On the contrary, Christianity as taught by Jesus opened the way to all Good. And Christianity as it was practiced in its early years was an idealized form of Socialism that benefited each and all. No one was wealthier than his neighbors, it is true—but neither was any poverty-stricken. Theirs was the creed of the Three Musketeers—"All for one, and one for all!"

"Ask and ye shall receive," said Jesus. "Seek and ye shall find." That was not directed to the rich alone. That was to ALL men.

Providence has never made a practice of picking out certain families or certain individuals and favoring them to the detriment of other people—much as some of our "leading families" would have us believe it. It is only man who has arrogated to himself that privilege. We laugh now at the "divine right of Kings." It is just as ridiculous to think that a few have the right to all the good things of life, while the many have to toil and sweat to do them service.

To quote Rumbold's last words from the scaffold—"I never could believe that Providence had sent a few men into the world ready booted and spurred to ride, and millions ready saddled and bridled to be ridden."

There is nothing right in poverty. Not only that, but there is nothing meritorious in poverty. The mere fact that you are poor and ground down by fear and worry is not going to get you any forwarder in the hereafter. On the contrary, your soul is likely to be too pinched by want, too starved and shriveled to be able to expand.

"The Kingdom of Heaven is within you." To me that means that Heaven is here and now. That if we want any happiness from it we must get it as we go along. I have never been much of a believer in accepting these promissory notes for happiness. Every time one of them falls due, you find you just have to renew it for another six months or a year, until one of these days you wake up and find that you have more promissory notes than you have collateral and you are left holding the bag.

The Cumaean Sibyl is said to have offered Tarquin the Proud nine books for what he thought an exorbitant sum. So he refused. She burned three of the books, and placed the same price on the six as on the original nine. Again he refused. She burned three more books, and offered the remainder for the sum she had first asked. This time Tarquin accepted. The books were found to contain prophecies and invaluable directions regarding Roman policy, but alas, they were no longer complete.

So it is with happiness. If you take it as you go along, you get it in its entirety. But if you keep putting off the day when you shall enjoy it—if you keep taking promissory notes for happiness—every day will mean one day less of it that you will have. Yet the cost is just the same.

The purpose of existence is GROWTH. You can't grow spiritually or mentally without happiness. And by Happiness I don't mean a timid resignation to the "Will of God." That so-called "Will of God" is more often than not either pure laziness on the part of the resigned one or pure cussedness on the part of the one that is "putting something over" on him. It is the most sanctimonious expression yet devised to excuse some condition that no one has the energy or the ability to rectify.

No—by Happiness I mean the everyday enjoyment of everyday people. I mean love and laughter and honest amusement. Every one of us is entitled to it. Every one of us can have it—if he has the WILL and the ENERGY to get out and get it for himself.

Joyless work, small pay, no future, nothing to look forward to—God never planned such an existence. It is man-made—and you can be man enough to unmake it as far as you and yours are concerned.

God never made any man poor any more than He made any man sick. Look around you. All of Nature is bountiful. On every hand you see profusion—in the trees, in the flowers, in everything that He planned. The only Law of Nature is the law of Supply. Poverty is unnatural. It is man-made, through the limits man puts upon himself. God never put them there any more than He showed partiality by giving to some of His children gifts and blessings which He withheld from others. His gifts are just as available to you as to any man on earth. The difference is all in your understanding of how to avail yourself of the infinite supply all about you.

Take the worry clamps off your mentality and you will

make the poverty clamps loosen up from your finances. Your affairs are so closely related to your consciousness that they too will relax into peace, order, and plenty. Divine ideas in your spiritual consciousness will become active in your business, and will work out as your abundant prosperity.

As David V. Bush says in "Applied Psychology and Scientific Living"—"Thoughts are things; thoughts are energy; thoughts are magnets which attract to us the very things which we think. Therefore, if a man is in debt, he will, by continually thinking about debt, bring more debts to him. For thoughts are causes, and he fastens more debts on to himself and actually creates more obligations by thinking about debts.

"Concentrate and think upon things that you want; not on things which you ought not to have. Think of abundance, of opulence, of plenty, of position, harmony and growth, and if you do not see them manifested today, they will be realized tomorrow. If you must pass through straits of life where you do not outwardly see abundance, know that you have it within, and that in time it will manifest itself.

"I say, if you concentrate on debt, debt is what you will have; if you think about poverty, poverty is what you will receive. It is just as easy, when once the mind becomes trained, to think prosperity and abundance and plenty, as it is to think lack, limitation and poverty."

Prosperity is not limited to time or to place. It manifests when and where there is consciousness to establish it.

It is attracted to the consciousness that is free from worry, strain, and tension.

So never allow yourself to worry about poverty. Be careful, take ordinary business precautions—of course. But don't center your thought on your *troubles.* The more you think of them, the more tightly you fasten them upon yourself. Think of the *results* you are after—not of the difficulties in the way. Mind will find the way. It is merely up to you to choose the goal, then keep your thought steadfast until that goal is won.

The greatest short-cut to prosperity is to *LIVE IT!* Prosperity attracts. Poverty repels. To quote Orison Swett Marden—"To be ambitious for wealth and yet always expecting to be poor, to be always doubting your ability to get what you long for, is like trying to reach East by travelling West. There is no philosophy which will help a man to succeed when he is always doubting his ability to do so, and thus attracting failure."

Again: "No matter how hard you may work for success, if your thought is saturated with the fear of failure it will kill your efforts, neutralize your endeavors, and make success impossible."

The secret of prosperity lies in so vividly imaging it in your own mind that you literally exude prosperity. You feel prosperous, you look prosperous, and the result is that before long you ARE prosperous.

I remember seeing a play a number of years ago that was based on this thought. A young fellow—a chronic failure—

was persuaded by a friend to carry a roll of $1000 counterfeit bills in his pocket, and to show them, unostentatiously, when the occasion offered. Of course, everyone thought he had come into some legacy. The natural inference was that anyone who carried fifty or a hundred thousand dollar bills in his pockets must have a lot more in the bank. Opportunities flocked to him. Opportunities to make good. Opportunities to make money. He made good! And that without having to spend any of this spurious money of his. For most business today is done on credit. I know many wealthy men who seldom carry anything but a little change in their pockets for tips. Everything they do, everything they buy, is "Charged." And big deals are put through in the same way. If a man is believed to have plenty of money, if he has a reputation for honesty and fair-dealing, he may put through a transaction running into six or seven figures without paying one cent down. The thing that counts is not the amount of your balance at the Bank, but what others THINK of you, the IMAGE you have created in your own and in others' minds.

What do you lack? What thing do you want most? Realize that before it or any other thing can be, it must first be imaged in Mind. Realize, too, that when you can close your eyes and actually SEE that thing, *you have brought it into being*—you have drawn upon that invisible substance all about you—you have *created something.* Hold it in your thought, focus your mind upon it, "BELIEVE THAT YOU

HAVE IT"—and your Higher Self will pour its Vital Force into it and bring it into being.

God is but another name for the invisible, everywhere-present, Source-of-things. Out of the air the seed gathers the essences which are necessary to its bountiful growth; out of the invisible ether our minds gather the rich ideas that stimulate us to undertake and to carry out enterprises that bring prosperity to us. Let us see with the eye of the mind a bountiful harvest; then our minds will be quickened with ideas of abundance, and plenty will appear, not only in our world, but everywhere.

"As the rain cometh down and the snow from heaven, and returneth not thither, but watereth the earth, and maketh it bring forth and bud, and giveth seed to the sower and bread to the eater; so shall my word be that goeth forth out of my mouth: it shall not return unto me void, but it shall accomplish that which I please, and it shall prosper in the thing whereto I sent it."—Isaiah.

Remember that you are a Creator. So when there is something you greatly want, make a mental picture of it. Put that picture on paper, too, if you can. Then consciously draw upon all the Vital Force around you and put it into that picture—put it into the thought-mold that picture represents. Do that—know then that you HAVE this thing that you want—and you can confidently depend upon your Higher Self to bring it into manifestation. There is magic, you know, in BELIEVING.

CHAPTER XXI

THE SCULPTOR AND THE CLAY

Eternal mind the Potter is,
And thought the eternal clay.
The hand that fashions is divine;
His works pass not away.
God could not make imperfect man
His model Infinite, Unhallowed thought
He could not plan—Love's work and
Love must fit.

—Alice Dayton

When you step into your office on Monday morning, no doubt you have dreams of wonderful achievement. Your step is firm, your brain is clear and you have carefully thought out just WHAT you will do and HOW you will accomplish big things in your business. Perhaps the very plans you have in mind will influence your whole business career, and you have visions of the dollars that will be yours rolling into your bank account.

But do these dreams come true?

Are you always able to put through what you had planned to do—does your day's work have the snap and power you imagined it would have? Are you ever forced to admit that your dreams of big accomplishment are often shattered because of "fagged nerves" and lack of energy, because you have not the "pep"?

How easy it is to think back and see how success was in your grasp if only you had felt equal to that extra bit of effort, if only you had had the "pep," the energy to reach out and take it. The great men of the world have been well men, strong men. Sickness and hesitancy go hand in hand. Sickness means weakness, querulousness, lack of faith, lack of confidence in oneself and in others.

But there is no real reason for sickness or weakness, and there is no reason why you should remain weak or sick if you are so afflicted now.

Remember the story of the sculptor Pygmalion? How he made a statue of marble so beautiful that every woman who saw it envied it? So perfect was it that he fell in love with it himself, hung it with flowers and jewels, spent day after day in rapt admiration of it, BELIEVED in it, until presently his Higher Self poured its Vital Force into that image and gave it the breath of life.

There is more than Pagan mythology to that story. There is this truth in it—that any man can set before his mind's eye the image of the figure he himself would like to be, and then breathe the breath of life into it merely by keeping that image before his subconscious mind as the model on which to do its daily building.

For health and strength are natural. It is ill-health and weakness that are unnatural. Your body was meant to be lithe, supple, muscular, full of red-blooded energy and vitality. A clear brain, a powerful heart, a massive chest, wrists and arms of steel—all these were meant for you—all these you can have if you will but *know,* and *feel,* and *think* and *act aright.*

Just take stock of yourself for a moment. Are your muscles tough, springy and full of vim? Do they do all you ask of them—and then beg for more? Can you eat a good meal—and forget it?

If you can't, it's your own fault. You can have a body alive with vitality, a skin smooth and fine of texture, muscles supple and virile. You can be the man you have always dreamed of being.

You who envy the rosy cheek and sparkling eye of youth, who awake in the morning weary and unrefreshed, who go to your daily tasks with fagged brain and heavy tread—just remember that Perfect Youth or Perfect Health is largely a state of mind.

There is only one thing that will put muscle on your bones. There is only one thing that will keep your organs functioning with precision and regularity. There is only one thing that will build for you a perfect body. That one thing is your subconscious mind.

Every cell and tissue, every bone and sinew, every organ and muscle in your entire body is subject to the control of your subconscious mind. As it directs, so they build or function.

True, that subconscious mind accepts suggestions from your conscious mind. Hold before it the thought that the exercise you are taking is building muscle upon your arms or shoulders, and your subconscious mind will fall in readily with the suggestion and strengthen those muscles. Hold before it the thought that some particular food gives you unusual energy and "pep," and the subconscious mind will be entirely agreeable to producing the added vigor.

But have you ever noticed how some sudden joy (which is entirely a mental state) energizes and revitalizes you—*more than all the exercise or all the tonics you can take?* Have you ever noticed how martial music will relieve the fatigue of marching men? Have you ever noticed how sorrow (which is entirely a mental state) will depress and devitalize you, *regardless of any amount of exercise or health foods you may take?*

Each of us has within him all the essentials that go to the making of a Super-Man. But so has every acorn the essentials for making a great oak tree, yet the Japanese show us that even an oak may be stunted by continual pruning of its shoots. Negative and weak thoughts, thoughts of self-doubt, of mistrust, continually prune back the vigorous life ever seeking so valiantly to show forth the splendor and strength of the radiant inner self.

What is it that accounts for the miracles of healing which take place at shrines all over the world? What is it that gives revivalists, faith healers, practitioners, power to dispel sickness, power to "make the blind see, the deaf hear, the lame walk"?

All of these wonders do occur—make no mistake about that. At St. Anne de Beaupré, at Lourdes, at thousands of shrines, at hundreds of meetings like those of the practitioners of the Mental Sciences, the sick have been, and every day new ones are being, cured of their infirmities. Why?

It cannot be merely because of the power of the "healer" or the holiness of the relic, for in olden times thousands of so-called "relics" were no more parts of the bodies of the Saints they were supposed to represent than they were of yours or mine. Yet in many cases they proved just as potent for good! Why?

If you have read much of history, you know that the Kings in the Middle Ages were a pretty scoundrelly lot, yet the "King's Touch" healed hundreds every year. Why?

Religions which we piously regard as pagan have on record almost as many cases of miraculous healings as have we. Again, why? If we have the only truth, how is it that they, many of whom never heard of the Christ, should be able to use the truth in another form to accomplish the same result?

Why? Because the Laws of God are universal laws. Whether we follow them blindly or understandingly, they work just the same. They are as impartial as the sunshine. They require only conformity to them.

Everything in this universe is made up of energy. That energy manifests itself in three different states—solid, liquid and vapor.

When you want to change the form in which any solid manifests itself, you have only two methods open to you:

First, you can carve or break or burn off parts until the remainder is in the form you desire.

Second, you can break up the whole mass (by heat or mixing with liquid or vapor) until you have liquefied or vaporized it, and then mold it into the shape you desire.

Those methods are universal. They apply to wood or rock or iron or flesh. They are the only two ways known to man of changing the form of any solid substance.

How, then, are miracles of healing achieved? In the same way as miracles of turning lumps of iron into useful tools—by breaking up the solid mass, resolving it into its higher potential, then molding it into the form you desire.

But you cannot take your flesh and resolve it into liquid by putting it into a furnace as you do with iron. And you cannot break it up and mix it with water, as you do with wheat. What then, can you do with flesh and bone?

Liquefy it through EMOTION! The heat of a strong emotion is the only power that will resolve the cells of your body into a higher potential. Understanding faith that God's image of you is perfect, is the only power that will mold them into the pattern God intended.

It matters not what may ail you, it matters not how close to death's door you may be, fervent emotion can loosen all your condensed energy, faith can bring it back into the perfect mold. Mind you, by "fervent emotion" we do not mean hysteria or wild excitement. We mean deep feeling—*the conviction that you have received* the healing you are praying for.

Of course, *every* emotion has a tendency to raise the life in us temporarily to a higher potential. And every emotion has, at times, been used unwittingly to heal the sick and afflicted. Brown Landone, for instance, told of having been an invalid for seventeen years, his whole time spent in bed or in a wheel chair, his knees swollen as large as water pails, his heart organically diseased. Then one day the house caught fire, and this man who could not climb a flight of stairs without fainting away, not only ran up steps like an athlete, *but carried down one after another three heavy trunks!*

More conclusive even than this is an Associated Press dispatch recounting the unexpected visit of a boa constrictor to the paralytic ward of the Guayaquil Hospital in Ecuador. When the snake arrived—through the window—there were eight patients in the ward, all helplessly paralyzed. Ten seconds later, the snake was the ward's sole occupant.

Every bed was emptied, every patient "miraculously" cured! One, who had not moved from his bed in two years, leaped to a window, and then took easily the eight-foot jump to the ground. And in each of the eight cases, *a complete cure was effected!*

The dumb have been made to talk, the deaf to hear, just

by taking them in an airplane and doing "stunts" that worked them into a high state of excitement.

But an outside stimulus is in no wise necessary to stir the emotions. It can be done as effectively from within, through the stimulus of a strong conviction. Starting a fire or importing a snake to cure a paralytic is almost as wasteful as the old Chinese custom of burning down a house just to roast a pig. There are less expensive and more effectual ways.

Go to any of the more popular shrines, and you will see men carried in on stretchers or limping along on crutches, lifted to a high emotional pitch through preaching or music or just the contagion of the emotional excitement around them, then walking away as well and strong as you or I.

There is nothing miraculous about it, any more than life itself is miraculous. The miraculous part is that mankind has not long ago discovered the perfectly natural laws governing such "miracles."

Why are the Churches beautifully decorated, in rich colors? Why do they give us such wonderful music? Why do they have congregational singing? Because beauty and color and music and singing all appeal strongly to the emotions, have a tendency to awaken the dormant life in us, stirring it out of the congealed form in which sickness or accident has left it, giving us the chance to pour it anew into God's perfect image.

How did Jesus heal the sick? By first commanding the "devil" to get out of them. In other words, by first loosening the congealed life from its diseased form. Then it flowed easily into the perfect pattern He held of it. "Satan hath bound this woman," He said of one, and then proceeded to loosen the bonds.

Who is "Satan"? Who but the devils of fear and worry, who "bind" the life in so many poor souls into all manner of diseased forms. What is mankind's greatest enemy? Ask any doctor, and he will tell you—"Congestion!" And what is congestion but *congealed* life, life bound into constricting limits by worry and fear?

Dr. G. Dumas, of Paris, discovered that *writhing* acts as an anesthetic for pain. Why? Because writhing means strain, and strain has a tendency to make the muscles hard, to *congeal* the life in them, deadening it so there is no longer feeling in it. Continued strain brings unconsciousness or death. Why? Because the congealing process reaches the seat of the nerves or the heart, and it stops functioning. The "potential" becomes too low for life to act.

When that potential is raised by drugs or alcohol, the release is only temporary, for it is merely a chemical release. When the chemical reaction ceases, the particles of life will settle again, with the poison of the chemicals to trouble them in addition.

Treating with drugs is working upon conditions. To cure those conditions, you must go back to the parent cause. "Heal me, O Lord, and I shall be healed," prayed the Prophet Jeremiah. And when you work through Mind to reach the causes of your trouble, you are truly healed.

That is the way Jesus worked. He first preached. He gave His hearers the necessary understanding. He worked up their faith, their emotion—*then He healed them.*

Choose what you will be! Your responsibility is to think, speak, act the true inner self. Your privilege is to show forth in this self, the fullness of peace and plenty. Keep steadfastly in mind the idea of yourself that you want to see realized. Your daily, hourly, and continual idea of yourself, your life, your affairs, your world, and your associates, determines the harvest, the showing forth. Look steadfastly to your highest ideal of self, and your steadfast and lofty ideal will draw forth blessing and prosperity not only upon you, but upon all who know you.

For mind is the only creator, and thought is the only energy. What counts most is the image of your body that you are holding in your thought. If heretofore that image has been one of weakness, of ill-health, change it *now*—TODAY. Repeat to yourself, the first thing upon awakening in the morning and the last thing before going to sleep at night— "My body was made in the image and likeness of God. God first imaged it in its entirety, therefore every cell and bone and tissue is perfect, every organ and muscle performing its proper function. That is the only model of me in Universal Mind. That is the only model of me that my Subconscious Mind knows. Therefore, since Mind—God—is the only creator, *that is the only model of me that I can have!*"

CHAPTER XXII

WHY GROW OLD?

And Moses was an hundred and twenty years old when he died: his eye was not dim, nor his natural force abated.

Remember how you used to plough through great masses of work day after day and month after month, cheerily, enthusiastically, with never a sign of tiring or nervous strain? Remember how you used to enjoy those evenings, starting out as fresh from your office or shop as if you hadn't just put a hard day's work behind you?

No doubt you've often wondered why you can't work and enjoy yourself like that now, but solaced yourself with the moth-eaten fallacy that "As a man grows older he shouldn't expect to get the same fun out of life that he did in his earlier years."

Poor old exploded idea!

Youth is not a matter of time. It is a mental state. You can be just as brisk, just as active, just as light-hearted now as you were ten or twenty years ago. Genuine youth is just a perfect state of health. You can have that health, and the boundless energy and capacity for work or enjoyment that go with it. You can cheat time of ten, twenty or fifty years—not merely by taking thought of what you shall eat or what you shall drink, but through a right understanding of what you should expect of your body.

"If only I had my life to live over again!" How often you have heard it said. How often you have thought it.

But the fact is that you CAN have it. You can start right now and live again as many years as you have already experienced. Health, physical freedom and full vigor need not end for you at thirty-five or forty—nor at sixty or seventy. Age is not a matter of years. It is a state of mind.

In an address before the American Sociological Society some years ago, Dr. Hornell Hart of Bryn Mawr predicted that—"Babies born in the year 2000 will have something like two hundred years of life ahead of them, and men and women of a hundred years will be quite the normal thing. But instead of being wrinkled and crippled, these centenarians will be in their vigorous prime."

Thomas Parr, an Englishman, lived to be 152 years old, and was sufficiently hale and hearty at the age of 120 to take unto himself a second wife. Even at 152, his death was not due to old age, but to a sudden and drastic change in his manner of life. All his days he had lived upon simple fare, but his fame reaching the King, he was invited to London and there feasted so lavishly that he died of it.

In a dispatch to the New York *Times,* I read of an Arab in Palestine, one Salah Mustapha Salah Abu Musa, who at the age of 105 *grew his third set of teeth!*

There is an ancient city in Italy which can be approached by sea only through a long stretch of shallow water full of rocks and cross currents. There is one safe channel, and it is marked by posts. In the days of the Sea Rovers the city used to protect itself by pulling up the posts whenever a rover hove in sight.

Mankind has taken to planting posts along its way to mark the flight of time. Every year we put in a new one, heedless of the fact that we are thus marking a clear channel for our Arch-Enemy, Age, to enter in from the sea of human belief.

But the fact is that there is no natural reason for man to grow old as soon as he does, *no biological reason for him to grow old at all!*

Why is it that the animals live five to seven times their maturity, when man lives only two to three times his? Why? Because man hastens decrepitude and decay by holding the thought of old age always before him.

Dr. Alexis Carrel, Nobel Prize winner and member of the Rockefeller Institute, has demonstrated that living cells taken from a body, properly protected and fed, can be kept alive indefinitely. Not only that, but they *grow!* In 1912 he took some tissue from the heart of an embryo chick and placed it in a culture medium. It lived and grew for some thirty years, until they tired of tending it and threw it out.

Dr. Carrel showed a moving picture of these living cells before the American Institute of Electrical Engineers. They grew so fast that they doubled in size every twenty-four hours, and had to be trimmed daily!

The cells of your being can be made to live indefinitely when placed outside your body. Single-celled animals never die a natural death. They live on and on until something kills them. Now scientists are beginning to wonder if multicellular animals like man really need to die.

Under the title, "Immortality and Rejuvenation in Modern Biology," M. Metalnikov, of the Pasteur Institute, published a volume that should be read by all those who have decided that it is necessary to grow old and die.

Here is the first sentence of the concluding chapter of the book: "What we have just written forces us to maintain our conviction that immortality is the fundamental property of living organisms."

And further on:

"Old age and death are not a stage of earthly existence. . . ."

THE FOUNTAIN OF YOUTH

Four hundred years ago Ponce de Leon set sail into the mysteries of an unknown world in search of the Fountain of Youth, when all the time the secret of that fountain was right within himself.

For the fact is, that no matter how many years have passed since you were born, *most of the cells in your body are only eleven months old today!* Those cells are constantly renewing themselves. The one thing about them you can be surest of is CHANGE. Every one of the millions of cells of which your body is composed is constantly being renewed. Even your bones are daily renewing themselves in this way, and are believed to rebuild themselves completely every seven years.

These cells are building—building—building. Every day they tear down old tissue and rebuild it with new. There is not a cell in your body, not a muscle or tissue, not a bone, that is old! Why then should you feel age? Why should you be any less spry, any less cheerful, than the youngsters around you whom you have been envying?

The answer is that you *need not*—if you will but realize your YOUTHFULNESS. Every organ, every muscle, tissue and cell of your body is subject to your subconscious mind. They rebuild exactly as that mind directs them. What is the model *you* are holding before your mind's eye? Is it one of age, of decrepitude? That is the model that most men use, because they know no better. That is the result you see imaged upon their bodies.

But you need not follow their outworn models. You can hold before your mind's eye only the vision of youth, of manly vigor, of energy and strength and beauty—*and that is the model your cells will use to build upon.*

Do you know what is responsible for much of the difference between Youth and Age? Just one thing. Youth looks *forward* always to something better. Age looks backward and sighs over its "lost" youth.

In youth we are constantly growing. We KNOW we have not yet reached our prime. We know we can expect to continually IMPROVE. We look forward to ever-increasing physical powers. We look forward to a finer, more perfect physique. We look forward to greater mental alertness. We have been educated to expect these things. Therefore we BELIEVE we shall get them—and we GET them!

But what happens after we get to be thirty or forty years of age? We think we have reached our prime. We have been taught that we can no longer look forward to greater growth—that all we can hope for is to "hold our own" for a little while, and then start swiftly downward to old age and decay. History shows that no nation, no institution and no individual can continue for any length of time to merely "hold his own." You must go forward—or back. You must move—or life will pass you by. Yours is the choice. If you will realize that there is never any end to GROWTH—that your body is constantly being rebuilt—that perfection is still so far ahead of you that you can continue GROWING toward it indefinitely—you need never know age. You can keep on growing more perfect, mentally and physically, every day. Every minute you live is a minute of conception and rebirth.

You may be weak and anemic. You may be crippled or bent. No matter! You can start today to rebuild along new lines. In eleven months, most of those weak and devitalized cells, those bent and crippled bones, will be replaced by new, strong, vigorous tissue.

Look at Annette Kellerman—crippled and deformed as a child—yet she grew up into the world's most perfectly formed woman. Look at Theodore Roosevelt—weak and anemic as a young man—yet he made himself the envy of the world for boundless vigor and energy. And they are but two cases out of thousands I could quote. Many of the world's strongest men were weaklings in their childhood. It matters not what your age, what your condition—you can start now renewing your youth, growing daily nearer the model of YOU that is imaged in Universal Mind.

Arthur Brisbane said that at the age of eighty-five George F. Baker was doing the work of ten men.

That is what every man of eighty-five ought to be doing, for he should have not only the physical vigor and strength and enthusiasm of twenty-one, but combined with them he should have the skill and experience, the ripened judgment of eighty-five.

There is no more despairing pronouncement than the belief of the average man that he matures only to begin at once to deteriorate and decay, when the actual fact is, as stated by the eminent Dr. Hammond, *there is no physiological reason* why a man should die. He asserted—and the statement is corroborated by scientists and physiologists—that the human body possesses inherent capacity to renew and continue itself and its functions indefinitely!

Your body wear out? Of course it does—just as all material things do. But with this difference—your body is being renewed just as fast as it wears out! Have you damaged some part of it? Don't worry. Down inside you is a chemical laboratory which can make new parts just as good or better than the old. Up in your subconscious mind is a Master Chemist with all the formulas of Universal Mind to draw upon, who can keep that chemical laboratory of yours making new parts just as fast as you can wear out the old.

But that Master Chemist is like all of us—like you. He is inclined to lazy a bit on the job—if you let him. Try to relieve him of some of his functions—and he won't bother about them further. Take to the regular use of drugs or other methods of eliminating the waste matter from the body, and your Master Chemist will figure that your conscious mind has taken over this duty from him—and he will leave it thereafter to your conscious mind. Lead him to believe that you no longer expect him to rebuild your body along such perfect lines as in youth—and he will slow down in his work of removing the old, worn-out tissues, and of replacing them with new, better material. The result? Arteries clogged with worn-out cells. Tissues dried and shrunken. Joints stiff and creaky. In short—Old Age.

The fault is not with the Master Chemist. It is with you. You didn't hold him to the job. When a business or an enterprise or an expedition fails, it is not the rank and file who are to blame—it is the directing head. He didn't give his men the right plans to work on. He didn't supply the proper leadership. He didn't keep them keyed up to their best work.

What would you think of an engineer who, with the best plans in the world, the best material with which to build, threw away his plans when he was half through with the job and let his men do as they pleased, ruining all his early work and all his fine material by putting the rest of it together any which way?

Yet that is what you do when you stop LOOKING FORWARD at thirty or forty, and decide thereafter to just grow old any which way. You throw away the wonderful model on which you have been building, you take the finest material in the world, and let your workmen put it together any way they like. In fact, you do worse than that. You tell them you don't expect much from them any more. That any sort of a patched-up job they put together after that will be about as good as you can look for.

Man alive! What would you expect from ordinary workmen to whom you talked like that? Your inner workmen are no different. You will get from them just what you look for—no more, no less.

"Your time of life" should be the best time you have yet known. The engineer who has built forty bridges should be far more proficient than the one who has built only a few. The model you are passing on to your Master Chemist now ought to be a vastly more perfect model than the one you gave to him at twenty. Instead of feeling that your heart is giving out and your stomach weak, you ought to be boasting of how much better a heart you are now making than a few years ago, how much more perfectly your stomach is functioning than before you learned that you were its boss.

Of one thing you can be sure. God never decreed a law of decay and death. If there is any such law, it is man-made—and man can unmake it. The Life Principle that came to this planet thousands or millions of years ago brought no Death Principle with it. For death is like darkness—it is nothing in itself. Death is merely the absence of life, just as darkness is merely the absence of light. Keep that life surging—strongly.

In the Book of Wisdom, of the Apocryphal writings, you read:

"For God made not death; neither hath He pleasure in the destruction of the living.

"For He created all things that they might have being; and the generative powers of the world are healthsome, and there is no poison of destruction in them, nor hath death dominion upon the earth.

"For righteousness is immortal:

"But ungodly men with their works and words called death unto them.

"For God created man to be immortal, and made Him to be an image of His own proper being.

"But by the envy of the devil came death into the world."

"Whosoever liveth and believeth in me (understandeth me)," said Jesus, "shall never die."

And again—"If a man keep my saying, he shall never see death."

Universal Mind knows no imperfection—no decay—no death. It does not produce sickness and death. It is your *conscious* mind that has decreed these evils. Banish the thought—and you can banish the effect. Life was never meant to be measured by years.

I remember reading a story of a traveler who had journeyed to a land of perpetual sun. Since there was no sunrise and no sunset, no moons or changing seasons, there was no means of measuring time. Therefore to the inhabitants of that land, time did not exist. And having no time, they never thought to measure ages and consequently never grew old. Like organisms with a single cell, they did not die except by violence.

There is more truth than fiction to that idea. The measurement of life by the calendar robs youth of its vigor and hastens old age. It reminds me of the days of our grandparents, when a woman was supposed to doff her hat and don a bonnet at 40. And donning a bonnet was like taking the veil. She was supposed to retire to her chimney corner and make way for the younger generation.

Men and women ought to *grow* with years into greater health, broader judgment, maturer wisdom. Instead of becoming atrophied, and dead to all new ideas, their minds should through practice hold ever stronger images before them of youthful vigor and freshness. The Psalmist says—"But thou art the same, and thy years shall have no end."

No one need retire to the chimney corner, no matter how many years have passed over his head. Years should bring wisdom and greater health—not decrepitude. Many of the world's famous men did their greatest work long after the age when most men are in their graves. Tennyson composed the immortal lines of "Crossing the Bar" at the age of eighty. Plato still had pen in hand at eighty-one. Cato learned Greek at the same age. Humboldt completed his "Cosmos" in his ninetieth year, while John Wesley at eighty-two said—"It is twelve years now since I have felt any such sensation as fatigue."

You are only as old as your mind. Every function, every activity of your body, is controlled by your mind. Your vital organs, your blood that sends the material for rebuilding to every cell and tissue, the processes of elimination that remove all the broken down and waste material, all are dependent for their functioning upon the energy derived from your mind.

The human body can be compared to an electric transportation system. When the dynamo runs at full power every car speeds along, and everything is handled with precision. But let the dynamo slow down and the whole system lags.

That dynamo is your mind, and your thoughts provide the energy that runs it. Feed it thoughts of health and vigor and your whole system will reflect energy and vitality. Feed it thoughts of decrepitude and age, and you will find it slowing down to the halting pace you set for it.

You can grow old at thirty, You can be young at ninety. It is up to you. Which do you choose?

If you choose youth, then start this minute renewing your youth. Find a picture—or, better still, a statuette—of the man you would like to be, the form you would like to have. Keep it in your room. When you go to bed at night, *visualize* it in your mind's eye—hold it in your thought as YOU—as the man *YOU ARE GOING TO BE!*

The Journal of Education had the idea in their story of "The Prince and the Statue":

"There was once a prince who had a crooked back. He could never stand straight up like even the lowest of his subjects. Because he was a very proud prince his crooked back caused him a great deal of mental suffering.

"One day he called before him the most skillful sculptor in his kingdom and said to him: 'Make me a noble statue of myself, true to my likeness in every detail with this exception—make this statue with a straight back. I wish to see myself as I might have been.'

"For long months the sculptor worked hewing the marble carefully into the likeness of the prince, and at last the work was done, and the sculptor went before the prince and said: 'The statue is finished; where shall I set it up?' One of the courtiers called out: 'Set it before the castle gate where all can see it,' but the prince smiled sadly, and shook his head. 'Rather,' said he, 'place it in a secret nook in the palace garden where only I shall see it.' The statue was placed as the prince ordered, and promptly forgotten by the world, but every morning, and every noon, and every evening the prince stole quietly away to where it stood and looked long upon it, noting the straight back and the uplifted head, and the noble brow. And each time he gazed, something seemed to go out of the statue and into him, tingling in his blood and throbbing in his heart.

"The days passed into months and the months into years; then strange rumors began to spread throughout the land. Said one: 'The prince's back is no longer crooked or my eyes deceive me.' Said another: 'The prince is more noble-looking or my eyes deceive me.' Said another: 'Our prince has the high look of a mighty man,' and these rumors came to the prince, and he listened with a queer smile. Then went he out into the garden to where the statue stood and, behold, it was just as the people said, his back had become as straight as the statue's, his head had the same noble bearing; he was, in fact, the noble man his statue proclaimed him to be."

A novel idea? Not at all! Twenty-five hundred years ago, in the Golden Age of Athens, when its culture led the world, Grecian mothers surrounded themselves with beautiful statues that they might bring forth perfect children and that the children in turn might develop into perfect men and women.

Eleven months from now *you* will have an almost entirely new body, inside and out. Few of the cells, little of the tissue that is now in you will be there then. What changes do you want made in that new body? What improvements?

Get your new model clearly in your mind's eye. Picture it. VISUALIZE it! Look FORWARD daily to a better physique, to greater mental power.

Give that model to your Subconscious Mind to build upon—and before eleven months are out, that model *WILL BE YOU!*

CHAPTER XXIII

THE MESSAGE OF JESUS

How then shall man so order life
That when his tale of years is told,
Like sated guest lie wend his way;
How shall his even tenour hold?

Be true to Nature and Thyself;
Fame or disfame court not nor fear;
Enough to face the still small voice
That thunders in thine inner ear.

Spurn every idol others raise,
Burn incense to thine own Ideal;
To seek the True, to glad the heart,
Such is of life the Higher Law,
Whose difference is the Man's degree,
The Man of Gold, The Man of Straw.

—HAJI ABDU-EL-YEZDI

What was the real message of Jesus? What was the one unforgivable thing that He taught which brought down the wrath of the Jews upon His head?

—What one thing did He add to the teachings of Moses, of Amos and of Hosea that changed the whole current of history?

—What has since become the basis of all Democracy?

NOT the doctrine of the One God. NOT the new idea of loving one's neighbor and forgiving one's enemies. No—that was not why the Pharisees and Rulers hated Him and resolved to have His blood. But because He went up and down the length and breadth of the land, teaching that *all men are equally the children of God!*

Can you imagine what this meant to mankind in that day of slavery and oppression? Just think—if God is the Father of ALL men, then ALL are His children, equally entitled to the good things of life, equally dear to Him.

"No wonder," wrote Bruce Barton in *The Man Nobody Knows,* "the authorities trembled. They were not fools. They recognized the logical implication of such teaching. Either Jesus' life or their power must go. No wonder that succeeding generations of authorities have embroidered His idea and corrupted it. It was too dangerous a Power to be allowed to wander the world, unleashed and uncontrolled."

That is why the idea most of us have of Jesus is so far from the reality that lived and taught and worked wonders throughout Palestine some nineteen hundred years ago.

"This was the message of Jesus," Barton explained, "that God is supremely better than anybody had ever dared to believe. Not a petulant Creator, who had lost control of His creation, and in wrath was determined to destroy it. Not a stern Judge dispensing impersonal justice. Not a vain King who must be flattered and bribed into concessions of mercy. Not a rigid Accountant, checking up the sins against the penances and striking a cold, hard balance. Not any of these . . . nothing like these . . . but a great Companion, a wonderful Friend, a kindly, indulgent, joy-loving Father. 'Hold your heads high,' He had exclaimed, 'you are lords of the universe . . . only a little lower than the angels . . . Children of God.'"

Jesus did not come to call attention to Himself, to get people to believe in Him as a god or demigod; He did not come solely to reveal God to man; *He came to reveal man to himself.*

"Beloved, now are ye the Sons of God!" Not only did Jesus proclaim this in His words, but His whole life was given to teaching and showing the Divine Sonship of man. Thirty-seven times in the Gospel records He refers to Himself as the Son of Man. He never called Himself God. But He claimed *union* with God, and He claimed and demonstrated possession of the Father's power and all that the Father had. But He disclaimed this as a mere personal power. "It is not I, but the Father in me; He doeth the works."

Furthermore, He again and again assured His followers that this same power was in them. "If ye believe in me and my word abideth in you, the works that I do shall ye do also. And greater works than these shall ye do."

What, then, was the Message of Jesus? The greatest message ever brought to any planet! That man is the Son of God. That he inherits from the Father all of life, all of wisdom, all of riches, all of power.

God is the parent. And man's every quality is derived from Him. Not only that, but *man inherits every quality of the Father!* He has only to grow in knowledge, to learn the Father's ways, to lean trustfully upon His help, in order to be supreme "amid the war of elements, the wreck of matter and the crash of worlds."

Apart from God, man is a weakling, the sport of circumstance, the victim of any force strong enough to overpower or brush him aside. But let him ally himself with the Father and he becomes, instead of the creature of law, the ruler through law. Instead of the sport of circumstance, he makes circumstance. Instead of the victim of fire or water or sickness or poverty, he masters the forces of nature, demands health and prosperity as his birthright.

The God that most of us were taught to believe in was a huge, patriarchal Man-God, seated upon a throne high in the heavens. A King, stern, righteous and just—chastening His children mercilessly whenever He felt it was for their good; holding an exact scale between the good they had done and the sins they had committed, and dispensing penances or rewards to balance the two.

The King idea has gone out of fashion here on earth this many a year, and the idea of a God-King is fast disappearing from our conception of the Infinite. After 1900 years, we are at last coming around to Jesus' idea of a loving Father-God, a God that is in each of us, whose "good pleasure it is to give us the kingdom."

In the light of such an understanding of God, we can readily grasp how it was possible for Jesus to heal the sick, to feed the hungry, to bring forth gold from the fish's mouth, to still the tempest—and what is even more, to promise these same powers to us!

Man is the Son of God!

We start with that. How, then, shall we take advantage of our son-ship? How use the infinite power it puts in our hands? The purpose of life is to develop the Divinity that is in us. What is the first thing we must do? Where shall we start?

REACHING INTO INFINITY

The first essential is to find a point of contact with the Father. Benjamin Franklin sent a kite up into the clouds and brought down along its string a current of electricity. Through him, man learned to harness this electricity for his daily servant. Franklin made his contact with the Source of Power.

Thousands of years before Franklin—centuries even before the birth of Christ—men began to send up kites (figuratively speaking) trying to contact the Source of Life itself.

A few succeeded. A few great Prophets like Elisha, Elijah, Moses, contacted the Source of all Power, and whenever and as long as they kept that contact, nothing could withstand them.

Franklin caught the source of electrical energy, and by learning to understand and work with it, man has turned those terror-inspiring thunderbolts of destruction into man's greatest friend and servant. The electricity did not change. It is exactly the same now as aforetime. It is man's conception of it that has changed.

Uncontrolled, lightning is a curse to mankind. Through understanding, man has harnessed it to serve his needs. Touch a button, and it lights your home. Turn a dial, and it brings you news or instruction, entertainment or music, from hundreds or thousands of miles away. The mere throwing of a switch releases the power of millions of horses. Pulling it out bridles them again. Was there ever such a master servant?

Yet it is as nothing to the power latent in the Source of Life—the power of the Father of all things. Even now, ignorant as we are, we occasionally contact it, but we do it accidentally—*and we fail to maintain the contact!*

Remember "The Lost Chord," by Adelaide Proctor?

Seated one day at the organ,
I was weary and ill at ease;
And my fingers wandered idly
Over the noisy keys.

I know not what I was playing,
Or what I was dreaming then,
But I struck one chord of music
Like the sound of a great Amen.

I have sought, but I seek it vainly,
That one lost chord divine,
Which came from the soul of the organ
And entered into mine.

You know how often things have come to you like that—snatches of song, or speech, or verse such as man never wrote before. Visions of wonderful achievement. Echoes of great ideas. Glimpses of riches you could almost reach—the riches of the Spirit within.

If only you could tap that boundless reservoir at will, what success would not be yours, how puny your present accomplishments would seem by comparison! And you *can* tap it. You can make your contact with Infinity—if not at will—at least with frequency. All that is necessary is understanding and belief.

How to do it? How to go about it? Through your Higher Self, through the Holy Spirit within you, your part of Divinity. Why did the Apostles, after cowering abjectly in hiding for ten days after the ascension of Jesus, suddenly issue forth boldly and astonish the world with their preaching and their miracles?

Jesus had commanded that they should not depart from Jerusalem, but should tarry there "until they be endued with power from on high."

"And when the day of Pentecost was fully come, they were all with one accord in one place. And suddenly there came a sound from heaven as of a rushing mighty wind, and it filled all the house where they were sitting.

"And there appeared unto them cloven tongues like as of fire, and it sat upon each of them. And they were all filled with the Holy Ghost."

Just as the one great fact of the Gospels is the presence of the Son exalting and revealing the Father, so the one great fact of the Acts of the Apostles is the presence of the Holy Spirit inspiring all their acts.

"The Comforter, which is the Holy Ghost, whom the Father will send you in my name," Jesus had promised them, "he shall teach you all things, and bring all things to your remembrance, whatsoever I have said unto you."

That same Comforter will teach you, will bring to you any good tiling. He has all wisdom, all power. How, then, shall you contact him?

First you must clear away the obstacles that stand between

you and him, as explained in the previous chapter. Then you must have perfect trust, utter faith in him.

You have seen pictures of miners with lamps in their caps, the light from these illuminating everything in front of them. Picture the Holy Ghost as a "tongue of flame" over *your* head, illuminating everything that is dark in your path. Picture it as a Guardian Angel, leading you in the right way, guiding you, guarding you from all harm. Picture it as one interested only in your good, bringing you new ideas, new opportunities, new life.

There is nothing of good you can wish for that this Higher Self cannot bring to you. There is no ambition so great, no goal so high, that it cannot reach it.

Say aloud frequently—"The Holy Spirit within me goes before me and opens the way. Infinite Wisdom tells me just what to do." Say it—and *believe it!*

When problems confront you, when obstacles seem to bar your path, don't worry; don't fret. Put them up to your Higher Self.

Know that there is always some way over or around or through every obstacle. Know that when one door closes, another opens. So put it up to your Higher Self to find the way, and then go serenely about your work, doing those things that seem best to do, but not worrying about the outcome, KNOWING that as sure as there is a God in Heaven, your part of Him—your Higher Self—is working out the solution for you.

Remember this—whatever you fix your attention upon

with singleness of desire and faith, you compel to come into your life.

If you feel that you need increased supply, don't dwell upon your need, but center your attention upon the things necessary to satisfy that need. Concentrate on your blessings, be grateful for them, delight in them, and they will increase and multiply. As the poet so well expressed it—

Our prayers are answered; each unspoken thought
And each desire implanted in the mind
Bears its own harvest, after its own kind;
Who dreams of beauty has already caught
The flash of angel wings. Who seeks to find
True wisdom shall assuredly be taught,
But thorns of fate have thorny thoughts behind,
For out of our own hearts our lives are wrought.

"The soul answers never by words," said Emerson, "but by the thing itself sought after."

Have you ever seen the Hopi Indians' Snake Dance—their prayer for rain? It is probably the oldest religious ceremony on this continent, and it is said that it never yet has failed to bring the rains.

Speak to Him thou, for He heareth
When Spirit with Spirit doth meet;
Closer is He than breathing,
And nearer than hands and feet.

Scientists may talk learnedly of atmospheric conditions and natural laws, but the fact remains—the Indians send up their heartfelt prayers to the Holy Spirit in simple faith—and so far as is known, the rains have never failed to come.

There is in each one of us a Power that hears the cry of the human heart. There is behind us a Father "whose good pleasure it is to give us the kingdom." "Closer is He than breathing; nearer than hands or feet." You don't have to beg Him for the good things of life any more than you have to beg the sun for its heat. You have only to draw near and take of the bountiful supply He is constantly holding out to you.

So what is it you want of the Father within you? Whatever it is, you can have it. Whatever of good you ask for with earnest desire and simple faith, the Father will gladly give.

Do you lack a home? There is a perfect home for you already built in the Father's mind. Know this, realize it, then like Hagar in the wilderness, pray that your eyes may be opened that you may see this perfect home of yours.

But don't forget to DO SOMETHING to show your faith. What is the first thing you would do if you had that home you are praying for? Well, if you believe that you HAVE it, you will start DOING. You will prove to your subconscious that there is TRUTH in your affirmations.

There is a perfect position for you, a perfect mate, a

perfect work, a perfect idea of each cell and organism in your body. It is up to you merely to seek that you may find them, believe that you receive them.

You have the most powerful magnet on earth right in your own mind. Use it! Charge it with desire and faith. Speak the word that sends the Holy Spirit within you in quest of that which you want.

Let your daily prayer to the Spirit within you be that He manifest the divine design in your life—that He bring you to your proper work, your right place.

Say to Him each day, as F. S. Shinn suggests in one of her helpful books—"Infinite Spirit, open the way for the divine design in my life to manifest. Let the genius within me now be released. Let me clearly see the perfect plan."

And then, if you like, ask Him to give you a lead, an indication of the next step to take.

"Call upon the Almighty," says the Eastern Sage. "He will help thee, Thou needst not perplex thyself about anything else. Shut thy eyes and while thou art asleep, God will change thy bad fortune into good."

Over and over and over
These truths I will weave in song;
That God's great plan needs you and me,
That Will is greater than Destiny,
And that Love moves the world along.

However mankind may doubt it,
It shall listen and hear my creed,
That God may ever be found within—
That the worship of self is the only sin,
And the only devil is Greed.

Over and over and over
These truths I will say and sing,
That love is mightier far than hate,
That a man's own thought is a man's own fate,
And that life is a goodly thing.

—ELLA WHEELER WILCOX

CHAPTER XXIV

KEEPING THE TRACKS CLEAR

Many years ago, when the Grand Central Terminal in New York was being built, traffic there was fearfully congested. Thousands of trains coming in—thousands of others going out—tracks to be laid, building to be done, space to be found for vast quantities of material—and all the while the din of building, building.

Naturally, trains were delayed. Naturally, passengers were complaining. Naturally, good business was being lost.

And then a strange thing was noticed. Incoming trains were late—five minutes, ten minutes, half an hour and more, on every division *but one.* On that division, practically every train *came in on time!*

They checked up to find the reason. Trainmen smiled when they asked them—"Nothing in their way," they explained, "so they brought their trains in on schedule."

They traced it to the Superintendent in charge of that division—and there they found the answer. "Why," he told them, "it's simple enough. You can't bring trains in unless you first send out those that come in ahead of them. I just keep my tracks clear, that's all."

And for keeping his tracks clear they made him vice president and put him in charge of the whole terminal!

Men write asking me how they can tap the Universal Supply that is all about them, how they can get the money they require for some worthy enterprise or need.

How do you tap the supply of electrical current from the power house near you? Not merely by connecting your wires to the main current. That puts power into your wires, but of itself it serves no useful purpose. Before you can actually tap the source of electrical power, you have to *find an outlet for it!* You have to use what is in your house wires before more can come to you. The moment you stop the outflow—that moment the incoming current stops, too.

What is the surest way to bring business into a store? To first give out something—give out advertising, give out samples, give out special service.

What is the surest way to bring more water from the common reservoir into your pipes? To first draw out the water that is in them.

What is the surest way to draw upon the Universal Supply for more money? To first use to good advantage that which you have.

You don't depend upon the water in your pipes for your bath. You cheerfully use it to clean the tub, knowing there is plenty more behind, pushing its way forward, waiting to be used.

No more must you depend upon the money in your pocketbook or your bank account. Use it cheerfully, freely, for any good purpose, knowing there is infinitely more where that came from, merely waiting for you to make room for it.

The other day a friend told me of a time when he was in urgent need of a thousand dollars. All he had to his name was a $10 bill. And he found himself holding on to that $10 bill like a drowning man to a straw. For days he kept it, fearing to break it lest he should be lost entirely.

Then it suddenly occurred to him that he was pinning his faith to a lone $10 bill instead of to the Source of all supply—that he was damming the flow of money by keeping that little obstruction in the faucet.

He sat down at once, and to show his faith, he mailed that $10 to the first worthy charity that came to his mind.

Immediately his faucet opened and the supply flowed through abundantly, and never since has it failed to respond to the same treatment.

There is that scattereth, and increaseth! yet more. And there is that withholdeth more than is meet, but it tendeth only to want.

The liberal soul shall be made fat; and he that watereth, shall be watered also himself.

—PROVERBS 11:24

CHAPTER XXV

THE LAW OF LIFE

When Maitland and Hagenberger made the first Pacific flight from San Francisco to Hawaii, the one thing they suffered from most was hunger.

One of the officers at the flying field, hearing them mention this, went over their plane carefully and right beneath their feet, covered by a piece of tarpaulin, found stored a *full supply of sandwiches!*

Like the Amazon explorers who almost perished of thirst when blown out to sea by a storm, while all the time they were floating on a *sea of fresh water!*

But we need not smile. We are doing the same. We are floating on a River of Plenty, yet suffering by millions from poverty and lack. We are floating on a River of Life—yet dying by millions of sickness. Why? Because we don't know enough to let down our buckets! We think we have drifted into the salt sea of contagion or age or germs—and all the while, the River of Life flows serenely by.

The greatest Teacher the world has ever known came

to a people steeped in poverty and ignorance and disease. And what did he teach them? How to find riches in the ground? How to build ships or trains or flying machines? How to take from their more fortunate neighbors? No—none of these things.

He told them of a loving Father-God, possessing all life, all health and all riches, who would gladly give these to them in the exact proportion in which they believed in Him. They were not to doubt, they were not to fear. They were to ask, believing, and as they believed so it would be unto them.

He brought this message of hope and good cheer to mankind—that every man and woman is surrounded each moment with all of life and health and riches. That no matter how low he may have fallen, no matter how near his last gasp he may be, he has only to "let down his buckets" to replenish his ebbing life, his lost hopes.

Of the sinners He said—"It is not the will of my Father which is in heaven, that the sinner should die, but rather that he should be converted and live." Of the children, He told us—"It is not the will of my Father that one of these little ones should perish."

The River of Life is always by us, always available, but we must USE it! There is no limit to its power or willingness to help—no limit, that is, but the extent of our BELIEF in it.

That is the secret of all the success of Psychology, of all the cures of Metaphysics—that God is to each of us exactly what we believe HIM to be—a stern Judge, a blind Fate, an impersonal Principle, or a loving Father. It is up to us to choose which we shall have. But whichever we choose, that is what He will be to us.

Of course, God Himself doesn't change. It is simply that He has given us free will to avail ourselves of as much or as little of Him as we wish. When we experience sickness or other evil, it is not He that gives it to us. We have turned our back on Him, that is all—and just as when we turn our back to the sun, we see the shadows, so when we turn our back to God, we get the shadows of poverty and sickness.

He has all of life. He has all of health. He has all of riches. And in proportion as we believe in Him and His willingness to share these good gifts with us, in that exact proportion shall we receive. "As your faith is, so shall it be unto you."

CHAPTER XXVI

SQUARING THE CIRCLE

When Phillips Brooks was in college, his greatest ambition was to become a professor of mathematics.

He "majored" in mathematics, and as soon as he finished college, he took up the teaching of it as a profession. What was his chagrin, at the end of six months, to be told that he was no teacher, that his pupils had made no progress, and another would have to be found to take his place!

He was completely discouraged. He left his place downcast, sick at heart. For days and weeks he cast about trying to decide what he should do. At last, more as a forlorn hope than anything else, he picked the ministry.

After the usual preparation, he was "called" to a little church in Philadelphia.

Strange to say, this would-be teacher of mathematics made an immediate and spectacular success in teaching that most difficult subject—religion. People came from far and near to hear him. His church grew too small, and a larger one was built for him. He was called to the Holy Trinity Church in Boston. Presently he was made Bishop. He became one of the greatest preachers this country has known.

As a mathematics professor, he was a square peg in a round hole. As a preacher, he was in his right niche. It required only a little change, but that little changed not only his outlook, but his whole life.

Andrew Carnegie started as a bobbin boy and his highest ambition, until he was grown, was to be a telegraph operator.

Michael Faraday started as a preacher and became the greatest electrical wizard of his day.

Whitney was a Connecticut school teacher, yet he invented the cotton gin.

Bell was a professor of elocution, yet he invented the telephone.

Morse, Dunlop, Gillette, Eastman, Ingersoll, Harriman, Gary—the names of these square pegs who started in round holes is legion. Until circumstances forced them out of their wrong places, they got nowhere. As soon as they found their right niches, they went forward with giant strides.

The best thing that can happen to any of us is to fail and be thrown out of these tasks for which we are not fitted. If we can hold the faith, we will eventually find the jobs for which we are fitted. And then we will *show the world!*

But until then? Do your best with the work before you.

Dig into it. Make sure you are not overlooking any Acres of Diamonds beneath your feet.

And all the while keep the Man Inside You a-seeking of your goal. Lay before him every night your hopes, your fears, your knowledge, your drawbacks—then put it up to him to find the right work.

Lay the burden upon him in the implicit confidence that he HAS the answer—then depend upon him to give it to you at the right time, in the right way. And meantime, get ready. Do what is given you to do better than it has ever been done before. Who knows but it is the very thing that will lead to your great opportunity.

SIR GALAHAD
ALFRED TENNYSON

My good blade carves the casques of men,
My tough lance thrusteth sure,
My strength is as the strength of ten,
Because my heart is pure.
The shattering trumpet shrilleth high,
The hard brands shiver on the steel,
The splinter'd spear-shafts crack and fly,
The horse and rider reel:
They reel, they roll in clanging lists,
And when the tide of combat stands,
Perfume and flowers fall in showers,
That lightly rain from Ladies' hands.

How sweet are looks that ladies bend
On whom their favours fall!
For them I battle till the end,
To save from shame and thrall:
But all my heart is drawn above,
My knees are bow'd in crypt and shrine;
I never felt the kiss of love,
Nor maiden's hand in mine.
More bounteous aspects on me beam.
Me mightier transports move and thrill;
So keep I fair thro' faith and prayer
A virgin heart in work and will.

When down the stormy crescent goes,
A light before me swims,
Between dark stems the forest glows,
I hear the noise of hymns:
Then by some secret shrine I ride;
I hear a voice but none are there;
The stalls are void, the doors are wide,
The tapers burning fair.
Fair gleams the snowy altar-cloth,
The silver vessels sparkle clean,
The shrill bell rings, the censer swings,
And solemn chaunts resound between.

Sometimes on lonely mountain-meres
I find a magic bark;

I leap on board: no helmsmen steers:
I float till all is dark.
A gentle sound, an awful light!
Three angels bear the holy Grail:
With folded feet, in stoles of white,
On sleeping wings they sail
Ah, blessed vision! blood of God!
My spirit beats her mortal bars,
As down dark tides the glory slides,
And star-like mingles with the stars.

When on my goodly charger borne
Thro' dreaming towns I go,
The cock crows ere the Christmas morn,
The streets are dumb with snow.
The tempest crackles on the leads,
And, ringing, springs from brand and mail;
But o'er the dark a glory spreads,
And gilds the driving hail.
I leave the plain, I climb the height;
No branchy thicket shelter yields;
But blessed forms in whistling storms
Fly o'er waste fens and windy fields.

A maiden knight—to me is given
Such hope, I know not fear;
I yearn to breathe the airs of heaven
That often meet me here.

I muse on joy that will not cease,
Pure spaces clothed in living beams,
Pure lilies of eternal peace,
Whose odours haunt my dreams;
And, stricken by an angel's hand,
This mortal armour that I wear,
This weight and size, this heart and eyes,
Are touch'd, and turn'd to finest air.

The clouds are broken in the sky,
And thro' the mountain-walls
A rolling organ-harmony
Swells up, and shakes and falls.
Then move the trees, the copses nod,
Wings flutter, voices hover clear:
"O just and faithful knight of God!
Ride on! the prize is near."
So pass I hostel, hall, and grange;
By bridge and ford, by park and pale,
All-arm'd I ride, whate'er betide
Until I find the holy Grail.

CHAPTER XXVII

HOW PELTON GAINED 900,000 CUSTOMERS

Some years ago there was a young man in a small Connecticut town with a book—and an idea. The book was written for ambitious men—to help show them the way to success. This young man had an idea that he could sell it to every man who was willing to study and work for success. But selling takes time—and money. *And he had only a couple of hundred dollars to his name!*

In such case, what would you have done? Many a man, in the same circumstances, rails against fate—and does nothing. But above all else, this young man had courage. He believed in the book, he believed in his idea, and he was willing to stake his all on his judgment.

The question was—how to use his $200 so as to get the most out of it. As an appropriation for a publicity campaign, it was a joke. Bookstores? Posters? Circulars? *Mail order!* It would just pay for a page ad in one of the Current Events Magazines that was largely read by a high type of serious-minded man.

He took his problem to this magazine, and got its help and that of a good advertising agent in laying out his ad. Book men themselves, they knew the kind of copy that would most appeal to the book-buyer. And they helped him to put that kind of copy into his ad.

The magazine came out—and *nothing happened!* Two or three days passed—still not an order. Can you imagine the suspense, with his last penny staked in the venture? He had almost concluded that he must bid his $200 "Goodbye!"

Then a single order came straggling in. He welcomed it like a long-lost brother. Next day three or four. Then they started coming in bunches.

From that first ad, costing him $200, he got $2,000 worth of orders for his books!

The young man was A. L. Pelton, of Meriden, Connecticut, and that $200 was the start of his fortune. With the $2,000 received from his orders, he immediately placed more ads, and as the orders kept rolling in, branched out into other magazines. In the subsequent ten years this young man sold $5,000,000 *worth of books!*

And to show the quality of the books, more than half of that $5,000,000 represented *repeat* orders from pleased customers. After he staked his all on an idea, A. L. Pelton built up a list of over 900,000 customers and published more than twenty great inspirational works.

And all this from only $200 and an idea!

Of course, there will be some to attribute his success to luck, but if you have ever sold goods by mail (as I have), you know how small a share luck has in its success, and how great a part consists of careful planning, intensive thinking and hard work.

It is like the man who got up at a dinner to Dr. Alexis Carrel and ascribed the success of this famous surgeon to genius. Dr. Carrel looked at him sadly. "Here I work heart and soul for twenty years to get where I am," he answered, "and all the credit I get for my efforts is to be told I am a born genius." Genius is not born. Genius is acquired. And as Edison put it—it is 98 percent perspiration and 2 percent inspiration.

What is the lesson of Pelton's success? Simply this—that material capital is the least important of all the elements that go to make up success. The biggest successes have been built up from little or no money. The thing that counts—the thing without which any amount of money is useless—is the idea. And that can be the product only of mind.

You have a mind—as good a mind as Pelton or Ford or any other man who has built his fortune through his own unaided efforts. What are you doing with it? Are you developing ideas that will make men better or richer or more comfortable? Are you thinking in terms of service? Or are you just wondering how you can make more money?

There is only one man who will pay you money, you know—and that is the man for whom you do something—be that something the shining of his shoes, the writing of a book, the repairing of his car or the filling of his stomach. And the better you do it, the more he will pay you.

So think first in terms of service. What can you offer that people must have done for them?

Find the service—get the idea—then put into it everything you have—money and time and thought. In a few years, you, too, will be able to look upon your hundreds or your hundreds of thousands of satisfied customers.

CHAPTER XXVIII

FROZEN CREDITS

You have probably heard of that term used in bankruptcy—*"Frozen Credits."* Most men know what the term means—many of them to their cost.

When ice jams the Great Lakes in the Fall, when the "Soo" freezes tight and no more boats can get through, always there are a few cargo boats caught in the ice. Their gram or their coal or their ore remains perfectly good, but until the Spring thaw it is of no use. It is frozen in.

When you invest money in farms or lands not easily sold, when you tie up your capital in big stocks of merchandise that you can't get rid of, when you lend money to those who cannot quickly repay—then you learn the meaning of the term "Frozen Credit."

Your security may be ever so good, your debtor unquestionably honest—but if you can't lay your hands upon the money when you need it, the goodness or integrity of your investment doesn't do you a lot of good. It is frozen in.

All are agreed that God has infinite riches—enough to make every man on earth a millionaire and still have plenty left over. All are agreed that we are His children, heirs to His infinite wealth. But there most of us stop. We are heirs to infinite wealth. We know it is all around us. We can see it, feel it, taste it, smell it—it is in the very air we breathe—yet we can't lay our hands upon it. Why? Because to us, it is a "frozen credit."

And yet there are men to whom these same riches seem to flow so easily, so abundantly, without apparent effort on their part.

How do they succeed in thawing their frozen credits, when every effort of ours seems to leave them more tightly jammed?

How is it with a frozen river? Your ice jam is always in some narrow part, is it not—or where bridges or wharves pinch it together. Get it past these, get it into a wider channel, and your jam breaks up of itself.

The men to whom riches and abundance flow so easily are those who have widened their channels by looking for plenty, by expecting it and by preparing for it through continual and ever-increasing service. They never hoard. They never look for safety only. Their credits never have a chance to freeze because they keep them moving, working, digging their channels ever deeper and wider so that more and more keeps flowing in.

As the Scriptures put it—"He that hath a bountiful eye shall be blessed."

He that sees only plenty, he that expects only plenty, he that works with only plenty in mind, will by his very thought attract that plenty to him.

Basil King tells the story of a ship-wrecked sailor, struggling in the water, praying for a rock—any kind of rock—on which to rest. And a rock was all he found. Another, with greater faith, reached the shores of a pleasant isle.

The great River of Life is a river of plenty. Cast yourself and your fortunes into it confidently, believingly, and it will carry you on to the Isle of Plenty. Mistrust it, struggle against the current, and it will wreck you on the Rocks of Want.

CHAPTER XXIX

A NEW LIFE AT FIFTY

When is the time to give up? If Fate hands you a jolt in the short ribs, if Misfortune lands a "haymaker" in the ninth round, ought you to throw up the sponge and quit, or is there still time to come back and make good?

Mr. and Mrs. J.W.W., of Oklahoma, are living proof that there is.

Ten years ago, when he was fifty years old and she forty-nine, he failed in business and lost almost every dollar they possessed.

Too old to land easy jobs, too proud to ask financial aid from friends, they were faced with the necessity of doing something—and doing it at once.

It happened that, some years before, Mr. W. had bought a small equity in some undeveloped land in Western Oklahoma. It occurred to him that if they could exchange this for an equity in a little farm, they might be able to raise enough to at least keep them from starvation.

They advertised in several papers, and finally succeeded in making the exchange—but what a farm they got!

Sixty acres—but the three-room house was old and dilapidated. The roof leaked, the walls were crumbling. It really did not seem possible for anyone to live in it.

But they realized they must live there—or in the poorhouse—so they set cheerfully to work. They patched the roof and walls, they put glass in the windows, they cleaned—how they cleaned! Whitewash and soap and disinfectant—fortunately all three of these are cheap—and they used them with lavish hand.

Almost before they knew it, that little three-room shack had taken on the appearance of a home! It was clean. It was cozy. And it was livable! The house stood in a big ten-acre pasture, in a setting of beautiful old maple trees, and when they had finished cleaning and repairing it, they were so proud of the result that they named it "Maplewood."

Now at least they had a place to live. Remained only to find the means. They patched up the barn, which was, if possible, in an even more dilapidated condition, and fixed the chicken house. Then they bought a Jersey cow and some White Leghorn chickens.

With the proceeds of the milk and eggs, they were able to buy what groceries they must have. Luxuries were taboo—even though both had all their lives been accustomed to luxuries. They had the courage not only to start afresh and hew out their own home even as the early pioneers had done, but to stand the hardships of pioneer life as well.

Having no money for work teams or farming implements, they rented most of their sixty acres to a man who owned a small place near them.

For themselves, they picked up for a very few dollars an old horse and weatherbeaten buggy with which to carry their butter and eggs to the town, eight miles away.

There was no repining, no weeping over what might have been. They faced the world with courage and determination, and they faced it with a smile. And the world smiled back at them.

Their renter made a fine crop off their land, and their share of it came to enough to buy a good team of horses, plows and a wagon.

Their cow had a fine heifer calf. They set all the hens they could, and raised several hundred chickens.

One stormy night, a fine Collie dog came whining to their door. They took her in, warmed and fed her. She seemed to have come from a distance, for she was worn out and had evidently been starving for days. They made every reasonable effort to find her owner, but without success. She seemed just another gift of the gods. In the nights that followed, she earned her keep over and over again by driving predatory animals from the chicken house.

The next year, with the horses he had bought, Mr. W. was able to cultivate the farm himself, so there was more money from the crops. With it, he was able to still further improve the house and barn, increase the number and quality of his livestock, even put by a little money.

The Collie here still further distinguished herself by bringing in a litter of eight lovely puppies, which sold for $10 to $15 apiece, thus providing still another source of income.

The cow had another calf. The hens brought up a bigger brood of chickens than before. Dame Fortune smiled upon this old couple, who had the courage to smile in the face of misfortune.

And so the years have gone, each year seeing them a bit further ahead than the previous one.

Today, they have a fine new five-room bungalow, with bath and screened-in porch. From the lumber in the old house, they built a new barn. They have three substantial chicken houses, a garage, and a good, dependable car to take the place of that outworn buggy.

They have a sturdy team of horses and a fine herd of Jerseys. And five hundred Leghorn hens that pay for all their household needs.

They owe nobody a penny; they are independent, healthy and happy. Last fall they had worlds of grapes, peaches, plums and apples from the orchard they had planted. Rose bushes climb over their door and gates. A telephone connects them with their neighbors, a radio with the world at large.

Sunshine without, peace and comfort and contentment within. And all because they didn't know when they were licked. All because when Fate knocked them down, they refused to stay out. All because they had the courage and determination to fight on—and smile!

If you happen to know some middle-aged couple who are looking forward hopelessly to a dreary old age, who live in constant dread of losing their livelihood, show them this article.

There are thousands of abandoned farms scattered all over this great country of ours—abandoned because the young folks want the light and life of the great cities. Many of them can be bought for a song, or rented on shares. To the men and women who are willing to endure present hardship for future peace and comfort, they offer opportunity. They offer home.

CHAPTER XXX

YOUR RIGHT TO BE RICH

"Then shalt thou lay up gold as dust, and thou shalt have plenty of silver."

—JOB

For a long time I, and I fancy a great many of you, also, have had the wrong idea about money. In this iconoclastic age, when investigating committees are rampant, when biographers and other idol smashers are telling truths about people and things, I want to tell you the TRUTH about MONEY!

How many things have been said about it. It has been called "filthy lucre," "the root of all evil," and all sorts of names. No wonder that when we have felt the real need of money—because it is something we cannot live without—we have been afraid and ashamed to ask God for it. We have hemmed and hawed over our prayers, and have tried to make our wants known to our Heavenly Father in a roundabout way, asking for all sorts of things, hoping that somehow, in some way, we could get it over to Him, that the real thing we need is *money.*

WHAT IS MONEY?

Webster defines money as "the recognized medium of exchange of value for value received." Nothing evil in that. While we live on this planet as human beings, equity and honor in our relations to each other must be expressed through some tangible form that may be recognized by the physical senses of sight and touch. Money then is the recognized medium through which equity and honor are expressed between man and man. Now, equity and honor, integrity and confidence, are attributes of man's higher or spiritual consciousness, which express the best or divine in man. Then money in itself is the tangible form through which equity and honor, the divine spirit in man, expresses itself in the world of the outer and visible things.

Ceasing to look upon money as an evil, we see it as a symbol of God's abundance, and allow it to assume its rightful place in life. No longer used for selfish aims, for selfish accumulation is not the spirit of equity and honor, we can know money for what it really is—God's creative thought of abundance—manifesting itself in the material gold and silver and the precious stones of earth; and our right use of these riches constitutes a realization of a partnership with God, in which we become channels through which these spiritual riches are expressed in our business relations with our brother man.

As a matter of fact, we have no authority for condemnation of money. The first mention of the word occurs in Genesis after God had blessed Abraham with great abundance, "and he was very rich in cattle and in silver and in gold." When his wife Sarah died, he desired to buy a cave for a burial place for her "for as much money as it is worth," and when Ephron offered to give him the field with the cave, the grand old Patriarch declined to accept it as a gift, "and weighed unto him four hundred shekels of silver, current money with the merchant."

Solomon, when he had asked of God wisdom that he might rightly rule Israel, was also given riches and wealth and honor, above all kings. Having recognized the spirit of equity and honor, the material *things* were added unto him. Later Solomon says: "Wisdom is a defense, and money is a defense," linking together wisdom and money.

Jesus talked much of money and business methods. It seems strange that this phase of his teaching has been so little recognized. Jesus had great business wisdom and endeavored to unfold his knowledge to those in the business world at that time, but they could not comprehend him. And today, nearly two thousand years later, we are still suffering the disappointments and sorrows resulting from misapprehension of the Master's teaching, "My people are destroyed for lack of knowledge."

Business, as taught by Jesus, does not include the terrible burdens which have imposed themselves upon the world in which we live and work. Dominion over the earth is not something man has to struggle to acquire. It was given to him when he was placed on the earth. Jesus understood and made free use of this dominion given him by the Father. He strives to make us understand. "Why do ye not understand my words?" and "Greater things than these shall ye do." All that is demanded in the furtherance of business affairs is easily attainable in the Christ way.

Witness the conquest by Jesus over every earth condition. Never a need of any kind, that was not met by his understanding. He walked on the water, stilled the tempest, fed the multitudes, healed every disease, restored the dead to life. Weary fishermen, who had toiled all night in vain, were shown the way to attract supply in the form of a great "draught of fishes, insomuch that the boats could not hold them."

Jesus was endeavoring to teach us that the LAW *that produces* is greater than the production. He tried to make us aware of the substance at hand—at *your* hand—at *my* hand. When Hagar was in the wilderness, with her little son dying of thirst, she called unto the Lord for water. All that happened was that "God opened her eyes and she *saw* a well of water." Her consciousness was made aware of the supply at hand. Through her SELF within, she recognized infinite Power, and became a partner in business with the Father, and her needs were met.

THE NEW AGE

"Behold I show you a new Heaven and a new earth." Wise men do not sleep in the dawn of a new age. They are alert to the "all things" that are taking place about them.

Tired and discouraged men in the business world today, are you not weary of the age-old struggle? Are you not ready for the new and better way? Will you not accept the Christ way? Where are you? In the desert? There is no desert place to Him. Substance is everywhere, in the great earth depths, in the ether, overlying, underlying and encompassing you. The Kingdom of Heaven *at hand*. "I am come that they might have it *more abundantly.*"

You business men and women are needing to know that if you but cast your net on the *right* side, you will catch great draughts of success in your endeavors. You need to use your houses of business aright to have the abundance so great that you will have to call others to come and help draw the net to gather the rich return.

Jesus was not afraid to talk about money. He uses the talents, and the treasure in the field, and the pearl of great price, to illustrate the Kingdom of God. Those servants who increased their master's wealth by wisdom in trading received his commendation. And you remember his rebuke to the servant who was afraid to use the money. "Thou wicked and slothful servant . . . Thou oughtest to have put my money in the bank, and then when I returned, I should have had my own with interest." How simple he made the payment of the taxes, showing Peter the exalted way of fulfillment, understanding so fully the supply at hand that a fish could be made a party to the transaction.

"And I say unto you, *ask and you shall receive,*" and be given just that which satisfies your need, when you ask, and exactly that for which you ask. "If a son of any of you that is a father shall ask for bread, will he give him a stone? Or if he ask for a fish, will he give him a serpent? If ye then being evil know how to give good gifts unto your children, how much more will your Heavenly Father give good things to them that ask Him?"

THE ROOT OF ALL EVIL

"And Adam said I heard Thy voice in the garden, and I was afraid." And this serpent, "more subtle than any beast of the field," introduces itself into the consciousness of man, as the devil, or one evil, FEAR. And man has been trying to hide himself from God ever since.

What a complication! Trying to hide from his own consciousness of himself. And ever since that time our Father-God has been trying to make us aware of the unreality of fear and to lead us to discover our oneness with Him. "God is Love. There is no fear in love; but perfect love casteth out fear, because fear hath torment."

And we are afraid to trust our Father in money matters. He cares for the lilies and the sparrows and the fowls of the air, the great wide world with its beauty and abundance, the heavens with its millions of star-worlds, the suns, the moons of the inconceivable, vast universe, declaring the power and glory of God. Yet we are afraid! We are afraid to trust our brother man. He may by some means get our money away from us. We are so suspicious and afraid and try to hold on to it so tightly that we can neither enjoy it ourselves nor let others enjoy it. In this awful fear-evil, money ceases to be an expression of equity and honor between man and man;

it ceases to have spiritual values of confidence and love and peace and joy, which cannot be taken from us, and it becomes the tool of fear, "the root of all evil." "Where moth and rust doth corrupt, and thieves break through and steal."

When Samuel's sons walked not after his ways, but turned aside after *lucre* and took bribes and perverted judgment, the whole nation of Israel suffered. When Simon the Sorcerer made the mistake of thinking that "the gift of God may be purchased" and offered money for it, he received Peter's scathing rebuke, "Thy money perish with thee, for thy heart is not right in the sight of God." Paul in his Epistles to Timothy and Titus warns against "greed of filthy lucre," and in his exhortation to Timothy occurs the so misquoted "root of all evil" clause. "They that will be rich fall into temptation, a snare, and into many foolish and hurtful lusts . . . For the *love* of *money* is the root of all evil, which while some covet after, they have erred from the faith, and pierced themselves through with many sorrows."

IN GOD WE TRUST

"Thus saith the Lord that created thee . . . fear not . . . thou art Mine ... I will even make a way in the wilderness, and rivers in the desert . . . This people have I formed for Myself; they shall show forth My praise."

Have you ever closely examined the money of our government? The coins are of silver, nickel and copper. God's richness of creative thought is manifested in these wonderful metals. Every coin bears on its face the motto, "In God we trust." The coins are round, representing endless possibilities, never ending supply.

Underlying the motto on our coins, there is a great spiritual truth. If we truly enter into the spirit of this statement, it will uplift our thought concerning money. To trust in God truly is to cease to trust in the visible coin. Trust in God enables us to become conscious of the Divine Intelligence, which governs our affairs and eliminates all worry and anxiety regarding finances.

Money is a reward of service, and service is an outer expression of love. The reward for true service is sure and unfailing. "Whoever would be first among you, let him be servant of all." To serve best brings greatest reward.

Your right money is your reward for right service, and it represents your dominion which no one can take from you. Let no subtle thought of fear or doubt creep in to rob you of your rich ideas.

Faith in God's exceeding great and precious promises, faith in your brother man, faith in yourself and in your work, helps you to understand how to keep the channels open. Spiritual substance and its outward expression, money, flows; and the same channel through which it comes to you, must be kept open that it may flow through you to others. Thus blessing your money, you have become a co-worker with your Father, for this is the Kingdom of God and His right-wisdom, and all things are added unto you.

"I am become rich, I have found me out substance."

It is no small thing to partake of the understanding of

Jesus. It is not just an idle group of words but a feast of ideas, and we should open our minds and hearts for profound instruction, for "when He the Spirit of Truth, is come, He will guide you into all truth . . . and He will show you things to come."

You are a creator! What your mind can conceive, hold in consciousness, your mind can create. Every idea has always existed in Divine Creative Mind. The affairs of our earth life are those ideas already expressed or in process of expression. The Heavenly things are those ideas in Divine Creative Mind still to be expressed. The invisible is ever coming forth into the visible. Atom power, television and other marvels of today are among "those things hidden from the foundation of the world," which are now becoming visible, expressed or pressed out from Creative Intelligence. Atomic power had existed all these ages, until Divine Intelligence pressed out through the mind of a man an idea. This idea enabled man to harness the atom, and made it possible to use it.

"Eye hath not seen, nor ear heard, neither have entered into the heart of man, the things that God hath prepared for them that love Him. But God hath revealed them unto us by His Spirit"—substance ideas expressing themselves through the mind of man, that he may learn to cooperate with the Father within, to help do the things God wants done on the earth. It makes no difference what line of work you are engaged in. As soon as you realize your relation to the All-power, you have through this consciousness allied your SELF with the intelligence and infinite bounty of Universal Good. God is revealing to you through His spirit your own rare gifts of mind and soul. There within you they have been from the beginning to be unfolded in His service.

There is a definite requirement made of man before he can use atom power, to serve him as it does today. Laws concerning its action have to be learned or it will work to injure instead of to bless. So with the laws of supply, and the supply itself, that is ever about us to be used in the right way when we learn to regard it as Jesus did. When Jesus "lifted up his eyes and gave thanks," he fulfilled the law and fed the multitude. Lift up your spiritual consciousness and give thanks to the Father within.

THIS ONE THING

"And Jesus said unto him, what wilt thou that I should do unto you?"

What is your real desire? Not partially but wholly must you make your decision. You are generalizing in your thoughts. You want prosperity. You are not sure just what is your sincere desire. Your idea is hazy, wavering,

George C. Golden illustrated this for one who came to him for assistance. Standing at his office window and looking down on the street below, he called his attention to the large number of people who were walking there, going in various directions, with no common interest. Mr. Golden then dropped a coin from the window, and as it struck the pavement and rolled away, one after another stopped and looked, until in an amazingly short time they counted thirty people grouped together.

As long as your mind is an undisturbed thoroughfare, many thoughts are passing through, but you are not halting any of them. Take one idea, make a good distinct picture of it, and immediately your thoughts begin to group themselves, and you have the nucleus of your desire. This one thing you do, and ideas from the SELF within begin to collect around the one thing, and you open the way for your good to flow to you.

Watch your thought! Examine each thought that comes to you. It may be your call. Open your mind, be alert to the things that are happening about you; having eyes, see ye, and having ears, hear ye. Be interested in every person you meet, you may entertain an angel unawares. He may have a vital message for you, or you may have one for him. Watch for your work, recognize it, be ready for it. You wish to be a musician. The thought comes to you, then the desire grips you, then you make your decision. Now holding this one thing in your consciousness, you bend every effort to the achievement of your desire. You prepare yourself through application, study and arduous practice, until you not only become conversant with the laws of harmony, but are able to effectively apply them in your work. Every profession, business, or job, has its laws of harmony which you can apply if you desire.

Examine yourself and see if your mental attitude is one that will be conducive to your growth. Have you the desire and the wisdom to use in an unselfish way these things which will be added unto you? In your spiritual consciousness get the idea strong and clear that your part of the work is to cultivate the soil and to plant the seed, but the increase comes from your business partner, the Father within. Devote your efforts to attaining the realization that the Mind within is the source of your true growth, and that the outer expansion of your prosperity will keep exact pace with the spiritual development that takes place within.

Only as you are equipped for service can you serve; only as you serve are you of value to others; only as you are of value to others are you paid; and the gold and the silver and the treasures of the earth are yours to enjoy, for you are the child of God, and if a child, then an heir, and joint-heir with Christ.

CHAPTER XXXI

YOU CAN DO IT

Try to be somebody with all your might.
Find your purpose and fling your life into it.
"The iron will of one stout heart shall make a thousand quail."
" 'Impossible' is a word to be found only in the dictionary of fools."
"He who has resolved to conquer or die is seldom conquered."

I am constantly asked by men and women whether I think they really have enough in them to make much of a success in life, anything that will be distinctive or worth while, and I answer, "Yes, you have. I know you have the ability to succeed, but I do not know that you will. That rests entirely with you. You can, but will you?"

It is one thing to have the ability to do something distinctive, something individual, but doing it is a very different thing. There is a tremendous amount of unproductive ability in the great failure army today. Why did not the men who have it make something of themselves? Many of those men could be prosperous, successful men of standing in their community, instead of the dregs of society. They had the opportunity to make good. Why didn't they?

You say you long to make your life count; that you are ambitious to get on. Why don't you? What are you waiting for? What holds you down? Who is keeping you back? Answer these questions and you will find the reason. There is only one—yourself. Nothing else keeps you back. The opportunities are on every hand, infinitely better ones than thousands of men and women who have made their lives count ever had.

It is up to you to find where and what the trouble is. Is it physical or mental? Do you lack physical vigor? If you do, your vitality and your will-power are depleted. Is your education deficient? Is your training for your vocation inadequate? Do you know what shortcomings are responsible for your failure to accomplish what you dream of and long to do? Very often some apparently trivial personal trait or defect proves strong as iron bonds to hold a man back from the attainment of a worthy ambition.

Now, if your achievement does not begin to match your ambition there is something wrong. If you are dissatisfied with the result of your efforts up to the present time examine yourself carefully, take stock of your mental and physical assets; and see where you have been slipping, falling down, where you have made your greatest mistakes or failures. You know the strength of a chain doesn't lie in its strongest link, no matter how strong, but in its weakest. Find your weak link, and then strengthen it.

MANY LACK THE WILL TO SUCCEED

Do not hide behind such silly excuses as that you have no chance, nobody to help, nobody to boost you, to give you a pull, to help you to capital, nobody to show you the way. If there is something in you, if you are worth your salt, you will make a way if you cannot find one.

"Despite all the cries of lack of opportunity which are being so frequently voiced in various ways, the hardest task today for us employers of labor is to get in sufficient numbers, boys and girls—with a *thorough* knowledge of three R's."

This is the recent utterance of the manager of one of the large department stores in New York City. He puts the blame for the state of things he describes partly on our public school system, and partly on the boys and girls themselves. Indeed, the most serious part of his indictment deals with them. His conclusion, based on experience with thousands of public school graduates, is that they are not only poorly equipped for business, but that they are also *"lacking in energy and the will to succeed."*

Now, without the energy and the will to succeed, no amount of education, no power on earth outside of one's self can push or lead or boost a person into success.

It is the difficult things in life that develop our mental and moral muscle, that build up courage and stamina.

In tropical countries, where man's food practically grows on trees ready to eat, and where there is little or no housing or clothing problem, the people are naturally indolent, slipshod, and slovenly. They are brutal in their passions. They know little of self-mastery or mastery of conditions, adaptation to a severe climate, or the conquest of a hard and stubborn soil. Consequently these people have contributed but little to civilization. The things which make life worth living: the achievements, the inventions and discoveries, the noble deeds, the advancement of industry, science, and art, have been contributed by men who have struggled with hard conditions of Nature, who have fought and conquered obstacles, who have lived in the temperate zones, and have experienced the rigors of cold and the enervation of heat.

It is doubtful whether any territory in the world ever generated more noble qualities, more sterling character, more civilizing forces than has the stubborn, hard soil and severe, inhospitable climate of New England. It was the surmounting of obstacles strewn in the path of these sons of New England, which early bred fortitude, persistence, and those allied traits which lead to preeminence and success.

The man who waits for favorable conditions and favorable circumstances will find that success in any field is never a walkover. It is the man who wins in spite of circumstances, in spite of adverse conditions, the man who wins when other people say he cannot, the man who does the "impossible," the man who rides over obstacles, who gets on in this world. And why? Because the very struggle to overcome the obstacles in his way develops the power that carries him step by step to his goal.

WILLIAM OF ORANGE

"As well can the Prince of Orange pluck the stars from the sky as bring the ocean to the wall of Leyden for your relief," was the derisive shout of the Spanish soldiers when told that the Dutch fleet would raise that terrible four months' siege of 1574. But from the parched lips of William, tossing on his bed of fever at Rotterdam, had issued the command: *"Break down the dikes: give Holland back to the ocean"* and the people had replied: "Better a drowned land than a lost land." They began to demolish dike after dike of the strong lines, ranged one within another for fifteen miles to their city of the interior. It was an enormous task; the garrison was starving; and the besiegers laughed in scorn at the slow progress of the puny insects who sought to rule the waves of the sea. But ever, as of old, heaven aids those who help themselves. On the first and second of October a violent equinoctial gale rolled the ocean inland, and swept the fleet on the rising waters almost to the camp of the Spaniards. The next morning the garrison sallied out to attack their enemies, but the besiegers had fled in terror under cover of the darkness. The next day the wind changed, and a counter tempest brushed the water, with the fleet upon it, from the surface of Holland. The outer dikes were replaced at once, leaving the North Sea within its old bounds. When the flowers bloomed the following spring, a joyous procession marched through the streets to found the University of Leyden, in commemoration of the wonderful deliverance of the city.

Who can keep a determined man from success and how can it be done? Place stumbling-blocks in his way and he takes them for stepping-stones, and climbs to greatness. Take his money away, and he makes spurs of his poverty to urge him on. Cripple him, and he writes the Waverly Novels. Lock him up in prison, and he writes the "Pilgrim's Progress"; leave him in a cradle in a log cabin in the wilderness, and in a few years, you find him in the White House.

"All the performances of human art, at which we look with praise and wonder," says Johnson, "are instances of the resistless force of perseverance."

Adverse circumstances spur a determined man to success.

The degree in which a man sees insurmountable obstacles and impossible situations in his path will measure his success ability. To some people the way ahead of them is so full of obstacles, so full of difficulties and impossible situations that they never get anywhere, while another man feels so much bigger than the things which try to hinder him, so much stronger than the obstacles which try to down him, the stumbling-blocks which try to trip him, that he does not even notice them.

We are all familiar with men who are continually up against something that they think is impossible, they are sure cannot be done; and yet there is generally somebody near them who manages to do this very impossible thing.

I have in mind a man who has such a habit of thinking that things cannot be done that almost any kind of a difficulty downs him. Unless he can see the road clear to his destination he is afraid to move a foot forward. If he sees any obstruction ahead he loses courage, even to undertake what he longs to do. If you ask him to do anything which is at all difficult he will say, "Well, now, I don't believe I can do it. In fact, it simply cannot be done." The result is he makes no progress in any direction and he never will.

If our ambition is merely a weak desire to obtain a certain thing provided it does not cost much effort, if we would merely *"like* to have" a certain thing, there is no magnetism in such a milk-and-water purpose. The ambition must be backed by the willingness and the determination to do anything that is within human power to accomplish the aim. This is the mental attitude that wins.

The habit of being a quitter before the battle begins is fatal to all distinctiveness. It is the death-blow to the development of originality and strength of character; and without these no man can be a leader. He must remain a trailer always; he must follow someone else's lead.

YOUR OBSTACLES MELT AWAY

If you are trying to get a start in the world but don't feel able to remove the many barriers that block your way, do not get discouraged. The obstacles that look so formidable at a distance will grow smaller and smaller as you approach. Have courage and confidence in yourself and the road will clear before you as you advance. Read the life stories of great men who from the start have cleared their pathway of obstructions which make yours look puny. Magnify your faith in yourself and you will minimize the obstacles in your way.

The whole science of efficiency and success in life consists in the vigorous, persistent affirmation of our determination and our ability to do the thing we have set our heart on. It consists in setting our face like a flint toward our goal, turning neither to the right nor the left, though a Paradise tempt us, or failure and disaster threaten us.

If your determination is easily deflected, if any persuasion can separate you from your life resolve, you may be pretty sure that you are on the wrong track.

Ill health or personal deformity may sometimes hold one back—though there are numerous instances of success in spite of them—but in the vast majority of cases where people fail in getting a good start in life or in ultimately reaching their goal it is because there is no energy in their resolution, no grit in their determination. They peter out after a few rebuffs. Two or three setbacks take the edge off their determination. They do not realize that success in anything worth while is the result of tremendous resolution, vigorous self-faith, and work, work, work—steady, conscientious, wholehearted, unremitting work. Light resolve, half-hearted efforts, indifferent, intermittent work have never yet accomplished anything and never will.

"Mere wishes and desires but engender a sort of green sickness in people's minds, unless they are promptly embodied in act and deed," says Samuel Smiles. "It will not avail merely to wait, as so many do, 'until Blucher comes up,' but they must struggle on and persevere in the meantime, as Wellington did. The good purpose once formed must be carried out with alacrity and without swerving. He who allows his application to falter, or shirks his work on frivolous pretexts, is on the sure road to ultimate failure."

Get busy, then, and work with all your might. There is no such thing as failure for the willing, ambitious worker.

Work, which many have called a curse, is really the salvation of the race. It is the greatest educator. There is no other way of developing power, calling out the resources, building stamina and breadth of character. Work is the great savior of the race. Without it we should be a backboneless and staminaless, characterless race.

Emerson says: "Men talk of victory as of something fortunate. Work is victory. Wherever work is done victory is obtained."

The man

Who breaks his birth's invidious bar,
And grasps the skirts of happy chance,
And breasts the billows of circumstance
And grapples with his evil star

will tower above his fellows.

Energy of will distinguishes such a man as surely as muscular power distinguishes a lion.

"He who has a firm will," says Goethe, "molds the world to himself."

"People do not lack strength," says Victor Hugo, "they lack will."

JULIUS CAESAR

Of Julius Caesar it was said by a contemporary that it was his activity and giant determination, rather than his military skill, that won his victories. The man who starts out in life determined to make the most of his eyes and let nothing escape him which he can possibly use for his own advancement; who keeps his ears open for every sound that can help him on his way, who keeps his hands open that he may clutch every opportunity, who is ever on the alert for everything which can help him to get on in the world, who seizes every experience in life and grinds it up into paint for his great life's picture, who keeps his heart open that he may catch every noble impulse, and everything which may inspire him—that man will be sure to make his life successful; there are no "ifs" or "ands" about it. If he has his health, nothing can keep him from final success.

No tyranny of circumstances can permanently imprison a determined will.

The world always stands aside for the determined man. Will makes a way, even through seeming impossibilities. "It is the half a neck nearer that shows the blood and wins the race: the one march more that wins the campaign: the five minutes more of unyielding courage that wins the fight."

CHAPTER XXXII

DON'T PUT IT OFF AND DON'T GIVE UP

HOW "PUTTING OFF" LOST A WAR

The British War Office has made an important decision.

In order to crush the American colonies, it is decided that General Burgoyne, in Canada, shall march south to meet, at Albany, the forces of General Howe, who is to march north from New York. Through the union of these two forces the American colonies will be cut in two and further resistance will be impossible. The letter of instructions to Burgoyne has been forwarded by Lord George Germain, the British Secretary of State for the American colonies, and the letter to Howe is in preparation.

The weekend comes. Lord Germain has planned to make a visit to his country estate.

On his way out of London—by horse and carriage—he stops at his office, to take care of important last-minute business. The most important business is to sign the letter of instructions to General Howe. He finds, however, that his under-secretary, D'Oyly, has forgotten to write these instructions.

"If you will wait just five minutes," says D'Oyly apologetically, "I'll write a few lines."

"So!" cries Lord Germain angrily, "my poor horses must stand in the street all the time, and I can never do anything as I plan it. The letter will just have to wait till I get back."

And with these words he leaves in a huff—to take care of his poor horses—and to get to his country place.

Not only are the instructions not sent on time, but they are never sent—for upon Lord Germain's return to town both he and his secretary D'Oyly have completely forgotten the matter.

Howe *never* gets these instructions, and not knowing what else to do marches southward.

Largely because of lack of Howe's aid Burgoyne suffers total defeat and the capture of his entire army by the Americans at Saratoga.

Because of this great and decisive victory Benjamin Franklin is able to induce the French king to send aid to the American colonies.

Because of this aid Washington is able to bottle up Cornwallis at Yorktown and force his surrender. With this surrender England has forever lost her American colonies.

The American colonies won their independence because of their own courage and love of freedom—but it is also true that Britain lost the colonies because of stupidity and blundering on the part of her generals and statesmen. Had it not been for Lord Germain's procrastination *regarding Howe's instructions, the result of the war might have been far different.*

Among those who have the ability to succeed, the one greatest cause of failure is procrastination. Through waste of time:

Duties go unperformed.
Important decisions are never made.
Opportunities fly by ungrasped.
Engagements go unmet.
Trains are missed.
Life itself slips by unlived.

Whatever is being done—*all* that is being done—in this vast teeming world of ours is being done *now. Today.* Nothing has ever happened *tomorrow.* What you are going to be—what success you will reach—is being decided by the action you are taking *now.*

The procrastinator fools himself into thinking he has more time than he has, puts off deciding until it's time to act, because of fear decides to do that important job next week, forgets to keep accurate check on his time, tries to solve a big problem without enough facts or without analysis and ends up by not solving it at all, postpones unpleasant tasks until tomorrow.

The smart man has a definite schedule and follows it. He keeps a fresh list of jobs to do and then does today the things that need doing today. He makes a definite decision to keep all engagements on time. He starts preparation early enough so that when the time arrives to act he will be ready. He has an accurate timepiece and keeps an eye on it. He divides his big problem into little problems and solves them one at a time in order. He knows beforehand so thoroughly what he is going to do that he starts unafraid.

Cut out procrastination today.

Below are listed several suggested courses of action. Choose the one that fits you best and follow it out *now.*

1. Schedule your routine duties.
2. Set down the things (outside of routine) that you have to do and want to do—and set a definite time to give them your serious attention.
3. If you are undecided whether or not to do a certain thing, sit down and figure out the situation honestly. *Decide whether* you will do it or not. If you decide *not* to do it, *forget it.* If you decide to do it—*fix a definite time to do it.*
4. Plan to take up only one problem at a time till completion.
5. If your procrastination is the result of fear—*put fear aside—risk failure.* Put fear aside by telling yourself that while you *may* fail if you make the move you desire, your failure is certain and automatic if you *don't* make the move.

6. If you procrastinate when faced with a big difficult problem, *analyze*, break the problem into parts, and handle one part at a time.

ANSWER THESE QUESTIONS

1. Is there something I know I ought to do, and haven't done?
2. Is there any good reason why I don't do it right now?
3. Do I have and follow a schedule of my daily routine duties—so as to avoid procrastination because of petty indecisions?
4. Do I crowd my calendar with so many appointments that I cannot possibly meet them on time?
5. Do I wait till 10 o'clock to prepare for a 10 o'clock appointment?
6. Do I waste time by inability to decide which of two courses of action to take?
7. Do I let small problems pile up on me while wasting time trying to decide on some big problem?
8. Do I waste time thinking vaguely about courses of action I will probably never take up?
9. Do I procrastinate because of some big problem

which, because of my failure to analyze, seems impossible to solve?

10. Do I procrastinate in important matters because I let fear or distaste turn me aside from decision and action?

Break through the cobwebs of indecision. Whenever you are faced with these questions:

Shall I do this or not?
Which of these courses shall I take?

and similar questions, remember that perhaps the biggest danger is in the *procrastination* resulting from your indecision. *Decide, act,* and you have a fighting chance for success—while indecision and procrastination can have no possible result but failure.

THE VALUE OF PERSISTENCE

A serene moon shines down on a calm sea.

But a roar fills the air, and the salt odor of the sea is smothered under the acrid fumes of gunpowder.

Broken masts, and spars, and fragments of sail float about—with here and there a man struggling frantically.

There is a lull in the firing from one of the ships—the one whose sails are nearly all gone, whose masts are jagged stumps, whose hull is shattered below the waterline. Has her captain decided to surrender? After all, with nothing but a sinking ship between him and the bottom of the ocean, he may well think it time to surrender.

The captain of the other ship notes the sudden quiet. Have the rebels decided to give up? he asks himself. If they have surrendered, their flag ought to be down, but through the smoke he cannot see what they are doing. He therefore cries out across the water:

HAVE YOU STRUCK YOUR COLORS?

And from the shattered ship the reply comes back, a defiant shout:

I HAVE NOT YET BEGUN TO FIGHT!

It is John Paul Jones, hero of the American navy. Far from admitting defeat, he is working out a new plan of attack.

Since his own ship, the *Bon Homme Richard,* is slowly sinking, the only way he can win is to *board the enemy ship* and fight the British on their own decks!

Slowly he maneuvers his unwieldy sinking ship closer to the enemy. Side scrapes side, and then drifts away again. John Paul's men make several attempts to grapple the enemy, but without success. Then, by chance, an anchor-fluke of the *Bon Homme Richard* catches in a chain attached to the other ship. The enemy is caught! A little quick deft work with ropes and the two ships are lashed firmly together.

"Board her! Board her!" shouts John Paul, and indomitable American seamen swarm across to the decks of the British frigate—*and start their fighting.*

Soon almost alone among his dead and dying, the British captain strikes his own colors, and John Paul and his exultant Americans sail away masters of the *Serapis,* while the *Bon Homme Richard,* a hopeless wreck, slowly sinks.

Without *persistence,* John Paul, instead of sailing back to France in command of the *Serapis,* might well have gone to a watery grave with the *Bon Homme Richard*—have been captured by the British and dangled from a yard-arm as a pirate.

You know, there's a peculiar thing about persistence. Most of us have much more persistence than we realize. We have great persistence—but do not exert that persistence in the *right direction. Persistence* is the expression of a man's *will to live.* We can either exert our persistence by pushing the world out of our way till we reach freedom or *success*—or we can exert it by *running away* from our problems and difficulties—and let the world crush us the first time we stumble. But persistence must be combined with intelligence. If at first you don't succeed, try, try again—but in different ways! Many a man, who objects that his persistence does no good in doing difficult jobs, fails because of persisting with the wrong method instead of using his persistence to find and use new and better methods until he *does* succeed.

Of two men, one brilliant and with little persistence, the other of average intelligence but great persistence, the second is far more likely to achieve great results—in science, in art, in the professions, in *business.* The Law of Averages will favor the man who persists. All of us have bad luck and good luck. The man who persists through the bad luck—who keeps right on going—is the man who is *there* when the good luck comes—and is ready to receive it.

Which way do you persist? If your heart ticks off the normal number of beats per minute, you have plenty of persistence. The question is, are you exerting that persistence in the RIGHT DIRECTION in connection with your work?

Here is a number of questions that will enable you to check on yourself. Answer these questions honestly, and thereby learn in what parts of your work you are lacking in the RIGHT KIND OF PERSISTENCE.

Man fortunately has it in his own power to change the direction of his persistence if he will only make an honest, intelligent effort to do so. Change the direction of your persistence where you are now using the wrong kind, and you will be able to make many gains you are now losing.

1. Reviewing my own life, can I cite definite cases in which I have achieved something I wanted just because of unusual persistence on my part?
2. Since I achieved success in those instances simply because of my PERSISTENCE, isn't it

logical to believe that the steady use of persistence in my work day in and day out, will pay me real dividends?

3. Do I persist doing the work every day that I know I ought to do to achieve the ends I desire?
4. Do I persist more in running away from difficulties—or in overcoming them?
5. Do I persist in studying my business or work to try to better my knowledge of it?
6. Do I persist in studying my work to try to improve it?
7. Do I have people who I KNOW need my work—and will possibly suffer loss if I don't persist until I see them?

DON'T GIVE UP! Many men who have achieved great success modestly disclaim the possession of genius, brilliance, or unusual intelligence, attributing their success to an average intelligence coupled with great persistence and will-power.

Others, still more modest, attribute their success to luck.

When John Paul Jones was attempting to lash the *Bon Homme Richard* to the *Serapis* so he could board the latter, it was pure luck that an anchor-fluke of his ship caught in a chain of the British frigate. But if he had not persisted in fighting *long after apparent defeat,* this "luck" would not have come to him.

Luck is chance, and most of us have an equal share of both good and bad luck. But many of us fail to enjoy the good luck that ought to be ours simply because we do not have the necessary positive persistence to carry us through the bad luck that happens to hit us first.

"They are fools whose hearts are set on riches but whose souls admit defeat."

CHAPTER XXXIII

YOUR PROBLEM CAN BE ANSWERED

DREAMLAND

Q. Some time ago I purchased a little set of books—"The Secret of the Ages." I want to take this opportunity to tell you how much I enjoyed reading your books. Whatever your advice to the public, whatever you write, seems to instill so much courage and assurance that life is really worth living. You shine out like a light urging me to have heart and forge ahead.

—Miss A.L.T., New York, N. Y.

A. That's a mighty nice letter of yours and I appreciate it. Did you ever see the movie called "Peter Ibbetson"? It was the story of a man unjustly convicted of murder, who had to serve all his life in prison. Physically, he led a miserable routine existence, but mentally he lived in dreamland—the happiest dreamland imaginable.

It's a beautiful picture and there's only one thing wrong with it—if one can live in that realm of dreamland, he presently finds that the dreamland becomes a reality, and the drab reality vanishes.

The great thing to realize is that wealth is just as plentiful, just as free as the air you breathe. For what is gold made of? Electrons and protons, just like the air about you, only in gold they are differently and more densely arranged.

God—the Father—has all this wealth, and you are His son—not only heir to Infinite supply, but He definitely gave you dominion over the earth.

What you must do is realize your sonship, realize the power it gives you; then command this Man inside You to turn to gold whatever amount of electrons may be necessary for your present need, leaving to Him the channel through which He will bring it to you.

In your business deals, don't worry about the commission end of it. Think rather of what you can do to serve your customers best. There are always new and better ways of developing districts. Try to find these rather than struggle with your competitors over the little business that seems now available.

And when difficulties confront you, baptize them OPPORTUNITY and set the Man Inside You to finding the way to turn them from difficulties into opportunities.

CAPITAL

Q. I have read and reread your books and am just as far away from success as I was when I started. If you can help me out, you are the man I am looking for.

I have an invention which is a wonder. If I could only

get $10,000 to manufacture and market it! No matter how bright things look to me, if I plan to do something, just as sure as fate, they will go the reverse. What is wrong?

—M.F.H., LOS ANGELES, CALIFORNIA

A. The first thing that you need is not $10,000 but a change in your mental attitude.

If you had $10,000 now and felt as you have done in the past, it's only a question of time until you'd lose it. You've got to lose your jinx before you get any money. Recently I read an article about a young foreigner, which showed how he started a machine shop 20 years ago with a discarded foot-lathe and a boiler salvaged from a junk heap, in an old barn that cost him $1 a month rental. Today his plant is valued at $750,000.

The important thing in starting any business is not the money, but the idea and the spirit behind it. Our files are full of letters from people who, with little or no money, started businesses that have made good. These are not Fords or Rockefellers. They are tales of ordinary men and women like you or me, and what they can do, you can do.

So my advice is to get started even though your start be no bigger than this man's. Once started, the capital will come your way.

SUPPLY

I have received the set of "The Secret of the Ages," and although I have read only three of the books, I have decided to keep them. I am perfectly satisfied as to their actual cashable value to me. They are just wonderful! And I know they are going to be everything you say about them, and I feel sure that all who read and study the marvelous teachings therein will be brought in touch with the higher things of life—into a new realization of the life abundant, that which Jesus meant when he said—"I am come that they might have life and that they might have it more abundantly." Your books show your readers how to unlock the latent-energy in the atom and give to us our divine heritage and birthright, and this new life is just waiting for our recognition of it.

May your many readers, amongst them myself, be able to discover and work out the marvelous truths given in your books and so be wondrously blessed with all the success we need in life. And this I know is your greatest wish and desire, that all may have such an abundance.

—MISS S.D.T., LOS ANGELES, CALIF.

THE RIGHT JOB

Q. After reading "The Secret of the Ages," I set about trying to put into practice what I had read. I was in a chaos of distress at the time, yet my absolute needs were met. In a week a job came "out of the blue" which enabled me to pay in advance for a very comfortable little furnished apartment.

A Scotch family nearby possesses a secret formula for a healing wax which was brought over from Scotland. They talk about commercializing this wonderful healing wax (they say lockjaw has been healed by it, and cases of blood-poisoning, galore). A friend of mine says he will back me to a modest extent if I undertake to make and market this wax. Believing entirely in your teachings, I am not reconciled to the idea.

Would it be wrong or destructive for me, believing as I do, to engage in such a business?

A. I am delighted to hear that you've made a good start toward demonstrating prosperity once more. That, I know, will give you the courage and the confidence to demonstrate further.

There is a right place for you, there is a work you can do which no one else can do as well; so send your subconscious a-seeking of it.

And don't be looking for it a month from now or six months from now. In mind everything is in the now. So know that this job is for you now. It is yours. Claim it. Be thankful for it. Then go ahead in the confident knowledge that the lead is on its way to you.

That miracle wax strikes me as being a step in the wrong direction. It's all right. It's being done every day. And it's certainly a lot better than many of the nostrums that are making fortunes for their owners. But just sit down and ask yourself—"on whom or on what am I depending for life and all that is good in life? Would Universal Mind approve of my placing my dependence on a nostrum?"

Look to God alone for your right job and He will find it for you.

A TERRIBLE STATE

Q. I have read the book, "The Secret of the Ages," that you so kindly sent me, not just once but ten and more times; it's a wonderful book, and as far as personal improvement is concerned, it is the truth—by the means outlined in this book, which I knew years ago, I was able to recover from arthritis, after doctors all said I'd never walk again.

But: these principles fail to work, when an attempt is made to improve one's financial situation. I think the reason is this: While one's subconscious is able to improve one's physical condition and is all powerful in *that* respect, being able to build perfect health, increase one's mental ability and so on, it meets opposition from all the race the instant it tries to add to one's material prosperity—*everyone else has a subconscious* mind too, and all of society is quick to do everything possible to deprive the individual of everything they can. I've never known any people who meant me anything but harm of one sort or another; what few kindnesses I have received, have later proved to be just "bait" to get me in the proper attitude of mind to be victimized.

One's subconscious can't "buck against" the whole human race, powerful though it may be, because everybody else has a Subconscious too, and they intend to take advantage of you in any and every way possible.

One other flaw in the book: "All men are of divine origin." Then so are the apes; watch a group of children at play; the only other animal that is as noisy and ill-behaved, is the monkey or ape! A flock of other animals don't act so cussed! People certainly came from ape-like ancestors, and *descend* is the correct word to describe their evolutionary progress *(downward!)*.

The human race is *NOT* in any way divine or God-like—it is *contemptible,* and *evil,* and *you* know it! The human race has done everything it could think of to destroy the earth, which it has infested too long already!

One main reason for not believing in a *personal* deity is this: if He was what Christians think He is He couldn't put up with the rotten human race: He would blot it out.

I grant you there is a Universal "Mind" or "Absolute" back of creation—but why does this "Mind" condone evil?

I suppose the little whelps who rob bird nests, and try to kill all song birds, as well as try to destroy everything of beauty they can get their dirty paws on, are made in "His" image! Such a belief makes me mad!

Humans are the most depraved, rotten, dishonest and contemptible animals on this earth—a *just* "God" if He existed, would exterminate them instantly. Armageddon is long overdue.

I've never known any honest, truthful or "good hearted" humans, except *one—you did* try to help me by sending your book!

—E.G.B.

A. Thank you for your letter. In some respects you are right and in some I would beg to differ. It is true that very few people have the faintest resemblance to a real Son of God. But that is, of course, because man has strayed so far from the path of God and no longer is interested in hearing God's voice. It is only because of the great Love of God that He had not exterminated man long before this.

The use of Mind Power certainly can bring financial benefits. We have files and files of letters from people telling us how they have benefited financially from reading our books. Many churches can tell of many instances where prayer brought wealth.

I can tell from your handwriting that you are not easily discouraged, you maintain a hopeful attitude and you are ambitious to get ahead. You show thrift and careful judgment in making purchases. You have a feeling of independence and a critical mind. You have a forceful attitude and idealism is present. You have the ability to concentrate, your manner is reserved and you do not push yourself forward aggressively. You are serious and have a deliberate mind.

I think that if you think only of mean people, you will attract the same. I have found most people very friendly, helpful, and generous. I would like you to read Dale Carnegie's book "How to Win Friends and Influence People."

A SKEPTICAL STUDENT

Q. I have not been in practice for ten years now. Financial limitations made it necessary to discontinue.

Selling calendars and advertising specialties has been my day occupation while holding a steady job at night, first as a production operator on offset presses, then C-54 plane assembler during the war, followed by a round in the plastic molding field and spring, coil spring, grinding. The past two years as a watchman in a food flavoring plant, where I am at this moment typing this letter. Some sixty-six hours' time is taken up including transportation, then several hours three to four times a week in selling to business firms.

One time my faith in affirmations was very strong but since I failed to make it work and began thinking of the many who were devotees of this New Thought not making any outstanding success, I became a bit skeptical. Some lecturers and writers have emphasized that if one concentrates daily and has faith in due time will be able to "tune in" on God and obtain such knowledge direct as he may desire. That sounded good to me too. Then I began to think that these advocates should have had more personal power and been inspiring individuals doing great things akin to what Jesus could do, but none such gift seems to be demonstrated by them. So I found myself stranded sort of on a fence, meanwhile aiming to do what I could by work and application; the more of it the better would result in greater accomplishment.

The monks who belong to the American cults that begin the day with four hours of prayer and who give themselves over to God's will and deny themselves all worldly pleasure (as told in a recent Coronet magazine) should show better results from their efforts. This organization has been functioning since the sixteenth century and they have five or six institutes in the U.S.

I think there is nothing like action and organized action to bring about reforms and improvements which I am most interested in.

A plan has occupied my thoughts for now fifteen years, a most gigantic undertaking but begun in a very small way. My many sad disappointments and failures have taught me to be cautious and to know what to expect before making any radical leap into an untried movement.

This drug addiction, rape, lawlessness, among youth is no surprise to anyone who has made a study of causes. "We reap what we sow" is still up-to-date and we have been sowing cigarette smoking, liquor and freshen-up-beverages for quite some time. We have been feeding the kids hero stuff via movies and then top it off with colored ads on back pages, bill boards showing pictures of these "heroes" and "heroines" and why they smoke certain brands or why they prefer certain drinks. And now Cook County alone has four thousand drug addicts we are told by a newspaper recently, and a juvenile Judge is alarmed by the number of youths who appear before him on drunkenness charges.

These are few of the many evils pouring down upon the neglectful heads of the ministry, welfare organizations, city administrations, and many organizations that have concentrated on relieving effects via hospitals, insane asylums, prisons, charity institutions, and courts.

—H.S.

A. Thank you for your letter. I am much interested in what you say. I agree with you that we cannot neglect the physical entirely for the spiritual. I have seen too many cases of this, God will not help those who do not help themselves. A body loaded with poisons from the soft civilized diet cannot respond to healing treatments except in unusual cases. I knew Brown Landone and knew of Dr. Robinson.

It is true that the majority fail in their efforts to make the LAW work. The main reason for this is that they do not pray to find God's Will for them in any matter. It is only what THEY want and not what God knows is best for them. Thus they do not receive the POWER that they need for externalization of their thought patterns. Another reason is that most people are only studying Truth for what they can get out of God, with no thought of giving God all their love and praise and blessings, and glory which are due HIM. When they are ready to give God this, then He is ready to reward them accordingly. If you will seek constantly for a consciousness of a closer relationship with God, so that He will become a living Reality to you, then you will receive the power to gain your wishes. The Law is unfailing and just and the fact that most people are unable to make it work for their benefit does not detract from it in any way. They DO make the Law work every minute of the day, but mostly to their disadvantage, as they externalize their thoughts of poverty, illness, and misfortune.

THOUGHTS THAT "SHOUT FOR JOY"

I prize the "Collier Books" more than I can tell you, and never fail to recommend those I already had to my friends all over the U.S.

Mr. Collier's thoughts simply "shout for joy" and sink deep into the consciousness of those of us who are sincerely seeking a more understandable way of life. I've been a Truth "researcher" for the past twenty-five years, found good in most all the teachings I've investigated, but few of them hit the jackpot like Mr. Collier's do. It's the acquiring the necessary amount of faith and believing *before* the actual realization that seems so hard for me to grasp, yet I have a feeling inside me that this is the only way to get what we pray for. You see, I was "brought up" in the Orthodox Church, and was taught that we should pray to God for things, but should *not* try to dictate to Him just how it was to come—if at all! Too, I was given only a *very vague* idea of just what God is other than a somewhat personalized individual "spiritual" being as shown in the pictures but which none could exactly explain. When I asked sensible questions, I was told that I shouldn't question these things, as "in due time all would be revealed." None of this satisfied. I know now that you will understand how I appreciate what Mr. Collier has to say.

—A.B.C.

IS THERE A DEVIL?

Q. I have been reading your book "The Secret of the Ages" and I have found it to be a very challenging book. However, I have found a number of statements to be confusing and misleading, as I am a Baptist in my Religious Beliefs and of course it is hard for me to understand or agree with a lot of the statements in your book. You make the statement that Mind is the only power, "that there is neither good nor bad, thinking makes it so" (Shakespeare). You give a lot of statements from the Bible, and yet a lot of the statements in your book seem to contradict many Scriptural Truths. For instance, your book says, Mind is the only power, yet the Bible refers to the Devil, to evil and wickedness in many places. In the sixth chapter of Romans, reference is made to Sin and Righteousness, and we are exhorted to be dead unto sin, but alive unto God through Jesus Christ our Lord. Now if there be no such thing as sin or the Devil or unrighteousness, why do we have so many references to such in the Bible? You see I am an honest, sincere seeker who wants to know the real truth. I do agree with your statement that Christians ought to have a lot more power than most of us possess today. I do believe in Christ's Power to heal, although thus far, I have been unable to demonstrate it.

Now here is another matter I am very much interested in—the New Church your book refers to. It says, "A new Church has been founded on the words of James: 'Faith without works is dead.'" It teaches that Jesus meant all that He said about healing, casting out demons, etc. Just what Church do you have in mind? Christian Science or Unity? Or do you have reference to any particular Church? Although at the present I am a Baptist, yet I believe the Church ought to be able to do these things too.

I will appreciate any information you may be able to pass on to me about such matters.

—J.L.D.

A. Thank you for your letter, which denotes that the writer has a keen, intelligent, and inquiring mind. I will endeavor to answer your questions to your satisfaction.

Now in regard to the Devil and his cohorts . . . God, as a Creator, cannot create a devil (He can create only good); and man, as a secondary creator, in turn cannot create a God (he, as a mortal, can only create evil).

We need to examine these two statements very thoroughly for two extremely valid reasons; First, because of the mistaken beliefs they can eliminate for man who accepts and understands them, and Second, so that our Heavenly Father may be freed of the stigma man attaches to Him when he thinks of "Satan" as God-created to tempt man.

There is the "devil" of course, but THE DEVIL IS THE SUM TOTAL OF THE MORTAL MINDS AND WILLS ON THIS EARTH (AND IN THE INTERMEDIATE) as opposed to the Will and Mind of God.

But, man says, are not some "the devil incarnate"? Yes, and no. If man (or woman) falls low enough to have no mortal goodness(?) of any kind in him—just lust, viciousness, murderousness, hate, evil in every form, then he might, with some grain of truth, be called a DEVIL INCARNATE. However, it is well to remember (for the sake of further tries on that one for ultimate salvation) that in every man and every woman—there is some Perfect Good awaiting to be loosed—The Works of the Holy Spirit when accepted as a working partner.

A Devil—to be a REAL DEVIL—would have to be wholly evil, and such a one God could not create, because all beings brought forth by Him were BORN IN HIS IMAGE AND LIKENESS, and no evil therein.

The Devil which has been created, and which pretty much runs this world at this time, is STRICTLY MAN-CREATED, and the evil which has fallen upon man is entirely of his own devising.

Even when he tries with all that is superficially good within him to plot out an existence that will save his soul, he will fail unless he is under God's Will. So you see that it is impossible for God to bring forth evil.

In regard to the "New Church"; that does not mean any particular church at all. It refers to any church that practices healing as demonstrated by Jesus Christ.

In fact, one does not have to go to church at all. In the silence of his own room he may come face to face with his God and so be a member of the "New Church" of God.

May God bless you as He does all who strive after Him.

"IT WORKS!"

I enjoyed "Secret of the Ages" so very much and I think it may interest you to know that the science has really worked for me. Last year I was a struggling cartoonist whose initial income from cartooning was just a poor $500, not $5000, but *$500*. Not much of an income, was it? Well, upon reading "The Secret of the Ages" just prior to the holidays, things began to change. This year, in the month of January, I've gotten $500 from cartoons, and my success as a cartoonist is rapidly building up momentum. Yes, in one month I made what I did last year. If you want, you can use this testimonial in your ads. The whole science is unusual, almost fantastic but it works, by golly, it works.

—J.G.

"WHAT IS THE SECRET OF THE AGES?"

Thank you and bless you for writing THE SECRET OF THE AGES!

I have studied many of the Unity books within the past four years and have a fine foundation in metaphysics, and your book says all the story in one volume, says it simply and with the punch of a top salesman! When I finished it I let out a long slow sigh, "Wow! What a salesman I!" My husband looked up and across at me. He is in the sales field and what I had said was the highest kind of a compliment.

Mr. L______ commutes by train from ______ ______ station, which is slightly more than eighteen miles from our farm, and the first morning he had your book tucked under his arm to digest en route, the title was turned outward. One fiftyish gentleman passed him three times, his lips moving as though forming words. Mr. L______ scrutinized him, thinking perhaps the chap thought they knew each other yet was not sure enough to greet him. On the fourth passing, "Pappy" kindly helped him out of his misery with a cheery "Good morning."

Whereupon the gentleman swung around, looked directly into Pappy's eyes and shot back, "WHAT is the secret of the ages!"

And they sat together all the way to ______ talking of your book. And every day for a week, the whole length of time he has carried the book, someone has sat next to him and has started a conversation that always got back to your book!

As a couple and individually we have each been living in a more universal sense than ever before, and now your book is the wonderful, enjoyable dessert to a splendid meal. May the ripples of its good spread far and wide.

—E.L.L.

"LIKE A LUCKY CHARM"

Several months ago a post-card offer to buy your book came to me in the mail and I accepted and paid the postman the necessary $5.00. This letter is to tell you that I have never had a moment of regret for spending that $5.00 even though my husband objected and considered it an extravagance which we could not afford at the time.

I travel from ______ to ______ five days a week by bus to work in the offices of the ______. It is not easy commuting but after three years I am beginning to enjoy it. We commuters get acquainted and enjoy each other's conversation and often exchange books. A little lady had been despondent over her daughter's unfortunate marriage and discord in her home since the daughter and unruly husband moved in with her. Lending your book to her so took this mother out of her usual thought pattern that she seems now like a new woman. She took command of the situation in her home so that now she says the son-in-law is no problem at all and is planning a home of his own within a few months. The little commuting mother is so happy and greets me so very cordially and praises that wonderful book I loaned her. I felt that I had fully repaid her for secretly sending me a gift subscription of "Weekly Unity."

But about the Book—every time I take it with me on the bus or to work, something nice happens to brighten my day. Am I getting superstitious about it? It is like a lucky charm. My worst enemies are within myself, of course, and, I realize that they are named Doubt, Discouragement, and Distraction. But your book is showing me how to keep from backsliding into the power of these negative states. My rather embittered and disillusioned husband rarely escapes their power either, and his influence of limitation has been holding me back these past three years. However, we love each other, and through applying all you have presented in this book we are beginning to make progress and feel that we shall come into our right places. We, in our hearts, would like to do God's Great Work as admirably as you are doing it!

—MRS. E.L.L.

SELLING

Q. It seems that I am most unable to attain my heart's desires which I believe are just and not too much to ask. One is to attain success as is measured by the company I represent. Work as hard as I may, each individual I call on, with but few exceptions, is so pressed for funds that it is utterly impossible for him to carry anything more at this time.

I have tried to vision upon retiring, the consummation of some large contract with a prospect I honestly feel and believe needs the service I can render, but upon my presentation, it seems that I am intruding and usually get no encouragement whatsoever.

A. If you've read "The Secret of the Ages," you know that there is around us a Universal Mind of which we are all a part, and to which we are each an outlet.

Now when you want anything, you have to impress that want upon Universal Mind—you've got to SELL your want to the mind of all.

Try to picture yourself in the Yale Bowl with 100,000 people gathered in the stands above you. They're not listening especially to you. They have their own interests, their own thoughts. So if you want to get something from them, you've got to impress your want upon them in some unmistakable way.

You can't merely ask some selfish request and expect them to heed it. You've got to sell them a real idea, a real service, before they're going to pay much attention to it. You've got to believe in it very thoroughly yourself before they're going to believe you. You've got to be absolutely sold before you stand much chance of selling them.

But when you can come through with some arresting idea with real service, real value behind it, you'll find your outlet not in one man or in a few, but in that whole great mass of people.

Your problem is to find an arresting idea that you would feel confident of selling to the great majority of people gathered in the Yale Bowl, if you were allowed to talk to them between halves of a football game. Do that and you'll be not in the $400,000 class, but in the $1,000,000.

WRONG THOUGHTS

Q. Have just finished "The Secret of the Ages." It gives such a clear idea of the subconscious mind and its immense importance—and has helped me very much.

Am writing to ask if, from your standpoint, the individual work of the conscious mind can entirely overcome wrong thoughts put into the subconscious by those about us? Can we protect this completely in our business?

A. Thank you for your good letter and for the nice things you have to say about "The Secret of the Ages."

As to your questions—yes, it is possible to shut out from the subconscious or else to neutralize the wrong thoughts that come to us from all around.

What you must realize is that there is but one power, and that power is God. While you hold on to the good, no evil can harm you. While your mind is filled with good, no evil can enter it, for you can't pour water into a vessel already full.

God never takes the good from us. It is we who separate ourselves from Him by erecting barriers between us of sin, or worry, or evil. The moment we tear these down we find the good waiting there to enter, like the sunlight on the outside of a shaded window.

FAITH

Q. Taking you at your word, I am drawing on you for $2500. I do not want this as a gift but a loan to be repaid to you, or whomever you might designate, in six months. I had about given up hope of being able to keep my family together, but your books have given me a new angle on life and I know that $2500 for six months will put me in a position to render real service to my fellow-men.

A. The suggestion I'm going to offer you will take a good deal of faith to carry out, but if you can manage the faith, it will work.

As I understand the Bible, God gave to us all of good. It is ours. The reason we don't manifest it is that for thousands of years we've been taught that nothing good can come to us without struggle. We've erected a wall around ourselves—a wall of unbelief that keeps the good out.

The thing we've got to do is to tear down that wall and let the good which is all around us reach us.

God is the Creator of the Universe. Everything of good in it is His. He knows where all the gold and silver and diamonds and other precious things are. God put them there.

We are His children. If He were an earthly father, what would we expect of Him? To share in all of His riches, would we not? And every good earthly father does share everything he has with his children. Do you think God is any less loving, any less generous than an earthly father?

You will agree, then, that God has all of wealth, and that as His children we share in this wealth. Why then do we not manifest it? Because we cut ourselves off from Him. We doubt His generosity. We don't believe in His willingness to give. We surround ourselves with doubts and fears and dam up the flow of His goodness.

Read that little talk of Jesus' in which He told His followers to "consider the lilies of the field how they grow." Then try to realize that all of good is yours—that you have it—that you've only to open up your mind and look always for good, expect only good, in order to receive it.

As things are now, you seem to be surrounded with want and all manner of bad things. Refuse to accept them as yours. Pick out every item of good you can see about you and claim only it. Be thankful for it. Plant that bit of good, nourish it, and soon, like the mustard seed, it will grow into a tree in whose shade you can rest for the remainder of your days.

A MOTHER'S PROBLEM

Q. I received your books and want to thank you for them. I feel as though a heavy load has been lifted from my shoulders.

My husband left me a year ago and took two of my children with him. I am willing to give him his freedom, but I want the children. As both of them are girls I feel they need a mother's care, regardless of what sacrifice I must make to care for them.

Could you suggest something I could do to support and still take care of them at home? Father Baker says that if I pray and believe, my prayers will be answered.

A. Father Baker is right. If you will pray and believe, your prayer will be answered. Read that little chapter on prayer in the books. It will help you.

But don't pray merely to get back your little girls. Pray for the right solution to your problem. Pray for the right way out for your husband. Try to bless him wherever he is and whatever he's doing.

Real love, you know, is selfless and free from fear. It pours itself out upon the object of its affection without demanding any return. Its joy is the joy of giving. And real love draws to itself its own. It does not need to demand.

As for finding an occupation, there are many things that even the mother of four children can do to earn money. People with no money, and little or no training, have built businesses of their own. You'd be surprised at the number and variety of these.

I received one letter from a woman with two children who found an hour or two a day in which to handle real estate, and who has built up a profitable business. I had another from a woman in Toronto whose husband failed in business and health and had to be sent to a sanitarium while she provided the means of keeping him there. She had no business training, but she did love gardens, so she went all through the suburbs, and wherever she found a yard that was untidy and unkempt, she went in and tried to sell the householder bushes and shrubs and show them the way to plant them. Now she's a member of the firm.

I had another from a woman who was left an orphan at thirteen with a younger brother and sister to care for. They'd always loved to make homemade candies and had made them unusually well, using, of course, rich cream and all the finest ingredients. They got the idea that if they would continue to make candy as good as they knew how, they could sell it at prices that would pay them a goodly profit.

Their first stand was a "Help Yourself" stand under the stairway of the Syracuse University. The customer helped himself to a box of candy and left the money. Today they have a business worth over $100,000.

It requires courage and faith, and the initiative to start something. With these you can go anywhere.

THE MAN INSIDE

Q. Have just completed your seven little books—"The Secret of the Ages." I am very glad to say that the books have given me more real facts than any book or books I have ever had the pleasure of reading.

I have pictured a certain line of business I want to build up, and I have visualized it and know the line I want to take on as a merchandising proposition. Now, should I make efforts to see if I can get the contract to cover this line of merchandise, or should I wait for my subconscious mind to bring about this result for me? It is true, I haven't the money now and have put the proposition up to the Man Inside to do the job. I am a little bit in the dark along this line and would appreciate your help.

A. Thank you for the nice things you have to say about "The Secret of the Ages."

About your problem: As I see it, the thing to do when you're faced with a difficult problem is to review it from every angle, go over every possibility you can think of, then throw the burden upon your subconscious self and ask it to give you the answer.

When you've done that, forget the problem for a while in the serene knowledge that your subconscious is working on it and will presently present to you at least the first step in its answer.

Sometimes, of course, it presents the complete answer at once, but more often it presents one step at a time.

Take that step, review the remaining problem and again put it up to your subconscious to give you the answer.

Don't be in a hurry, don't be fearful, and above all, don't worry about the outcome. Know that Universal Mind has the answer and that at the right time and in the right way, will present it to you. Ask for a lead. Ask to be shown the first step. Then take that step confidently, even though you can't see what is beyond.

IDEAS

Q. I am the fellow that had the nerve to walk in your office, look you in the eye, and take your hand.

If you recall, we discussed the necessity of something being done for the lumber industry. I have worked out a solution to this problem. It is all very clear, but I must have help. What is your suggestion?

A. Have you ever taken a cork and put it in the spout of a kettle so that the steam couldn't escape? Remember how, after a little while, that steam blew the top off with a nice big roar?

That's the way it is with ideas. Let them escape as they form, and they never accomplish much. Bottle them up for a little while, and they presently blow the top off things.

I think the only advice you need is not to work too fast. The ordinary man is pretty set in his ways, and especially in his ideas. He hates to change an idea because it means thinking, and there's no harder work than thinking.

So start small. Move your mountain a bit at a time. You get there in the end just the same, and you get there far more surely and with less damage to the feelings of your friends and associates, too.

If I can be of any help, call on me.

PERFECT IMAGE

Q. I have been reading your books with much interest. They have been a wonderful help to me.

I have been very successful in many things I have attempted, but the one tiling I most desire now is to reduce my weight which is difficult.

I know your wonderful understanding could solve my problem immediately, and I will thank you very kindly to advise me in this matter.

A. Have you ever seen the picture of Pygmalion and Galatea? If I were you, I would get a copy of it or of some beautiful statuette of a similar kind. Put it in your bedroom. Let it be the first thing you see on waking up in the morning, and the last you look at before turning out the light at night.

Then picture to yourself God as the sculptor Pygmalion, and yourself as Galatea. Have you ever known a sculptor to intentionally model an imperfect statue for all the world to see? God is a far more wonderful sculptor than any who ever lived on this earth, and He is far prouder of the work of His hand. He made your body in the most perfect image imaginable. That is the only image of it He knows. Therefore, it is the only image of it you can have.

What you must do is know that you HAVE this perfect image—know that it is yours—know that any other you seem to see is merely the distorted image of your subconscious mind, and that your only job is to change the image in your subconscious, not change the reality God made.

NEED A MAN BE SAINTLY?

Q. I returned by insured parcel post your books. Up to this good time I have not been able to get results, and, as I recall, you promised to answer questions relative to new principles set out or treated of in the books. I do not seem to be able to get the right contact with the subconscious mind. Does a man have to be absolutely godly or rather saintly in order to get results with the subconscious mind? If you do, then that settles it, for we read there is none perfect—no, not one.

I do not try to limit God's power. I believe He can do anything and that whatever He does do is right. I have no doubt but what the coin that Jesus found in the fish's mouth was a real coin of the realm and had been honestly minted: God's power just simply put that coin in the mouth of the fish, but He did not create it without regard for the Roman Law governing the minting of gold coins. Now I am not writing all this in a spirit of criticism, but trying to get at the truth of the matters treated. How shall I go about impressing my desires on Divine Mind?

A. I'm sorry you didn't find in my book the truth you were looking for. Under separate cover I'm glad to send you refund of your money.

Now as to your question: No, a man does not need to be absolutely godly or saintly in order to get results from the subconscious mind.

As a matter of fact, many men who are anything but that have received wonderful results in certain lines. Of course, the nearer you come to perfection, the easier it is to become at one with Divine Mind. But you don't need to wait for that to get results.

If you were a salesman and wanted a man to give you an order for a carload of groceries, you would know that the order must first be given you in the man's mind before ever you would get it on paper. It may be hours or days between the time he decides to give you the order and the time you get it, but from the moment the order is written in his mind, it is yours. The written order is merely the physical manifestation which you can show to your employers.

Just so it is with anything you want from God. The part that counts is His mental order for it, His consent to answer your prayer. When you get that, you can rest easy—the physical manifestation will follow in due course.

But you've got to make preparations for it. You've got to open your channels to receive it. I've written a little article about this part of it which I called "Keeping the Tracks Clear."

In the new set, the first two volumes of which you have, I've written a chapter on prayer which I believe will help you. One of the quotations in it is "In due season we shall reap if we faint not."

EVERYTHING GOING WRONG

Q. Everything I have been trying to do has gone wrong. Near the end of last year my health failed, I could scarcely breathe, and was sent to —. Disgusted with the place, so kept on going and have spent the past ten months traveling along the California coast.

Soon after I left Chicago, I was informed by my employer that as they had changed their system, my services were no longer required. A man of fifty, once out of a job, is OUT. No one will ever give him a chance to show whether or not he is of any value. "50 and you're out." That is the motto of all the young employment managers.

Likewise, I was informed that since the system was changed, the firm did not consider that they owed me the commissions I earned. $2,000 commissions on my sales still due me, and cannot get a dollar.

My fig and peach trees in California failed to come up to promise. The fruit was there all right, perfect, wonderful peaches and figs. But the growers went on "strike" until the peaches rotted in the orchard. Total loss. Fig growers and canners had an argument. Figs went to waste. Another loss of at least $800.

All those things are beyond my reach. I am in no way responsible for any of those calamities. It has taken the starch out of me—I have lost all ambition. I can't even sell goods, and I have always been able to sell, having worked my way through college by selling, newspaper writing and teaching, and having been in the selling game many years since.

Can you solve this enigma? I have thought and reasoned until my brain is in a whirl, but I cannot understand why every beautiful picture I see turns to dust, and why every apple I reach for crumbles to ashes. Why? Can you tell me?

A. There is something radically wrong with your thinking, because every man has within himself a powerful magnet which attracts to itself exactly the sort of substance with which it is charged.

Charge it with thoughts of evil and worry and disease and you will attract to yourself the very things you fear.

Charge it with belief in yourself, in your destiny, in your power to acquire all of the good things of life, and you will attract those things to you.

I'm sending to you under separate cover two of my latest books. Read them. Read especially the chapter called "The Lode Star." Then, if you like, return them. Or send $2 in full payment, whichever you wish.

But read the books. You need to understand the magnet within you.

MOTHER-IN-LAW PROBLEM

Q. I have a mother-in-law who is worse than any ever pictured in the comic papers. She is the devil. She has alienated my wife, and now she has gotten my baby away from me.

A. There's a brotherhood in India who never say "Good Morning" to each other. Instead, they say, "I salute the

Divinity in you." They do this even with the wild beasts in the jungle and they are never harmed.

If I were you, I would try to do this with that very difficult mother-in-law of yours. There is bound to be some good in her. Try to locate that good. Try to locate the God within her and bring it into its own.

As for your baby: Just remember that as you are one with God, so you are one with the love of this child which belongs to you by Divine right.

Repeat to yourself frequently: "There is no separation in Divine Mind; therefore, I cannot be separated from the love and companionship of my child which are mine by Divine right."

If you can repeat this to yourself with faith and belief, depend upon it, your problem will work itself out.

SONS OF THE RICH

Q. Why did Jesus, with all His power, not take the riches that were offered him and use them to do good? Couldn't He have done more good with them than poor as He was?

I have a boy and I have often wondered whether I ought to try to leave him anything or not. Seems to me the sons of the rich are pretty worthless, on the whole.

A. I think that Christ felt the greatest need of His day was not to take money or power and show what could be done with it, but to convince the common man that he is not a mere worm to be trodden under the feet of the rich men and rulers; not a slave, but a son of God, heir to all the earth. That it was he that God had in mind when he gave man dominion over the earth.

It is true that the sons of great men seldom do amount to much, but I think that the reason for it is not our artificial standard of values—not merely in the fact that their parents have too much money.

What does happiness consist of? Mostly in looking forward to greater happiness, a day or a month or a year from now. What does ambition consist of? In looking forward to something bigger, greater, a day or a month or a year from now.

A thousand years ago, China was centuries ahead of the Western powers. Then she got far behind them. Why? Because instead of looking ahead, she looked backward. Her religion was ancestor-worship.

In a lesser degree, that is the trouble with the rich men's sons of today—they worship what their fathers have done instead of looking ahead to the doing of greater things themselves.

CHAPTER XXXIV

BENEFITS RECEIVED

A GREAT CHANGE

No book that I have ever read has so completely changed my life for the better as has Robert Collier's book. I find so many friends who need to read it that I keep it on the road all the time, and my copy is getting quite dog eared.

So many wonderful things have happened to the people who have read my copy, and every one of them has rushed right out for a copy of her own. I wrote a book I'd planned to do for a long time because of the inspiration I received, another friend found courage to leave a job she hated and launch out on a brand new career, it kept another girl from killing herself, and the last one to read it has been using it to regain her health after several operations.

Bless you for publishing Collier's books.

Mrs. D.K.C.

FROM THE UNITED STATES SENATE

I told Senator ______ the other day that if one would winnow from my own writings with reference to the relationship of the mind and body, that I would be another witness to the truths you so ably present. It has always been heartbreaking to me to see people try to get health by the taking of pills and medicine out of the bottle. We have within ourselves the forces that make for or against health.

On the fly-leaf of my Grandfather's Bible I discovered this: "The world we inhabit must have had an origin; that origin must have consisted in cause; that cause must have been intelligent; that intelligence must have been efficient; that efficiency must have been supreme, and that which always was and is supreme we know by the name of God."

Apparently my Grandfather was thinking along the same lines that we are thinking. The trouble with us is that we don't make use of our intelligence, because it is not really efficient. In any event, let's keep on trying to make the world better by thinking good thoughts. By right thinking and right living we can revolutionize the physical existence of man.

Yours truly,
Senator ____

FROM THE COMMONWEALTH OF THE PHILIPPINES

SUPREME COURT
Manila
April 25, 1936

Sometime in 1929 I purchased from you two interesting sets of books written by you, entitled "The Secret of the Ages" and "The Secret of Gold" and "The Life Magnet." I was also one of the early subscribers to your magazine "Mind, Inc."

The magazine and the set of books have been of incalculable value to me. They have acquainted me with my hidden forces, and have instilled in me a sense of power and security that makes me a "Happy Warrior," fighting my battles for success and righteousness with a smile on my lips and a feeling of self-assurance. Since then I have forged constantly ahead, have finished my schooling, and been admitted to the practice of law. Lately, I was persuaded to accept the position of Secretary to Supreme Court Associate Justice of the Commonwealth of the Philippines. Your works have been my "talisman" all the time.

J.P.M.

FROM THE UNITED STATES SENATE COMMITTEE OF THE JUDICIARY

Please let me assure you that no time will be lost between the arrival of the short pamphlets to which your very acceptable letter of the fourteenth day of April refers and my reading of what you have said.

Indeed, I can not recall that I have ever failed to read anything from your pen that has ever become available to me. And I can now recall no page of your large literary output that, in my opinion, could be annihilated without distinct loss to humanity.

May I not again urge you to give me the pleasure of becoming better acquainted with you in the event of your being in Washington for any purpose before the adjournment of the Congress.

Since I last wrote you I have improved my every leisure moment by reading the excellent pamphlets entitled "The God in You." Indeed, night before last I was reading one of them at five minutes till two in the morning—and I do not mean by daylight saving time.

I hope that I may sometime have the pleasure of telling you "face to face" of an additional case, in which the book mentioned in our previous correspondence seems to have wrought what would ordinarily be considered a miraculous result.

Sincerely wishing you long life and unlimited success and happiness to the end of your days, I am, as always,

Yours truly,

Senator _____

$50,000 FROM READING A BOOK

Dear Sir:

Some fourteen years ago I bought a set of your books, "The Secret of the Ages."

Believe it or not, these books were responsible for my present position, which has meant more than fifty thousand dollars to me during this time.

I am a great hand to lend books to despondent persons: usually getting them back, but the last one I loaned this set to "forgot to return them."

I would like to get another set of the books.

Yours very truly,
G.A.M.
Waco, Texas

A BIG SALE

The literature on your book recalls to mind a letter I received ten years ago. At that time I was a writer on Specialty Salesman Magazine in Chicago, writing interviews with salesmen. I had a letter from a salesman in—, in which he told me of his successes as well as previous slumps. He said at one time he was just about down to zero when he happened onto a copy of your book. He continued that shortly after reading the copy he went out and within a half hour had sold over $1500 worth of cooking oil. His sales continued at an astounding rate. He sold cooking or salad oil to restaurants, hotels, wholesalers, etc. He told me how he sold to dealers who had previously turned him down. I still have this letter among my papers.

At the time I was so surprised at such a statement that I asked him if he could send me the brochure but he no longer had it, having let it get away from him in lending.

Nor did he know where to get another copy. If that letter is worth a copy of your book I'll be glad to send it on to you or if I am unable to locate it, will gladly pay you for a copy for I have not forgotten my desire to see a copy of your book.

K.I.

PRAISE

It suddenly dawned on me that perhaps you, too, would like a word of "p-raise" now and then. You probably get trillions of letters like these, but add this one to the pile!

I picked up your book at my brother-in-law's last July, opened it in the middle and started reading about love. I took the book home with me. At the time, I was just about the most self-pitying, depressed individual anyone could imagine! I was in the midst of an unhappy love affair, dissatisfied with my job, envious of others who seemed to have all the good times while I slaved away and came home each night to a hot apartment where I just sat feeling sorry for myself. Brother, I was really down! Fortunately, and thanks to your book it was to be for the last time! True, I do sink down even now, to pretty deep "sloughs of despond," but they don't last long, and each time I sink a little less deep and come up a little faster, and the times are getting more and more infrequent.

What can I say, except "God bless you" and "thank you from the bottom of my heart!" I am contributing my bit of cash each day at noon, and the amazing part is, I've already sent about $40 off to various deserving people, and am about to send one of the books to a man who is paralyzed, and yet, I seem to have more money than I ever had before. Every day, I find some new miracle in the world about me. I have developed the "expectant" attitude, and I look forward to each day, for I know that wonderful things have been planned for me. I have also sent the book to a friend of mine in Arizona whose husband is an Army captain. He is going to use it in some of his work with the GI's. My friend and I "meet" each day at 11, noon time, 3 P.M. and 8 P.M. Already, many of the things we have thanked God for "in advance" have come to pass. I wish I could shout your praises from the housetops! I had a woman's program once, but it was taken off the air. I never knew why. I received a lot of favorable fan mail and was promoting United Nations stuff toward the last. However, the "powers that be" decided that they didn't need the show any more. If I still had it, believe me, I would tell all the women listening about the book. I cannot begin to tell you what it has meant to me. I have so many blessings I'd be ashamed to go on being the complaining, griping, self-pitying fool I was before. Among my blessings I count your book. I write children's stories myself, and have been trying to get some of them published, and I know that I will now. Before, I took the defeatist "oh, that would never happen to me" attitude. Consequently, it never did!

This is terribly long-winded, but I sort of go overboard when I start talking about the book. Once again I say, "thank you, and God bless you a thousand times over!" What a pity we cannot all begin living by the law of love this very minute. The munitions plants could become apartment buildings and wars would cease!

G.C.

FROM CEBU CITY, PHILIPPINES

Dec. 1941

I know that you must be waiting for news; news about the good the book has done or is doing for me. Of course, at present I cannot say much, but I am sure you will have a deep feeling of satisfaction when I tell you: In a tiny spot ten thousand miles across the sea, and down into the heart of a soul lives "THE SECRET OF THE AGES"; yes, there it lives to bring cheerfulness and encouragement, love and hope, faith and life, all good—GOD! That soul was once downhearted and consequently fretful and cross—almost a wreck. But a wonderful transformation—a metamorphosis—has taken place. That miserable, despondent soul is now no more. That soul has come to the glorious recognition and unconditional acceptance of its oneness with GOD. Today that heart goes about radiant with joy, secure with a firm faith that all prayers will be heard, all yearnings satisfied, all desires fulfilled. And that heart and soul are mine.

May "THE SECRET OF THE AGES" reach the homes of millions all over the world that it may do for theirs what it is doing for mine!

I would be doubly glad if I can express my eternal

gratitude to the Colliers in person for bringing this priceless book into my life. Would you two and Mr. Collier join me in my prayers that I may have enough or rather plenty of money in order to realize this end? Would you? Well, I hope so!

THANKS A LOT. In the meantime I will be jotting down notes about my further progress in the course. AND you will always know about the bigger things.

A.A.T.

PROSPERITY PLUS

Dear Mr. Collier:

I have derived so much good from your books that I'm most anxious to have any new books you may have put out. About five years ago when I "hit bottom" and was seeking for something to steady my thinking, I came home one night without a dime in my pocket and without a loaf of bread in my home; a truly deplorable situation that gives one a very empty feeling.

Today I have my own business with twenty-nine employees; my own home and car; have traveled both ways in Masonry and am a Shriner, a member of our Country Club, the Civic Association, the Kiwanis Club and have a very desirable credit rating not only here but in Minneapolis, Chicago, St. Louis, New York, Pittsburgh, Washington, D.C., Great Bend, Kansas, Fargo, Sioux Falls, and other points where I have occasion to trade.

This may sound fantastic, and indeed it sometimes

seems so to me, except as through continued readings of the above books I have come to believe that the above conditions are those which have been promised us under certain conditions. Surely, you can at least understand my desire for "further enlightenment" if it is available.

Yours truly,
W.C.L.
Aberdeen, S.D.

$60,000 RECEIVED!

Dear Sir,
You may be interested to know, that I loaned most of Robert Collier's books to a very warm personal friend, in the east, and he was negotiating a business deal which required considerable capitalization. He was at a loss as to where he could obtain the funds through a private source, when one of my books reached him, he decided to try out the knowledge in this book, and Lo and Behold, a thought was inspired, which prompted him to board a train, to visit a friend who not only guaranteed financial assistance, in the amount of $60,000, but also offered my friend an opportunity to engage in a proposition which overshadowed the one for which the funds were required!!! I have documentary proof of this.

Sincerely yours,
F.P.
Kingman, Ariz.

SPREADING THE GOOD WORD

Dear Mr. Collier:

I have heard and read of many evangelists who have preached the gospel and have undoubtedly done a great deal of good among their fellow beings in inculcating into their minds an understanding of religion. However, I doubt if any man ever lived other than our Savior, Jesus Christ, who can be credited, like you, with bringing their fellow being to a real practical understanding of religion and the law of nature such as you have so completely accomplished through the various publications you have written.

Sincerely yours,
R.W.H.
Chicago, Ill.

LIKE ALADDIN'S LAMP

Dear Mr. Collier:

Aladdin and his lamp couldn't have done more for me than your book. As I wrote you previously, my husband had been unemployed, for seven months and conditions were really tragic. My parents had turned us out saying that they had asked us to stay with them temporarily but it had turned out to be quite permanent so we would have to leave.

Every chapter in your book seemed to fit our case, so,

absolutely unafraid I put the matter up to God and now, all in this short time, my husband has found employment and we have a little furnished apartment.

Surely you and your writings should have the blessings of the world. May God bless you, and the wonderful work you are doing.

Thankfully yours,
L.M.K.
Port Townsend, Wash.

FEAR GONE

Dear Mr. Collier:
I wonder how one goes about expressing gratitude so great it fairly oozes from every pore.

There seems to be tragedy in life every way you turn, and yet, to one with the newly-found realizations you give in your books, there seems to be no tragedy at all except to "wake up" and find it was only a dream. I do not think anything that can happen in life will bother me very much now. Gone is all fear of the future and a zest for living life daringly for all it is worth has taken its place.

I am sure you receive so many letters such as this that it is probably an old, old story to you but it is also possible that you are glad to know of one more you have helped to live fully. I thank you from the bottom of my heart for your great message. I start every day and close every day with your books and I feel I am helping others much by doing so.

Again, with gratitude, I am,

Very sincerely yours,
A.A.H.
San Antonio, Texas

A TEXTBOOK FROM NOW ON

Dear Mr. Collier:
I have just finished reading "Secret of the Ages" and I don't know when I have read anything that moved me so profoundly. It is beautifully and simply written in understandable language, and I shall use it as a textbook for living from now on, I can assure you. As I mentioned above, I have just finished reading it, but it will be re-read many, many times and assimilated, I hope.

I am enclosing a check for another copy.

Yours sincerely,
E.D.
New York, N.Y.

ABSOLUTE NECESSITY

Dear Seer and Soothsayer:
In seventy-six years I haven't found a volume that snuggled so comfortably into hand and mind. You put the world into a nut-shell, and crack it so we can get at the kernel.

Through the years I have read a great variety of things written by savants and word-mongers in general, but none, by-and-large, that presented their subject matter in such a cogent, concise yet universally comprehensive manner as you do. You don't obscure the forest by trunks full of printed leaves. The book is one of the absolute utilities.

In His Name,
J.L.
Los Angeles, Calif.

$500.00 EXTRA IN TWO WEEKS

My dear friend:
I read and reread the book; it told me many things I should have known, appreciated and applied—but had not.

Would it surprise you to know that certain ideas and principles of your book enabled me to definitely help myself in a number of ways, and that it brought me about $500.00 extra in two weeks after I had the book.

I am,

Yours cordially,
J.G.H.
Atlantic City, N.J.

FINANCES STRAIGHTENED OUT

Dear Mr. Collier:
I believe you will be interested in hearing how my affairs have straightened out since I received your letter of April 12th.

In your letter, you advised me to put everything—

myself and my affairs—in God's hands, to STOP RESISTING and to know that all things were working through me for good. Well, I did that very thing. I made an affirmation of that paragraph of your letter, and every time I began to worry over conditions, I would immediately start my affirmation:

"I put up no resistance to conditions that seem to overcome. Rather I BLESS them! I know all things are working together for my good, and I am working with them in the wisdom and power of the Spirit. I put myself and all of my affairs lovingly in the hands of God, with a childlike trust. That which is for my highest good will come to me."

I began using this affirmation on April 16th. On April 23rd, a friend of the family (who by the way is a director on the board of the bank which holds the mortgage on my home) came out to call bringing with him his wife and daughter. We spent a pleasant afternoon, though nothing was mentioned regarding any financial affairs.

The following Saturday, just two weeks after I began my affirmation, and when I had not one cent, this same friend phoned me from the Bank that he had arranged with the Bank to help me to save my home. He said he had arranged to take a second mortgage on my home and that the loan would be large enough to pay my debts, pay the interest on the first mortgage, pay my back taxes and current ones, and at the same time establish a small trust fund to care for me until something better presented itself.

I am so happy and grateful for this assistance, for it not only saves my home, but it also proves to me that *God in me has heard my prayers.*

I want to thank you, Mr. Collier, for your help in showing me the right way to pray to God.

Very sincerely,
Mrs.J.B.C.
Warsaw, Ind.

ABOUT THE AUTHOR

Born in St. Louis, Missouri, in 1885, Robert Collier trained to become a priest early in his life, before settling on a career in business, achieving success in the fields of advertising, publishing, and engineering. After recovering from a chronic illness with the help of mental healing, Collier began studying New Thought, metaphysical, and success principles. He distilled these principles into a popular and influential pamphlet series, collected into a single volume as *The Secret of the Ages* in 1926, and later revised by Collier in 1948. He died in 1950.

Look for These Prosperity Favorites from TarcherPerigee

Think and Grow Rich by Napoleon Hill
The landmark guide by the champion wealth-builder of all time—now revised and updated for the twenty-first century.
ISBN 978-1-58542-433-7

As a Man Thinketh by James Allen
The beloved classic on the creative potential of the human mind—available in a beautiful early replica edition. ISBN 978-1-58542-564-8

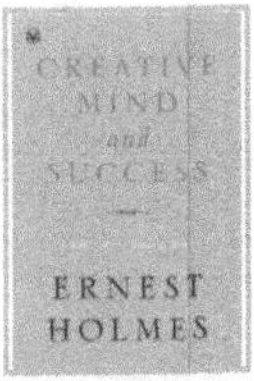

Creative Mind and Success by Ernest Holmes
A slender volume of immense power on the mental principles to success, by the author of *The Science of Mind*. ISBN 978-1-58542-268-5

Your Magic Power to Be Rich! by Napoleon Hill
The ultimate all-in-one prosperity bible, featuring updated editions of Hill's great works *Think and Grow Rich*, *The Magic Ladder to Success*, and *The Master-Key to Riches.*

ISBN 978-1-58542-555-6

Relax into Wealth by Alan Cohen
One of today's top life coaches explores the hidden key to success: Being yourself.

ISBN 978-1-58542-563-1

The Circle by Laura Day
The treasured guidebook that shows how the power of one simple wish can transform your entire life. ISBN 978-1-58542-598-3